To Travel Hopefully

Footsteps in the French Cévennes

CHRISTOPHER RUSH

RDR Books
Berkeley, California

To Travel Hopefully

RDR Books
2415 Woolsey Street
Berkeley, California 94705
Phone: 510-595-0595
Fax: 510-228-0300
E-mail: read@rdrbooks.com
Website: www.rdrbooks.com

First United States edition

ISBN: 1-57143-124-1
Library of Congress Catalog Card Number: 2005926741

Typography and cover design by Richard Harris
Cover photo: *Christopher Rush and Anatole
in Pradelles, France,* by Anne d'Esprémènil
Author photo by Scott Morris

Distributed in Canada by
Jaguar Book Group c/o Fraser Direct, 100 Armstrong Way,
Georgetown, ON L7G 5S4

Printed in Canada

First published in the United Kingdom, 2005, by
Profile Books Ltd, 58A Hatton Garden, London ECIN 8LX

Praise for *To Travel Hopefully* . . .

"As a human document it astounds me . . . and I marvel at its literary qualities . . . Nothing can shadow the stature of this book or how enriched I've been by reading it, or my admiration for Christopher Rush's achievement. It is to be treasured not just on the page, but in the heart — and spirit."

—Stewart Conn, Poet Laureate of Scotland

"An inspired Mozartian requiem, beautiful and terrible, wonderful and awful . . . As powerful a piece of writing as you are likely to read this year . . . [Christopher Rush's] books stick in the mind when others fade from the memory the instant one puts them down. A lyrical, passionate, sensuous writer . . . Think of George Mackay Brown, or Dylan Thomas."

—*The Sunday Herald*

"A work born of unquenchable art . . . It is difficult to convey the praise the book deserves. . . . The prose possesses an honesty that is fresh, still bleeding, yet shorn of the confessional guff that infests the modern media . . . The landscape is transformed."

–*Scottish Review of Books*

"Resonant, rich and raw . . . the master of lyrical lushness, firing every idea and image so luminously it could be picked off the page like a shard of ceramic . . . A harrowing, howling account from a man whose soul is steeped in literature, love and torment . . . A superbly readable and engaging travelogue . . . Rush is one of Scotland's literary stars."

—*The Glasgow Herald*

"The words marvellously possess a seismic force . . . writing that sings with tremendous descriptive richness and self-perception . . . I was twice moved to tears, yet constantly braced by the tensile courage of the enterprise."
—*The Scotsman*

"Quirky and colourful . . . moving and very human."
—*The Sunday Times*

"An astonishing pilgrimage from rage to redemption . . ."
—*The London Guardian*

"Desperately moving and beautifully written."
—*Time Out* (Book of the Week)

"A truly mesmerizing and beautiful book . . . rich with comic and disturbing detail . . . sweet, searching, devastating."
—*Scotland on Sunday*

"He writes brilliantly in this most evocative of books . . . No one who can actually read should be without it."
—Professor Derry Jeffares

"*To Travel Hopefully* is on a par with Joyce's *Ulysses*, though strikingly different, and it has even more passion than *Ulysses*. When I put it down, all I could think was, 'I want to give a copy of this book to every living person on this planet.'"
—Brendan Kennelly

"This is the most remarkable book I've ever read . . . a wholly absorbing account of a journey, a travel book of very unusual provenance."
—John Bayley

For Patricia

and for all travellers

'An inconceivably sweet longing, a yearning,
Drove me to roam through fields and forests.
With a thousand burning tears my heart was freed,
I felt another world rise up in me –
And I learned to live once more!'

Goethe, *Faust*

'A voyage is a piece of autobiography at best.'
Robert Louis Stevenson, *Travels with a Donkey*

CONTENTS

PART ONE

The Road to the Cévennes

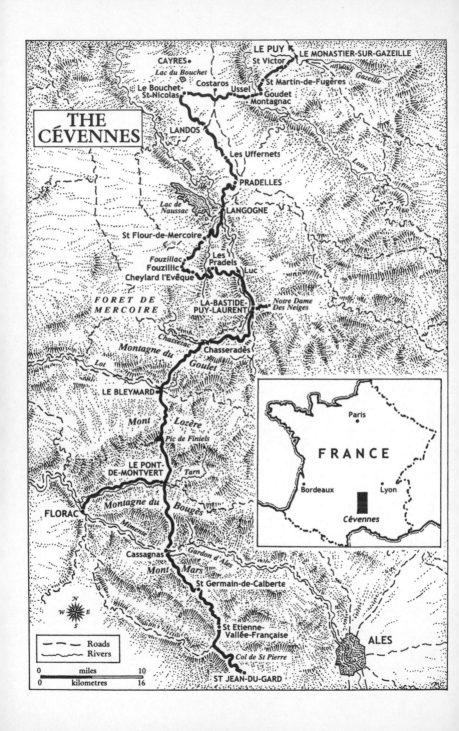

I STOOD IN the Place de la Poste of Le Monastier in southern France, staring at three hundred pounds of wet, steaming equine flesh with which I was now about to traverse some of the highest, wildest and remotest regions of the country, taking in four *départements* and scaling peaks of over five thousand feet, as well as sleeping when I had to *à la belle étoile*, a euphonious French euphemism for roughing it in the cold night air. Or in the pouring rain. It was late in the year, 22 September, and just before nine o'clock in the morning, with the rain bouncing off an inscribed plinth, which told me that Monsieur Robert Louis Stevenson had set off from this exact spot over a century ago, also with a donkey. He was twenty-seven at the time. I was forty-nine. And I wondered for a moment what madness had brought me here.

I knew the answer well enough. It was madness of a sort, virtual nervous breakdown, brought on by the sudden death of my wife the previous summer. As I watched the raindrops ploughing down the plinth, wetting the lettering of my hero's name, it was impossible not to live it all over again, like a drowning man, in those few minutes before I set off into the unknown. The sheer scale of the downpour encouraged the impression of seeing it all flash past, under a whelming tide.

The ditches were daubed with poppies at that time, the summer of '93, when we motored up from Edinburgh to catch the ferry to Orkney to visit a writer friend, George Mackay Brown. 'Motored' is another euphemism. We were late and the clapped-out old Cortina was coming apart. The exhaust fell off five miles out of Thurso. I tied it to the towbar with one of my wife's stockings and drove like the chariots of Jehu to the point where Scotland ran out of mainland and the Pentland Firth took over, white

3

with storms and treacherous with webs of tide. We limped on to the *Ola* making a racket like a tank in travail. Hard lumps of sea slammed us from all sides throughout the crossing. The ancient outsize tub took the battering with ironclad inanimation: the passengers proved less resilient and many threw up. By the time we reached Orkney Patricia was feeling unwell, but there was no reason to suppose that she was other than another victim of one of the most vicious stretches of water in the world. When we reached dry land she went straight to bed.

We were staying at Stenigar, the old boat-house studio of the artist Stanley Cursiter, friend of Peploe, and I was writing a novel, *Last Lesson of the Afternoon*, by its wide windows. Bullets of rain were rattling on the glass, the white fire of the surf glittering through the panes, between the sea-bleached houses, the soundless traffic of sails, the scribbling gulls. It was an easy place to scribble in, undistracted among the sleeping whales of the islands. The children played, Patricia rested in bed, I wrote on and on, unaware that another drama was being written, one that would dwarf my imagined masterpiece and deliver it back to the desk drawer, where it would wait its turn, await the passing of undreamed-of events. As a sad-eyed doctor said to me not three months later, 'The biology of this was probably written from day one.' Day one of what? Of time, possibly, though time is a tyrant whose jurisdiction runs out in Orkney. I had no notion of it as I headed up to the Braes Hotel with Mackay Brown to discuss the possibility of writing a critical biography of the prolific Orcadian. We drank beers and looked out over the roofs of Stromness to Scapa Flow, a bar of silver under the moon, precisely as depicted in one of George's poems. This, I thought, was an idyllic place for a writer. But the Orkney Eden, like all paradises, was already lost. It had a snake in it. Cancer.

4

The shadow of it, the sinister shark's fin, had never even crossed my mind till now. Not until our beautiful hostess, Shelagh Thomas, took me by both hands one evening after Patricia had yet again gone early and alone to bed. She gripped me hard and looked fiercely into my face. 'Something is wrong with your wife, my friend,' she said. 'This is not the Patricia I knew when you first came here.'

That had been nearly twelve years before, 1981. Catriona was three and Jonathan destined to be conceived on Orkney, as it turned out. Not as it just happened, though. It was a deliberate ritual. The wished-for pregnancy had failed to arrive in Edinburgh and Patricia had decided to come along with me on my next Orkney odyssey to see what the magical peace and silence of these islands might devise. At sunset we went to the Ring of Brodgar, the Temple of the Sun, and with Catriona between us, all three of us holding hands, we walked round with the sun and touched in turn each one of the circle of Standing Stones at Stenness. As we completed the circle she said to me with complete conviction, 'Tonight will be the night – you will impregnate me and it will be a boy.' Later we made love and I heard music streaming through the firmament. *For unto us a child is born, for unto us a son is given.* Both Handel and Patricia proved prophetic. By the time we came back to Edinburgh she was already carrying Jonathan.

All this came back to me while Shelagh was speaking. She saw the remembering look in my eyes and took my face between her hands. 'Listen to me,' she said. 'You have to do something about this at once. You have to take her to a doctor. You have to act *now*. Otherwise you will lose her, Chris. *You will lose her.*'

Fear, the black shark's fin, finally surfaced. And from that point on it was a dorsal-torn sea. On which I did lose her, just as Shelagh predicted. She refused to see a doctor in Stromness and we packed up and left Orkney early. The school holidays had barely begun.

All through the drive back to Edinburgh she was bleeding from the nose and gums and I knew then that the winter cough that had never calmed down, the spring tiredness that the Easter holidays had failed to heal, were symptoms of a darker workmanship happening craftily, inscrutably, somewhere in her body. I had no idea where. Little did I dream that she herself had known for months. Even so I searched for possible benign causes, my mind racing faster than the car, even with its gleaming new exhaust. I came hurtling down from Scrabster faster than I'd gone up. This was no mere ferry we were hurrying to catch. I thought of Charon, the grim ferryman of the Greek underworld, rower of the boat none of us wants to take. Styx or Jordan, the religion doesn't matter, we don't want to go there, and all the asphodel or milk and honey on the other side won't entice us. Not if we have a choice.

Choice? Sometimes you *can* choose your death, deliberately or unconsciously. But in most cases the choice is made for you. Cancer chooses *you*, it's a lottery – and it could be you, Wednesday, Saturday, any night of the week. Today was a Saturday, the last day of July. Exactly two months later we put her into a cold hole in the ground.

I was trying hard to expel images of cold holes in the ground but the shark's fin was now crossing and recrossing the bay of imagination. Even so, I told myself, there were all sorts of other probable reasons as to what was causing this. It had been a long hard year. Teaching Biology (for her) and English (for me) was the easy part. Or had been. But now the arteries of education were clogged up with excrement. There seemed to be a Miss Ambition and a

Lady Macbeth in every department, hard-jawed, hard-nosed hard sellers of themselves, products of the managerial revolution that had bureaucratized us and turned education into a service industry. I was busy writing a novel about it and exorcizing the angry ghost of the old educational system from my own. But Patricia had no personal escape mechanism and her disgust with it all had been building up. That could be part of it. Stress. She would need a good long holiday to relax and recover.

But that was the other problem. Even in her married life she had never been allowed to go on any holiday unaccompanied, even to our weekend sea-cottage in Fife. A special item of psychological luggage always had to be brought along – and that was guilt. An only child whose father had been killed in naval action during the war, she had suffered all her life from the demands of the narrow-nosed, whining widow whose special weapon from an armoury of blackmailing strategies was to fall ill during every holiday we ever had. This holiday had been no exception. Very probably the emotional strain was now telling on my wife as she stood torn between the need for freedom and the dragon in the doorway, with tongue of fire. Yes, that was it, without a doubt. A false alarm.

Then there was her time of life. Her periods had become erratic and the moon and the menopause might be in mad conjunction for all I knew. What I did know was that for many months she had lost all interest in sex. Ours was a marriage in which sex had quite simply got better and better until we'd reached the point where we both thought we'd explode. Then, quite suddenly, love-making had become constrained on her part, before ceasing altogether. A useless ignorant male, copping out, I had assumed it had something to do with hormones and that the difficulties would eventually pass. By the time we reached Edinburgh I had convinced myself that she'd be much better in the morning.

That conviction evaporated when I had to help her get to bed. She couldn't make the stairs. Unable to ascend on foot, even by clutching hold of the banisters, she was reduced to sitting down and hoisting herself up one step at a time. She refused to let me carry her. But when we reached the landing she had no choice in the matter. There wasn't a breath left in her body. The obvious thing to do was to ring for an ambulance, but once in bed she begged me to let her see the night out. Perhaps there would be an improvement in the morning after a night in our own bed. It's amazing what a breath of home can do.

Not too amazing. Morning brought blood – more nose-bleeds, mouth-ulcers, severe depression, intense panic. And absolute physical helplessness. Yet, following the logic of denial, secrecy and fear, she still refused point-blank to see a doctor and vowed she would never forgive me if I lifted the phone. I looked out of the bedroom window. It was the first day of August, and Arthur's Seat, Edinburgh's Acropolis, was ablaze with whinflowers, honey spilling from the extinct lion's side. Some words from the Bible flashed out afresh with total irrelevance, a form of mental displacement activity: *Out of the strong came forth sweetness, out of the eater came forth meat.* Was it cancer that was eating my wife? I pulled on my running gear, pounded to the top of the hill and in desperation howled aloud for help: to God, to Jesus, to my mother in eternity, to St Magnus in Orkney, to St Monan of the seagulls, over the blue firth to Fife, to the sea-girt fishing village home of my childhood. I am not a praying man, not formally. I believe that a good day's work is a prayer. And so is a kind action. Or even a soft word. Or a gentle thought. But with all of Edinburgh beneath my feet and the kingdoms of the world implicitly on offer, I gave way to the absurd temptation and asked for intervention. That's not asking for much, for Christ's sake! For my children's sake, God help them! The Bible's full of miracles, even if they're much thinner on the ground in these shallow times of ours. Still, let's have one for the road, I beg and beseech you! Let me come home and find my wife cured. Then I'll know for sure that you exist, and the remainder of my days will run a different course entirely, I promise!

An evil and perverse generation seeketh after a sign. I could almost hear the answer coming out of the clouds. It was waiting for me in any case when I reached home. She was lying on the floor, racked by pains in the joints and spitting blood on the carpet. She had wrenched the telephone out of its socket. Still wearing my running gear I raced the half mile to the surgery, burst into Reception and demanded to see the family doctor. I was advised, quite correctly, that I would be required to make an appointment, in common with the rest of the world. I began to lose control. But this is an emergency! An emergency? In which case you dial 999. They didn't understand. How could they? I didn't understand myself and in desperation I broke down in front of a line of patients. At which point Dr Fiona MacLaren emerged and swept me into her office and with strong arms and hands pressed me into a seat. It all came pouring out.

'And why won't she see me, do you think?'

'Because, doctor, she thinks she's dying.'

Dr MacLaren leaned forward and put the next question to me with extraordinary force.

'Do *you* think she is dying, Mr Rush?'

It was the first point at which I had been forced to

confront the possibility rationally and it had the sudden effect of momentarily calming me down.

'Yes, doctor, ' I heard myself answering, 'I believe she is dying.'

She wasted no time. I went on ahead of her and had to break into the bedroom. Patricia had read my movements and had locked herself in. So she knew what was coming when the doorbell rang. All the same she burst into tears when Dr MacLaren's face appeared round the splintered door.

'I've been so stupid, doctor, so utterly bloody stupid!'

'You haven't been stupid at all, you've been ill. And you're ill now, I can see that even before I examine you.'

The look of a certain faraway fear returned to my wife's eyes. Faraway but coming closer.

'I don't want you to examine me.'

Fiona MacLaren sat down on the edge of the bed and took one of the trembling hands in both of hers. She seemed to fill the room with that palpable sense of security, direction and control that is induced by the arrival of the police or fire brigade in time of crisis. To me she was a saint with a sword in hand, ready to take charge and fight off the hobgoblins of evil and despair.

'Why?' she smiled. 'Why won't you let me examine you?'

She looked as if she knew the answer. I knew that I didn't and I felt my bowels turn to ice when I heard my wife's next words, spoken very quietly.

'Because you don't have to examine me. I can tell you right now exactly what you'll find.'

The doctor nodded.

'Which breast is it?'

My wife bowed her head and the tears rained down on to the duvet cover, splashing the patterned blue flowers. I remember thinking how ridiculous, for some reason, they seemed, those particular flowers, and just for a second I got it whole, sensed the solving emptiness that lies just underneath our lives, under everything we ever do. I was preparing to teach the poetry of Philip Larkin next term and words to that effect came to the rescue: more mental displacement. And not for the last time. I had to struggle hard to break free from the relief of those verbal images and return to the scene in the bedroom.

'Which one is it?'

'The left one.'

'How long have you known?'

'Months.'

The doctor saw the look on my face and put up a hand for silence. I should stay out of this part of it, obviously. This was one woman talking to another.

'How many months?'

How many? She'd lost count. When the first suspicion of a lump had appeared she'd left normal time behind and had slipped into a dimension governed by denial, not by months and minutes. Three months then? suggested the doctor. Six?

Six, yes, easily. Maybe more. Maybe even nine.

It all came out. She could give the doctor no notion of the external symptoms – she herself had no idea of how the breast actually looked. From the moment she'd felt the lump she had stopped looking at herself. She had bathed and showered, dressed and undressed with her eyes shut, staying away from mirrors. 'I felt like the bride of Dracula,' she said later.

'And that's why I wouldn't let you touch me properly,' she said, turning to me, 'not because I'd stopped loving you. You know I always will.'

My tongue dried up in my mouth. I couldn't find the

11

words anyway. The doctor was in charge.

'If you won't let me examine you, at least let me take some blood from you. We need tests urgently.'

'There's no point in blood tests either – I think we all know what the results are going to be, doctor.'

Dr MacLaren smiled again.

'And what do you think the results are going to tell us? Go on, say it.'

And she said the word for the first time. That hateful word.

Cancer.

Obscene as cancer, a poet once famously wrote. Bitter as the cud of vile incurable sores on innocent tongues. There I was, at it again, my head starting to drift, legs kicking out to find words under my feet.

'Well then, if it is cancer,' I heard the doctor saying, 'we'll have to see what we're going to do about it, won't we?'

A sad shake of the head.

'There's nothing to be done about it.'

'Now you *are* being silly.'

Dr MacLaren moved into brisk mode, opening her medical bag and taking out syringes.

'You're looking at a woman who *had* breast cancer,' she said, 'and I'm looking at you knowing that if you lie here like this much longer you're liable to suffer a massive haemorrhage with the state your blood is in. Then you'll be carted out of here like a sack of potatoes in a very undignified fashion, whether you want it or not. Wouldn't you rather go gracefully to hospital, if you have to?'

Between us we managed to extract blood from her – she hadn't really the strength to resist – and Dr MacLaren sped off to the Royal Infirmary. The interim was awful. I paced up and down inside a private torture chamber, waiting for her to return with the results. The doorbell rang in the middle of the afternoon. I knew at once from her face that things were bad.

They were worse than bad. I think I knew then that they were fatal.

'There's only one way to play this and that's absolutely straight,' she said.

And she marched up to the bedroom and informed my wife of the results of the tests.

'Your blood is in a shocking condition. The platelet count is dangerously low. You need a transfusion at once. Let's get you ready for hospital. An ambulance will come round and collect you.'

An ambulance. Oh God, no! She had the almost pathological fear of ambulances articulated so exquisitely by Larkin in that grim unwavering poem. Closed like confessionals, they are the bringers of death, like the priest and the doctor, running over the fields. None of the sanguinary glamour of *Casualty* on Saturday night television, they are only one step away from the hearse, bitter-sweet chariots of hellfire, and they are driven by angels – not of mercy but of death. No, she would crawl to hospital rather than be taken by ambulance but at least she agreed to go by car. The doctor left and we began the journey to the bathroom so that she could wash before being admitted to the infirmary. We locked the door and she stood before the mirror. And said that the moment had now come when she could confront the truth.

'We'll look at it together, shall we?'

She spoke in a whisper. Not because she was speaking low. A hoarse croak in the throat was all that was left of her voice.

I stood beside her and slipped off her nightdress. How often we'd performed this exciting action as a prelude to passion. *Your gowne's going off such beauteous state reveals . . .*

Now it was a grim business. We both felt it, as if the nightdress were a shroud, as if we were unwrapping the bandages from something out of Egypt. She kept her eyes tight shut as I slid her arms through the sleeves and looked on my wife's nakedness for the first time in many months. I too had lost count.

I was standing behind her and stared straight over her shoulder at what the mirror had to tell us.

Mirror, mirror, on the wall . . .

She listened to my silence and still with her eyes shut asked:

'Is it bad?'

I had no answer.

She opened her eyes and looked straight into the glass. She gasped at what she saw. Her face had been slightly flushed from the temperature the doctor said she was running. Now a white wave seemed to pass through it – she lost all colour in that single moment. Her last strength was also drained from her and her legs buckled under her and she fell to the floor. I managed to catch her and prevent her from hitting her head on the basin. We knelt together, facing one another, the breast between us, an alien thing that seemed to have nothing to do with the still perfect and alluring specimen on the other side. The diseased breast was purple and blighted and black, like a bruised and ruined fruit that had festered for months in a beautiful but forgotten bowl. It was swollen and lumpy, and the cancerous growth glared from its surface as if it were ready to erupt and spew out its mortuary juice into our horribly altered lives. Yet the right breast, immaculate, still hung like a lovely pregnant teardrop, mourning its companion.

We looked at each other as if across a vast distance.

'You've lost me, my love,' was all she could say, 'you've lost me.'

And she kept repeating it.

We got her into her clothes, and before inching our way downstairs she looked at me and said she was sorry. I stared. Sorry? What on earth did she mean? I asked. You know what I mean. I'm going to die. No matter what they say, no matter what hopes they hold out, that's what's going to happen in the end. And it will be soon. You know it and so do I. And it's my fault. It's not just my breast that's destroyed, it's this whole family. Through my stupidity and fear. You can see it coming, can't you? You've all lost me, all of you. And I've lost you.

She was breathless and still white with shock and started tearing off her clothes, saying there was now no point in going to hospital. A degree in medicine was hardly necessary to see that this could go only one way. All she wanted was to be allowed to stay at home and die quietly. But I forced her to dress again, pulling back on clothes that she was by this time too weak to take off. Then I practically dragged her into the car, people staring at us in the street, and raced for the infirmary, my hands trembling on the wheel. My chest was pounding with panic, my skull bursting and I began to imagine aneurysms, haemorrhages, heart attacks. Christ Almighty, the kids will be orphaned! Where to bury us? Who to look after them? The people passing in the streets suddenly seemed like blessed beings from normality, from the impeccably distanced dimension of the everyday. That man looking at the newspaper he'd just bought, that girl student clutching her books, that spry old lady with the white fluffy head, come straight from the hairdresser's, one of God's dandelion clocks. The surly bus drivers, the mean-faced traffic wardens. How beautiful they all looked now, now that we were no longer one of them, no longer part of their world but on our way to some other world, what and where exactly we weren't sure but the signs were bad. No brave new world, then, that much was certain. People en route to execution saw their last earthly sights with enhanced perception as scenes of indescribable beauty, sharply realized, things they had always taken for granted. The first frost on cabbages, on the fields, on rooftops. Raindrops falling. The world never seemed sweeter than from the tumbrils. Even that swag-bellied drunk was a soul in bliss, a creation of Michelangelo. That's how it goes.

And so we came to the Royal Infirmary, where she was received with enormous care, compassion and understanding. And patience and skill. She allowed the doctors to examine her and we learned the worst: advanced carcinoma with liver malfunction, blood disorder, the disease in the lymph and bone marrow, and secondaries God knows where. No hope of cure, one of the doctors assured me. Only of a remission that might grant us some last weeks together, maybe even months. My God, less than a month ago we'd just gone on holiday. Now I found myself suddenly shopping for female things, floundering in the Saturday stream of humanity that surges through Princes Street, looking for new knickers and nightdresses among loud noons of ladies, all of them hellishly healthy. All I could see was the wild white face I'd left in the infirmary. Staring at me from above that cancer-bitten breast.

Then I returned, bearing my Marks & Spencer carrier bags and my headful of Larkin, to The Building: that neutral ground on which we humans all get caught at some point or other, our homes and names and loved ones suddenly in abeyance while we sit and wait to make our confession: that something has gone wrong. And that it must be error of a serious sort, seeing how many floors and files are needed to fix it, how many staff, how much money and equipment. It's frightening. And beyond it all – the wish to be alone.

But I step inside, trying to walk naturally, trying to look composed – and pass someone weeping on the stairs, hurrying from a room where a life has flickered out. The doctors are with Patricia, I am told, examining her again, and can I come back in half an hour? I wander about, as one does, and end up in Out-Patients. Even the smell that hangs in the hall is frightening, hitting you as soon as you enter: the mingling of mince and antisepsis, death-tainted food, and those weak wasteful propitiatory flowers. And there's something else, something that animals would sense – the scent of fear. Fear itself is frightening. In spite of the queues, sitting and shifting, the paperbacks on sale, the vending-machines, telephones and uniforms, in spite of all that it's not the smell of an airport lounge, where you can almost scent the lions, the long white beaches, the odour of excitement and expectation, arrivals and departures, meetings. People are thinking instead of the longer journey – the one that doesn't end in beaches and bars but in something far beyond these bewilderingly many doors, leading at last to a room where all choice ends, beyond the reach of any hand from the ranks of the healthy, any worldly touch – closer to the white congregations. You know you are going to die. Not yet, of course. And not here necessarily. But in the end certainly – and somewhere like this.

And there's another thing. As you sit or stroll there, participating in the big silence, the enormous hush of nerves on edge, you look round and notice something about the general appearance of this reluctant and somewhat furtive fellowship. Some are young, quite a few are old, but most are of that vague age that adds to their anonymity, and it strikes you that quite probably this is how you yourself must look to them. You're still wearing

17

that battered blouson leather jacket you bought in the sixties when you were a student, and maybe you've come in Levi's and desert boots – but that fools no one, least of all you. Soon it will be your turn to sit in the queue, to be conscripted into that anxious army of out-patients. Sooner than you think you may be an *in*-patient. And by the time you are seen by the cardiologist, the cancer specialist, the skin-slitting surgeon, all that desperate sartorial kiddology will be bundled up and crushed into some narrow locker, and you'll be standing like a medieval martyr, bound for the block in a white gown, deliberately oversized to make you stumble and look and feel ridiculous as you go up the final steps. Under that gown skulks your even more absurd carcass, entering its Prufrock stage. Your hair is a grey ebb-tide, your teeth a lead-mine, your belly a sack of sand – not much left in the hour-glass either. You have to peer outward over a sheer drop of paunch to check that you are still a man. Your chest is going bumpy, your thighs flabby, while all around your imprisoned self the birthday suit that God gave you crumples and coarsens in the sand-laden wind of time, increasingly refuses to respond to exercise, drinklessness, diet. Once that obedient daily dress that followed the brash changing fashions, now it lets you down by refusing to fit, turns instead into the muddy vesture of decay that grossly closes in. Prepares for its parchment days. And burning. In the whitening globe of your head the voices whisper to you – theatrical home-truths about the frail house of flesh you now inhabit. You're a box of worm-seed, a little crudded milk, fantastical puff-paste. What are you but a corpse waiting to be washed? Such are the thoughts that people the corridors, those awful wards. Feeling grotesque between my Marks & Spencer bags, dangling from either arm, I check my watch, find that an hour has passed, and make my way back through the maze, passing the open doors, the mad white hairs spread out on pillows, the staring eyes, the gaping jaws, the stretched necks, the vacancy, the absence of smiles. Laughter is for the young. I get hopelessly lost and by the time I find my wife's room she is surrounded again by a circle of white coats.

This is the point at which the hand of Miss Havisham touches all the clocks and we enter an eternal present from which there is no escape. The hand of Auden will come later, silencing the pianos, putting out the stars, dismantling the sun. Soon enough, the doctors say. They take over from clock time with their measured pronouncements, their slow-drip certainties, their opaque caution, while the nurses flit past us at a faster pace, all trimness and tenderness and teeth, dispensing the illusions of hope but emptied of all anxiety, as has to be their way. A matter of training. I long to join them in the unclouded heaven they seem to inhabit, angels of attention, of keen professional concern. The objective attention rubs off, helps us to stand on the edges of our own lives, inhabiting an area outside active involvement. We become spectators, split persons, looking in on the arena of anguish where our parts seem to be played by actors, doubling for ourselves. Distance keeps us sane. We discuss what is happening but it's as if we were talking about some other person, not the real Patricia. She is some kind of absent friend.

So I look hard at her, devour her, the woman I have obviously failed to study closely enough all these ignorant months. There is a frantic need to get behind the veils that kept me from the truth, to break the sacred seals of self-deception. It wasn't all concealment on her part. I was too wrapped up in my writing, inhabiting that solitary world all authors know, where you don't see what's in front of you, looking instead right through the solid surfaces

19

of life, seeing only the world you are creating, while all around you the real world, the one you have left behind, is being undermined. Something is rotten in the state of Denmark and you don't know it.

Searching for someone to blame I confront my guilty self at last. We all live selfishly, artists especially. Gradually the veils are stripped away, the seals undone. I recall all sorts of things now – the meals she missed, saying she'd eaten earlier, the television programmes she'd stopped watching, stopped laughing at. Her sudden whim to adopt two kittens for the kids. ('It will be something for them to transfer their affections to if anything ever happens to us.') I remember her fear of death. She had a biologist's wonder at the beauty of the human body but a corresponding horror of its vulnerability and the scope for error, illness, age – and the only end of age. It was not so much death that frightened her as the business of dying. She hated the idea of her body becoming an object to be invaded by strangers and she had never been in hospital except when the kids were born. This is what happens to you, I told myself, when your mother sleeps with you until you are sixteen – a mother who never discussed the workings of the body to her fatherless child, never opened up on sex. Maybe this was the seventh seal.

Or was it the death of my father? He had developed throat cancer a few years earlier, was heavily operated on, the voice box removed, and spent a year and a half of silent hell before dying, a miserable memory of the man he'd been. 'If it ever happens to me,' she'd said, 'I'd never go through all that pointless suffering. I'd rather die quickly – let the cancer do what it has to do.' How could I have forgotten this? He'd died just over three years ago, the wisp that was left of him. Thirty months later her cancer had probably started. Yes, this was the seventh seal.

20

I come back from my thoughts to look at her again. She is a thing of fragile beauty, caught at the centre of a web of tubes and wires, a new medical universe, a point of convergence for the monitorings of space-age machines, the probes of house doctors, the elliptical orbits of consultants, coming like slow comets by the blue moon, objects of wonder and dread. And for a time I hide behind their immaculate shield of science. She is now neither wife nor mother but a case, a set of statistics in which I keep up a fierce quotidian interest, fanatically devoted to the daily bulletins of temperature, platelets, haemoglobin counts, the units of blood, the mils of chemotherapy administered, the degree of patient response. It feels safer this way. And somewhere in the middle of all this I try to focus on the fierce frail identity of the woman I love, the woman who is slipping away daily on a dark tide of disease. A tide that ebbs inexorably towards death. She has been stopped at death's door, only to be lodged in the vestibule, the unreal ante-room where she waits to be admitted. It's a matter of time. Most things may never happen, but this one will, we know it for a certainty. We have been told to expect the worst and we do. Hope keeps on trying, though, to break through and contradict the facts, to prove the doctors wrong and make medical science blind. Hope springs infernal. Why won't the bastard die? Why won't it leave us in peace? Hope is not sweet, it is cruel. A thing of torment, an instrument of torture. Better be with the dead . . .

Than on the torture of the mind to lie in restless ecstasy.

The quotation drifts through my mind like a stray bird from the golden world of teaching Shakespeare, reminding me that the holidays are now draining away and that I am going to have to contact colleagues, the school authorities, and advise them that the Biology Department will be one member of staff short at the start of the new term and will be needing a temporary teacher. Even as I frame the news in my brain I tell myself to leave off pretending and get the thing right. It will be no temporary appointment, however much the school will make the kind, comforting, protesting noises. I might as well be clear about this with them. My wife will not be returning to work. Not ever.

For me the return to work is a kind of relief. For the children too, trapped until now in a holiday gone hellishly wrong. The hardest task of all is to tell them that their mother is terminally ill.

I choose my moment, gliding like a ghost downstairs and into the front room, where Catriona sits in the sunlight, sketching – a preparation for painting roses. She is at that lovely age where girls start to become their mothers' sisters and friends, wearing their clothes, sharing their confidences. But she and her mother are not going to have the time to explore the new relationship. I have come to nip that precious flower in the bud. I tell her and her face crumples. *O, Rose! thou art sick.* The flowers in the vase seem to turn away from her, tactfully, like tender, patient minds. They know all about the invisible worm that flies in the night, in the howling storm, destroying young lives with their dark secrets, corrupting the beds of crimson joy. I put my arms around her, watch the tears falling from her bowed face, blotting the pad. Two rose petals lie where they have fallen, at the ginger-jar's blue edge. Emblems of a stilled life. Now I know what Blake's poem is all about. It's about cancer, what else? Everything is.

Jonathan's turn next. He is watching us through the window, from the driveway, where he is kicking a football into the garage doors, savagely, relentlessly. He knows what's coming. He can see his sister's head buried in my chest, soaking my shirt, can see me stroking her long, distressed hair, mouthing the words. I go out to him and break the news. Or rather I give voice to the worst of thoughts, bring them out into the open. The ball smashes into the door, rebounds, and is driven back again, pulverizing the blistered paintwork. The pitiless assault is his only response, trapped as he is inside his eleven years. All he can do now is lash out. The tears will come privately, the mintage of grief.

Meanwhile it's done. Their world falls apart. The brutal stupidity and sheer irrelevance of this sudden intrusion into the household is something far beyond their imaginings, their comprehension. They have absolutely no notion of how to handle it. Inwardly the suffering starts. I am left feeling that somehow I have failed them on a massive scale. I ought to have taken better care of her, after all. I ought to have foreseen and forestalled this catastrophe. It's what fathers are for. It's what partners do. We should be careful of each other, we should be kind. While there is time. And I let too much time go by, let their mother down, seriously, irrevocably. I can feel their sense of betrayal, their huge anger, their suffocating grief. So in this sense the start of school is an escape from the torment.

But not for long. Soon the pressures begin to build up, the rounds of shopping, cooking, washing, ironing, phone calls, letters, activities, assignments – and the endless meetings and mounds of correction. Beneath it all, desire of oblivion runs. Yet even this is sweetness itself compared with the hardest horror of all, dealing with the dreadful mother-in-law, the Grim Granny, now deep in her seventies and still bitterly alive, still complaining and still demanding. For decades she has been dying (on a diet of gin and neat brandy and sixty cigarettes a day) but now her daughter has upstaged her with cancer and she is no longer the centre of attention. Like a miracle in reverse she loses the power of her legs and I am suddenly needed to see to her shopping and to transport her to hospital. She lives in a mouldering Georgian barn down in Portobello on the very edge of Edinburgh, where the sea air bites at her doorstep and she bites back with ill-fitting false teeth and a throatful of venom. *You're a heartless bugger and you care nothing for me!* I take the telephone off the hook during the night only to hear myself start to laugh in my sleep, a mad giggle coming up from the gut. Breakdown on the way? Hold hard there, Rush, you know you can see it through. This is only the beginning. There's a long, long trail a-winding, mate, just you wait and see.

Waiting is what we do.
We all know what we are waiting for.

A miracle? No, not that. There was the brief reprieve, only apparent, while the blood transfusions did their work and made her smile and put lipstick on for our daughter's sixteenth birthday. But it was the usual cruel rally, setting up false hopes that had no basis in any medical expectation. There was no other kind of expectation. This was a cancer matter. Arrangements were made to transfer her to the Western General's breast cancer clinic.

In the Western General there began a bout of more specialized treatment, 'to knock the cancer cells on the head' as one doctor put it, making it sound simple and crudely effective, like going after them with a rolling pin. Down wantons, down! But already she was a stage frailer, her eyes unnaturally bright, the mind occasionally abstracted, the voice vague. I felt a friend slipping away from me, sensed the start of a spiritual surrender to the forces that were fighting for possession of her body. And soul. Her will was almost moribund. Only that steady shining of the eyes, where once there had been a sparkle. God, I thought, I don't want her eyes to shine like that. I have seen this light before. It's a candle in the dark, the light of cancer, burning with the fatal lassitude of those who have let go. I don't want her to let go. I don't want her to be turned into an object. Far from the exchange of love to lie unreachable inside a room. Yes, I'm actually teaching Larkin through all of this, now that I'm back at school; and the suffering voice of the poet keeps me company, keeps me sane. What can be said except that suffering is exact?

Nature used to be the healer, the educator. Not any more. Putting out the bins, I glance up at my old allies, the stars, and suddenly see what Hamlet saw: a foul and pestilent congregation of vapours. The friendly faces have gone, leaving a skyful of sterile dust, like the quintessence of human dust, the epitome of life. So much for the majestical roof fretted with golden fire. A bin-liner bursts, and ashes and eggshells spill all over my shoe and into the road. How bloody ironical! An eggshell – the most worthless object Hamlet could think of. Eggshells and ashes. The dustman cometh. Will this help me teach the thing tomorrow? I go back inside and plunge into my books, plundering the poetry section like a drunken bee. This used to be a matter of self-conscious posing. But now it's for real and I'm desperate, with nowhere to turn. So poetry has to be the healer now. Seeing as there is no God.

I find an entry in my poetry notebook which tells me that if the days of our years are threescore and ten, then they may be seen for convenience's sake as a simple week, each of its seven days corresponding to a decade, beginning with Sunday and ending on Saturday. The Bible according to Larkin, the poet of death. And I reflect that school-teaching is a double-edged sword, because if you teach for thirty or forty years, all your youngsters are permanently at Monday, like leaves returning to the trees, while you plod on through the week. A middle-aged schoolteacher, I know that it's now tea-time on Thursday and that I die the day after tomorrow. A fine paradigm to focus the mind on futility. But my wife won't even reach the weekend. She dies today. Maybe even literally.

But she goes up and down like a boat in a storm. A small boat. A brutal storm. One that involves the mental torture of knowing you are going to be wrecked but not knowing when the moment will come, only that it is inevitable. This is one of the faces of cruelty, I tell my pupils, when lecturing on *Macbeth* with my mind elsewhere. This is how they torture the sea-captain. *Weary seven-nights nine times nine, shall he dwindle, peak and pine.*

And the dwindling goes on, inexorably. Internal bleeding, sickness, depression, loss of appetite, more tests. The results are death sentences handed down from on high on the breaths of the big chiefs, the white-coated ones. They are the masters now. We are in their hands. And we go home through the twilight, the kids and I, with the lamps coming on. As soon as we get through the front door the phone shrieks at us. The Grim Granny is close to starvation, cigarettes and brandy top of the list, and she needs me down there now. Not in the middle of next bloody week! While I am dealing with this the doorbell rings raucously. Christ, why are people so kind? Well, you said it, Rush: for Christ's sake, quite probably for Christ's sake, though it's hard to hold on to that medieval notion.

Easier to hold on to tomorrow's realities. Sodden rugby kit to be unmuddied and washed, missing PE kit to be located, sewing materials required for a Home Economics class, lunchpacks to be made up, last night's dishes to be washed. Something has to give. The plates don't get washed. They lie in their cold grime in the sink and we pile more on top. The dishwasher has broken down, of course. The centre cannot hold. This is clearly the time when things fall apart. I go to bed in a coiled spring, which sleep fails to loosen because of the wheel of dreams on which I'm broken nightly. *O, full of scorpions is my mind, dear wife!* Still teaching Shakespeare in my sleep.

Sleep. I long for it. True sleep. Sleep that knits up the ravelled sleeve of care, the death of each day's life, sore labour's bath, balm of hurt minds. Yes, I understand Macbeth better than ever now, especially as I dread sleep too, the nightly descent under the sea, where you lie floundering in slow motion, a prey to all the monsters of the deep unconscious mind. All night it goes on, broken only by more mad giggles coming up from the gut. There is the feeling of sheer physical exhaustion, the certain knowledge that you can't see it through after all; that not only is she going to die soon but that this nightmare is going to tighten its clutch and will go on for years and years, for the rest of your life. Then you curse yourself for this wallowing in wimpishness. Get up, you weak-kneed bleeder – you realize that you have spoken aloud, that the talking to yourself has started, but you carry on. Go on, get up, and take the fucking punishment, there's a lot more to come, best keep in training then, the big fight is still ahead.

And you stagger up, edge your way downstairs and lay out the lunch boxes, emptying the crusts and crushed crisps from yesterday, the sweaty uneaten apples, the untouched Mars Bars. The kids have lost their appetites too, poor little buggers. Nobody in this family of four is eating any more. An injection of coffee produces something vaguely resembling human motion. You take it back upstairs to bed and drink it ever so slowly, grudging every sip that diminishes the steaming circle, because you know that this is the best part of the day, the bubble-world of bed before the real day starts – free from the affliction of dreams. As you drink, you watch the clouds, stroked by Homer's rosy-fingered dawn, turn pink, and the windows across the back gardens brighten and catch fire, burn like autumn leaves. *Aubade*.

'What is an *aubade*, boy?'

'It's a hymn to morning, sir. A lyric sung by lovers, parting at dawn.'

'Very knowledgeable. You've been well taught. Who taught you last year?'

'You did, sir.' (As if I didn't know.)

'Really? Then can you tell me the difference between the *aubade* and the *alba*?

'Yes, sir. The *aubade* is joyful, whereas the *alba* is a lament, originating in Provence but inspired by Ovid. It comes from the Provençal word for dawn, and the irony is that dawn is breaking but that people who love each other have to say goodbye.'

'Indeed. You've learned well. They have to say goodbye. In spite of the dawn of another day, they have to say goodbye.'

So the days pass like funerals, jump-started by the four a.m. coffees, when I watch from bed the city windows burst into sudden flame, the unbearable dawns bleed through, like roses blossoming, and sense that unbeatable daily destiny start up in the streets, the one that's out to get you. Ah, yes, you did wake at four to soundless dark, watched the wardrobe materialize like a coffin and went through the whole thing again: the time torn off unused, the sure extinction that we travel to and shall be lost in always. Not to be here, not to be anywhere. And soon. Unresting death a whole day nearer now. But now it's nearly seven, you're under control, just, and the kids have to be nagged into getting up to face it all, while those dark towns heap up on the horizon, none of them concerned with us or for us, and all the uncaring intricate rented world begins to rouse. Is there a moment of sanity in it? Only in my diary, my paper priest, my white confessional. I tell it everything, like an adolescent whispering into the mirror. I tell it the good news, that she is being allowed home now. Of course we know it's a lie of sorts. We know it's only to die.

Still, that's how September started. A clear cold dawn, breathless blue silence, the sharp still sound of the dead seasons filling our ears – and mum coming home in the afternoon. We drove down to the sea first, so that she could see over the firth to Fife, where the unharvested yellow rape-fields winked blindingly at us, like squares from a Van Gogh canvas, borrowed from Arles for the day: vibrant against the impossible powder-blue of the sea, sweet and meaningless and not to come again, never such innocence. But it wasn't just for the day. The month was merciless in its unfolding autumnal beauty, a classic catalogue of designer days, on display. Patricia saw it all from the car window on that particular day and shook her head and cried. She knew she would never be in Fife again, at the cottage, at the seaside, even in the open air. This was the homecoming nobody wanted. Not like this.

The school tells me I should give up work now to be with her, and so I should. But that would be to bring out into the open the admission, that there is no hope, and that we are simply seeing out the end together. So I find myself sitting alone in my classroom. They are all at Morning Assembly. Only a mile away across the city she lies in another room, our bedroom, the woman who has been the centre of my existence for a quarter of a century. The bell rings. The maroon-clad armies are on the move. A switch clicks on in the brain. Macbeth rides again. Tomorrow and tomorrow and tomorrow. Right on, Will. Creeps in this petty pace from day to day. Got it in one, sir. Right on the nose. There's a divinity that shapes our ends, rough-hew them how we will. 'Tis a mad world, my masters. The pupils blunder in, their uncaring roughness unaltered. Brainless as ever. Between classes I take to hiding in the English Department's Resource Base bolt-hole, drinking coffee at a rate which ought to kill me before the end of each day. I prefer this cold black hole of Calcutta to my own sunnyside room. It has high windows through which nobody can see me and come in to drink a cup of kindness. Only the blue light pours in: cold, beautiful, eternal. Utterly empty, utterly meaningless. Comforting, therefore. It is relaxing to stare through this glass at nothing, just these luminous blue oblongs, broken only by the mind-free gulls. Now I understand more about high windows, and the sun-comprehending glass, and beyond it that deep blue air that shows nothing, and is nowhere, and is endless.

But my employers insist on compassionate leave – they are a caring school. And the decision is compounded when my daughter cracks up during class and is taken to Matron. A doctor from a hospice comes to counsel her. His large sorrowful eyes look as if they have taken in a few tragedies. Catriona is curled up like a foetus on one of Matron's beds. He takes two hours to uncurl her while I sit around helplessly. Apparently I can explicate a Shakespearean tragedy but I'm not trained for a real-life one.

30

This one is our very own and I don't know what to say. I feel irrelevant, utterly useless. But my talents are no longer required in the Colinton Road trenches, George Watson's College, up Lancer's Alley. It's time I fought on the home front. Time to look beyond the black-stockinged nurses and join the palsied old step-takers, the hare-eyed clerks with the jitters, the wax-fleshed out-patients, still vague from accidents. And the characters in long coats, deep in the litter baskets. Time to leave work and go among them, with time on my hands. Time to watch the bread being delivered.

So the house husband now doubles as the male nurse, taking charge of the ordeals involved in showering and going to the bathroom. The cancerous breast, now grossly swollen, lies on her, she says, like a rotten turnip, heavy and horrible. Her steps have become tottery, her breath shorter, her voice weaker, her eyes increasingly empty, or putting out again that unnatural glow that is the flag of the fatally ill. Be positive, the doctors say. How useless the injunction sounds. We all know it's a dead end and it's no go my honey love. She'll not see Christmas. And next month her mother is going to chalk up yet another useless birthday. Meanwhile Catriona, my poppet, cracks up repeatedly at school and has to be brought home.

Home? It's no longer a home. It's a place to dump our clutter, it's where we take our shoes off. A place we happen to eat in and doss down in. A platform waiting-room where we sit and wait for some train that's never going to arrive. It's a hospital outpost, a cancer ward, a potential funeral parlour. This is a house where mum lies dying. There is nothing left of what we thought of as home. Thank you, cancer, for wrecking our lives. Unmendably.

Down in the garage there is a forgotten old punchbag of Jonathan's, a long sausage-shaped thing, lying near the log pile. I take a thick black marker pen and in secret scrawl across the outer canvas covering: CANCER: THE BASTARD! This I rope up to a hook in the rafters and begin to punch. I punch faster and faster till my fists and arms and legs are trembling. Fuck you, cancer! Fuck you! Fuck you! Fuck you! Maybe the vibrations from my hatred will be felt in those obscene cells upstairs that chemotherapy can't kill. I'll try anything, including sympathetic magic. Prayer didn't work. Why should it? The punching lasts several days till the stuffing falls out of the bag. I come back inside to watch the predictable enough stages: weight loss, hair loss, loss of all hope; the wheelchair, the commode; a path paved with bedpans and bedsores; pneumonia possibly, the old man's friend, and the inevitable end. My God, is all this yet to come? Aye, sir, all this is so. I hear a mocking voice from somewhere inside my head, assuring me that the cancer has a long way to go before it has done its worst. It's a matter not so much of time as of intensity. Watch and see.

I watch one morning as she goes to the bathroom in slow motion, insisting I let her travel the distance by herself. It is dawn and her silhouetted legs are two sticks in the doorway, like something out of Africa. Her skin is wrinkling, the pelvic bones are showing through, the once plump bottom caved in on itself, the left breast a bombsite. Yet still she has a perfect right breast, as lovely as ever and as capable of attracting. It's hard to get my head round this. One side of her is killing her: on the other she looks like my young lover, the girl in mini-skirt and knee-length leather boots whom I proposed to at the end of the sixties. Outside the trees heave and creak and sway like ships in the wind, rehearsing for the equinoctial gales. In here there is a tempest in my mind that the punchbag couldn't wear out. Meanwhile the sun is at it again, the

32

busy old fool, peeping in at our windows and curtains to check that we are awake, churning out another round of its optical illusions of happiness.

By the middle of September she had become a complete prisoner in the upstairs bedroom, never coming down at all. The cats, Pushkin and Paloma, prowled about her restlessly, Paloma watching with knowing, serious eyes, Pushkin sitting on the pillows and licking the prisoner's hair, washing her steadily, lovingly, methodically, something he had never done before. Cats know things about people, was all she said.

Going to the bathroom was now an agonizing odyssey. Once she fell and hurt herself – not badly, but it panicked her and made her realize that we could no longer cope at home. Our nights of talking in bed were over. It had become still more difficult to find words at once true and kind. Or not untrue and not unkind. So she took the decision. That the last stages should be played out among the white coats and the green screens, where all would go smoothly because it had all been scripted and rehearsed a million times before. I said I could ring the hospital but still she refused an ambulance, insisting that I take her by car. When the moment came to leave she looked around our bedroom and said, 'I never want to come back here.' Words that made me turn quite cold. And during the long, slow journey out of the house she said, 'I know I'll never come back here in any case. I'll never see the cats again, the view from the study, the kitchen, the garden, the pictures on the walls.' Look at them for the last time, then: the pictures and the cutlery, the music in the piano stool. That vase.

This was it and she knew it, the long goodbye. She was taking her final farewell of our home, the house we'd brought Catriona to as a baby only sixteen years ago. And Jonathan eleven years ago. Eleven years. Fuck it all, they were too young to lose their mother. She was too young to die. But Peel Terrace had seen the last of her. All that was left now was the hospital. And the screens around the bed.

They were reluctant to take her in at the Western.

'Couldn't you think about somewhere like St Columba's Hospice?'

'Dear God,' she whispered. The doctor back-pedalled.

'I meant for their *recreational* facilities,' he said quickly. 'I'm not saying it's the end of the line.'

It was exactly what he was saying. Taking that finally on board she turned now and faced the new direction, the only one, the one not on the compass. She admitted she was giving up, resigning herself to a fate which she hoped would come soon, for the sake of those around her, who loved her so much that she couldn't bear to continue causing them so much pain. For the first time I read in her eyes complete absence of hope. It was appalling. Leaving the hospital I had to stop the car several times when the blinding tears made it impossible for me to drive. When I reached home the house was empty and cold. I'd never felt lonelier.

As I sat on an upright chair, staring into space, the cleaning lady arrived and I bolted to the Grange Cemetery and stayed there in the September sunlight to hide for an hour among the urns and angels, the Greek weepers, the stone doves, the scythes and hourglasses of earlier times. A good place to be serious in, if only that so many dead lie round. But all I need is a little peace. So I sit there quietly under classic Babylonian clouds, the muted hum of the traffic hardly real. This, I tell myself, is the eye of the storm. Around it revolves the city in which people are busy working, dying, voting Labour or something else, reading Brief Histories of Time and Accounts of Years in

34

Provence, and somewhere near the edge of that storm of life my wife is about to be flung off into endless space. Why am I sitting here instead of being out there with her? I don't merit this momentary peace. They've told me I don't have to wait for visiting hour. Knowing our time together is short. I'll go early then, as soon as I've bought some stamps and posted off that pointless mail.

But even in the short time I have been away from the hospital, things have taken another turn. Incontinence has come and a catheter has to be fitted. And along with incontinence the first signs of mental derangement. The doctors mutter that it could be the steroids. There is another possibility. The cancer has done its tour of the body and has arrived at last at the brain. This is the point where I start to lose contact with the woman I know, the woman I love, as she drifts into a sort of muddled despair. And there is something else that alarms me, the way her fingers are now fumbling with the bedsheets. A tiny thing, but the behaviour instantly calls to my hopelessly book-anchored brain the death of Falstaff as described in *Henry V* by the tearful hostess of the Eastcheap tavern. When she saw him start to fumble with the sheets, she said, she knew there was but one way. Shakespeare must have seen it or heard of it from life and put it into his art. Now here it is coming back from art to life to disturb me, one more example of the increasingly rapid ebb to extinction. Still haunted by those feckless white fingers and the unseeing eyes fixed on some unknown strand, I go to bed with hell in my head, dreading the call in the night.

It doesn't come.

The year reaches the equinox and the world stands poised, perfectly balanced between darkness and light. Darkness is the door ahead. The only door. *Now the leaves are falling fast, nurse's flowers will not last.* In headaches and in worry vaguely life leaks away. But for a few minutes she too seems to achieve an equilibrium, an impeccable calm, a lucidity and serenity that are awesome. 'Promise me one thing,' she says. 'Don't become a crusty old bugger. I hate to think of you living out the rest of your life on your own. Promise me. Find someone, be happy, live life.'

I make the promise, not believing it.

Another night passes. And another dawn comes.

That morning there was a vacant calm about her that I neither liked nor trusted. Her voice was soft and ingenuous. When I came away I felt it wasn't my wife I was saying goodbye to – not all of her. Something was missing. And yet her last words to me were: 'Don't say goodbye, just say "I love you".'

I said 'I love you' and left with a heavy heart. As I turned round in the doorway to blow her a kiss she winked briefly at me as she often used to do – the last flicker of her old spirit and of the friendship between us.

The very last.

On the final day the cancer spread like a forest fire through the brain, and her stream of consciousness ran chattering away from me, into a distance that stood beyond my comprehension. The children were brought in to say 'Hi' but they knew it was to say goodbye. The brainfire spared her the full knowledge of that at least. In the last hours she lay and raved. My pathetic words were occasional stones thrown into the stream, scarcely disturbing the turbulent flow for more than half a second at a time, mostly never at all. But there was a part of her that kept fighting to stay in control. For one whole hour she did nothing but count – forwards and backwards, sums in the head, days in the year, anything to clutch at reason before it broke down completely and deserted her.

She was a waning moon, only a sliver of her left. I stayed till eleven p.m. and decided I could leave the kids no longer – they were on their own at home. But when I returned I could see that Catriona was uneasy.

'Shouldn't you go right back again?' she said. And she added, 'It may be your last chance.'

Brave daughter. That's my girl. I hurried back to the hospital, reaching it not long before midnight. Locked. I couldn't believe it. Locked? Impossible. How can they lock a hospital? I ran round the building hammering madly on big double doors, like a lunatic trying to get *into* an asylum. I was desperate to hold her once more before she died. Eventually I attracted some dubious attention and was led through a side door, far away from her ward. I was given directions but my head was in a whirl. I threaded my way through the green night silence. Theseus without a Minotaur. She was a May bird and her star sign was Taurus. I was seeking Cancer: The Crab. And I was trapped inside a gigantic fish tank. Once a rubber-booted surgeon with mask and bandana, like some deep-sea diver, walked past in soundless slow motion. He mouthed a hello to me and I watched for the bubbles to escape his lips and go streaming to the ceiling of this unreal city. All cities were unreal to me now – except the city of the dead.

By the time I reached her and took her in my arms she had talked herself into a deep exhausted sleep, a coma perhaps, nobody was there to tell me, and the breaths were slow and secret, emanating from a preposterous distance, so long between them that each one seemed like the last. And of course one was the last – it was impossible to tell which. A quiet and undramatic final exit, just as she would have wanted it, free from fuss. There was no response to my touch or to my saying her name. I tightened my arms around her, crushing her so hard that if she'd had any consciousness she'd have registered pain. Nothing. I put my head on her breast, listening intently. The soft fall and swell had ceased. A single drop of blood splashed her nightdress. And one tear stained her cheek, arrested halfway down. As if she knew. As if she wept for her own passing. It was over. I called the night nurse, and the experts on death moved in to confirm. 'Oh, yes, I think she's gone, poor love.' And they went off for the doctor while I laid my head on that poor ravaged breast and wept bitterly. Another kind nurse led me away to another room and tried to comfort me with arms and hands and words till the doctor came to confirm the death and its time. Then I waited.

Fifteen minutes later I felt a hand on my shoulder. I looked up into the quiet face of the doctor on night duty. No words. He squeezed my shoulder and with his other hand pressed something into mine and was gone. I looked down and unclasped my hand, found myself staring at her wrist-watch and her ring. Our wedding ring. He had registered her death as occurring officially at 00.15 hours, Monday, 27 September. Fifteen minutes past midnight. Fifteen minutes into Monday. But that is when the doctor arrived at the bedside. I who was there, holding her, knew that it was midnight. That's when the last breath came, when I waited for the next that never came. She did what John Keats aspired to do. She ceased upon the midnight with no pain. And they gave her officially an extra quarter of an hour of life.

So at 00.15 hours on 27 September I looked down dumbly at her watch, which was reading that time, and at our wedding ring. Then they led me back to see her where she lay – unringed in a bed of snow. She had been given a quick make-over, brushed hair and powdered face. But there was a strange sound coming from somewhere, a harsh and alien sound that hurt. It was the sound of sobbing. And then it came to me that I was the one responsible for it, the sound of sobs racking me, tearing me apart. It was the sound of a heart breaking. I remember seeing my scalding tears raining down on those blind – and blinding – white sheets they'd laid her in. The room was in darkness apart from the tiny puddle of light produced by the angle-poise lamp, directed sensitively away from the dead face. I remember holding that unringed hand on which I'd placed a circle of gold when we were in our twenties, more than twenty years ago. Two night nurses stood on either side of the bed, like bridesmaids. One of them said, 'She's at peace.'

So this was peace. I had now to drive back home and tell the children that their mother was at peace. I walked slowly upstairs. Jonathan had gone to bed and was lying with the light out, staring at the ceiling. I perched quietly on the edge, put my hand on his head. No words were necessary. He read my face in the dark. A single tear formed in the corner of one eye and rolled down his cheek. Then he turned his face to the wall.

Neither was there any need to say it to Catriona. When I came through the door she looked at my face and we fell on each other's necks and wept. I don't know how long we stood there in the hall together, holding each other up. But then we lay together in 'the big bed' as she used to call it when she was a toddler, asking to be allowed to come in and sleep between us. Not that we did much sleeping in those days. We didn't sleep much now either, and I woke two hours later to the first dawn without my life's companion.

The first day after a death the sudden absence is hard to comprehend. Then it dawns on you like the new day. The absence is eternal: it will never go away.

Bereavement brings letters, cards, flowers, friends. Neighbours you never even knew existed, all offering clichés of all kinds. (The clock has ticked, my friend. The moving finger writes.) And the undertakers. Sleek black cushioners of all the practical horrors – and the sudden questions you hadn't thought to have to answer yet. Cremation or burial? Sacred or secular? Flowers or no flowers? Elm or oak? Or shall it be mahogany? The head undertaker had a young face, if somewhat pale and wan – probably from years of contemplating corpses. I'd taught his teenage daughter, interviewed him as a parent. Now here he was interviewing me as a widower. Strange how our professions bring us together as our needs and circumstances alter and shift. I wondered if he'd bury me eventually. The Grange Cemetery is booked up, he was saying. It will have to be Mortonhall. Rather far out from the centre of Edinburgh, I'm afraid, sir, but consequently pleasantly private and quiet, of course, and affording a spectacular view of the city: Arthur's Seat to the north and the Pentland Hills to the south. A peaceful place, which she would appreciate. Would have appreciated.

I'm sure she would. And so a plot was booked in Mortonhall. To hold her to all eternity. And to contain me when the time came for me to join her there. In perpetuity. The funeral was fixed for the last day of September.

I watched the mourners come, drifting in quiet black waves through the open front doors of the house. The sunlight poured through the vestibule and into the hall, and the swirling motes peopled the slanting shafts. The family arrived first, a quiet clutch from Fife, my mother's folk. Others slipped in like shadows. No unnecessary words, the iron handshakes, the bearhugs, the kisses from the women, the special look in the eye that you see only at funerals – they said it all. The undertakers waited nervously for the latecomers, precision navigators of this last voyage.

40

Then we walked round two corners to Mayfield Church.

It was packed. With family, friends, colleagues – platoons of pupils. All eyes were focused on the coffin, up at the holy end, raised like an offering. Was my wife really in there? In that little box? She occupied so few cubic inches of space.

We followed her coffin up the nave of the church and out into the impossibly perfect day, the ironical blues and golds of September's swansong. Then we began that most heartbreaking of all journeys, behind the hearse, slowing the city's traffic all the way up to the high ground of Mortonhall cemetery, the one with the view, where we had arranged that she would spend eternity – there on the sad height. After she lost the battle. In spite of all my speeches. In spite of the prayers, the poetry. *Do not go gentle into that good night.* Rage, rage against the dying of the light. She had raged against it in her last hours, but by then it was no longer my wife raging – it was cancer cells in the brain, putting out the light of reason. The images and memories from nine thousand days of marriage came crowding in on me as we cruised along in second gear through south Edinburgh.

I had often encountered that black wave in the city traffic – who hasn't? – a funeral in progress. And slowed instinctively. Now we were part of that wave, an oil-slick, travelling adagio, through the colourful stream of cars. At mid-Liberton the lights were broken but we were given precedence, of course, the whole convoy, and bulky men at big wheels, men with sour cheeks, bush moustaches, beer bellies and stubbled jaws waved us on with meek submissive gestures instead of the two fingers we might have been awarded in other circumstances. But these were the ultimate circumstances.

All things give way, it seems, to death.

Up at Mortonhall the Pentlands towered over the city, a green wave arrested in time. Here the crows were coughing like parsons and the bees were cruising among the flowers. She was taken out of the hearse and into the sunlight for the last time before being committed to the ground: earth to earth, ashes to ashes, dust to dust. Fumbling with my coffin cord, watching her swing slowly down into that hole in the ground, I heard a voice in my head from the once safe world of art. *Lay her in the earth. And from her fair and unpolluted flesh may violets spring*. But her flesh was not unpolluted. It had been ravaged by an obscenity that nothing could cure. Now all that was left were the traditional words of consolation, booming over the boneyard. *And though worms destroy this body* . . . What were they talking about? This body was already destroyed. But not by worms.

The earth was scattered in three handfuls over her coffin. Somebody threw in a rose. I flung poppy seeds from Fife into her grave, scattering them over her coffin. Where I imagined their magical germination, thousands of little lamps surrounding her corpse. One day they would blow over her head, her favourite flowers. *Sweets to the sweet, farewell*. I remembered scattering petals across the wedding sheets when we came home after our marriage. When all was young. The last of the wreaths were laid around the graveside and the bees dived down at once and got busy.

And so we left her, safe now with the bees, and with the dead for company, her own kind. Safe in their alabaster chambers. Untouched by morning and untouched by noon. Rafter of satin and roof of stone. And not a man broke down. Not even me. King Lear would have had something to say to us about this.

O, you are men of stones.

42

She left behind her the Gulf Crisis, the Thatcher era, the Arab-Israeli conflict, Northern Ireland, pollution, perversion, mounting terrorism, a dwindling church, a punctured ozone layer, global warming, some green fields and the Third World. All of them a sight more lovely than those screens around her bed. She was too good for this life. Also a pile of clothes, a teacher's post needing to be filled, a daughter of sixteen and a son still in primary school. And me. One mind-blown man to record the hurt.

I went up to a bedroom blighted by her death, stared at the arctic sheets, lay down on her side. Where was she? Edinburgh had swallowed her up. She was the city's now and the entire earth's, part of its atoms. She was fire, she was air. She was weather. She had immortal belongings – the last-ditch euphemisms of art for what I now confronted. She was never coming back through that door.

Next day I had to go along to the Registrar and become a statistic, join the new class of citizen to which I now belonged and would have to answer to when completing forms: Christopher Rush, widower. The Registrar was busy with the endless traffic of birth and death, and with marriage somewhere in between. A couple held hands and giggled, planning married bliss. Another couple carried a tiny bundle that was making bird-like noises. But death was having the field day, it seemed, from the subdued talk around me, low words in cold cubicles where people sat in shock, facing officialdom and its necessary questions: who, when, where? And *why*? Why do people die? There has to be a cause. Didn't you know you should have come within three days of the death? Eternity lasts a long time, God is in no hurry, but public records are more precise. And we must be punctual. All extremely upsetting and confusing, but even grief has to be processed. I saw how easily she too got turned into numbers as we all do in the end, her entire existence reduced to a few facts, hammered out, astonishingly, not on a smart new computer but on a clapped-out old Remington. There was something bleakly satisfying about this, watching it do the business as it recorded the bare facts of her entry and exit, the part she played, schoolteacher, her roots and forebears, partner and progeny. And why. Why she went. It was something to do with death. More specifically a carcinoma. Was that the word? In under ten minutes she too was a statistic, on file forever. And I, a widower, stumbled out into the sudden sunshine, clutching my new identity and her processed life, entered correctly in all the boxes, signed and stamped and dated, all on one side of A4. Fine, I thought – now comes the rest of my life.

So I walk once more into Room 29 and sell Shakespeare to youth, well laced with Larkin, sensing the increasing irrelevance to the streetwise careers they have rightly planned, and to an education system now geared to the new Life Skills for which English Literature is a mere service industry. But I keep up the act, holding on grimly to the invisible ropes. I have invisible wires too, in my jaw, enabling me to speak without breaking down. I can actually feel them physically, these psychological implants. I don't know what put them there – some hidden iron in the soul which I didn't know I had. Dig deep, you bastard, and bite on that bullet. Sitting at my desk I hear a colleague out in the corridor asking my Head of Department, 'How's Chris?' Back comes the reply: 'Held together by elastoplast and sellotape!' Right on, Harry. The pupils detect no difference in me, though. They don't know about the hammering in the chest, the churning in the stomach, and the pain produced by pulling on these wires when I formulate the words. They don't know that the man teaching them English Literature secretly wishes he were dead, and were lying with his partner up in Morton-hall, oblivious in eternity, or together in bliss. I'll settle for either, anything to stop the pain. There's no hell, though, in any afterlife. I know that now. Hell is separation from what you love, separation from love itself. Hell is here and now. Just keep on teaching, that's what you're good at, and the kids will think the old codger is enjoying himself as usual. What they don't know is that when they left the room he blubbed, yes, the old cock blubbed. Christ, this is not getting any better, is it? The book drops from the hand, music merely tells me what I've lost, whispering of desolation and despair. I watch couples on buses and in the streets, eyeing them narrowly, darkly and with bitter-ness. They belong to the old Eden, from which I'm now exiled, courtesy of cancer, the bastard, the serpent in the garden.

I give television a try. It turns out to be a Job's Comforter, a fabricator and purveyor of fantasy and lies. People around me are busy spending fifteen years of their lives watching it. It pours out horror stories of various world crises: wages, energy, unemployment, industry, overpopu-lation, depopulation, pollution, crime, ethnic cleansing – that's a good new name for genocide. Plutonium or Aids will kill us all off. Voting Labour will bring everything right again. Apparently. So the whirlwind of idiot hopes and idiot despairs comes spouting out of the pathetic little box, mixed up with all the soaps and meaningless froth of our sick society. Probably the pathetic little box is the real source of crisis, more powerful than any it mentions. It has the power to turn values upside down, to make fair foul and foul fair, to paralyse people into bored passivity for a quarter of their adult lives. Trapped in the triviality of everydayness, trapped in the treadmill of boredom and futility, they succumb. Or they look for an escape. Faust found it by reaching out to unseen forces, dabbling with the unknown. Most people settle for *EastEnders*. It's safer, though even more suffocating than the prison of personal consciousness. It's complete intellectual unconsciousness, the dead end of the human road, a cancer of the spirit. You just have to switch on this box and see a world rotten with lies and numb with mediocrity. Maybe the cynics and suicides have the right answers. I feel the sudden call of infinitely remote horizons, but I don't know what they are, just that they are out there somewhere. They say certain birds may navigate by sensitivity to some electromagnetic vibration originating in the Milky Way. I stare up at it – and catch nothing. Not a galactic heartbeat. Not a pulse.

Is Wells right? Is there no purpose whatsoever behind the aimless drift of evolution and is life a chemical process that originated in the seas of the Pre-Cambrian era and that will end miserably behind a windbreak in a cave?

Meanwhile Granny Graveclothes lives on and has to be minded: shopped for, cooked for, followed like a gleaner – picking up the abandoned cigarettes left lying lit and lethal in her wake. Why does the useless old whiner drivel on like this, deeper and deeper into a dementia achieved on sixty fags a day for three score years and ten, when her daughter, who never smoked a cigarette in her life, was handed a card marked for a grave decades before her time?

Now the October gales lash the gardens. That calm September sarabande that was the background music to her dying – it feels already like something that happened a century ago.

And I write for hours in my diary – which is addressed to *her*. You can't stop talking to somebody you love just because they're dead. The white page pulls me in. I tell it everything. Here I feel momentarily safe and tranquil, following the lines. Sometimes I look up with a shock to find myself sitting in what used to be our home. But I feel as if I'm visiting some museum. The house, with its once familiar arrangements of furniture, ornaments, domestic objects, gifts given over the years, has become a cold catalogue of the past. Yes, home is so sad. But where else is there to go?

It's not just that I've drunk a little too much, that I'm tired and I want to go to bed. There's something else. I, who loved wide open spaces, the big skies and the austerity of the ocean, am becoming agoraphobic, I think. I'm suddenly frightened by the lorries, sliding along the blank motorways, frightened by the tree-ringed skylines, the millions of acres of earth, the anonymous green grass covering the millions of vanished lives. Afraid of the land's end, the blue ploughlands of the sea, endless unfenced existence.

I know it's October. I heard someone howling in October. I know it's October because I wrote it down, how I heard this person howling, heard it while shaving in the bathroom: a deep harsh cry, torn from the abyss of ages. It made me stop and stare, the razor in the air . . . till I saw who it was. Me again, of course, that man in the mirror, staring back at me with soap on his beard and blood in his eyes. A madman howling savagely for his mate, emitting a cry loud enough to waken the dead. Would that it could. It never does, though. Never. My diary tells me that as well. This is not the first time I have howled.

It was a Sunday, I know that much. Useless things,

diaries. What does the day of the week matter? But a Sunday it was, for the record. The night before, I thought I met her on the stairs, when I went up to the attic for something in the semi-darkness of Saturday night. It was on coming back down that I detected her perfume, the one I bought for her when she was in hospital. I stopped halfway down the steps. 'I know you're there, love,' I said. She didn't answer but her fragrant spirit lingered and so did I, motionless for some moments in the middle of the stairs. Now it's cold morning and the October sun admits no ghosts, my love, no warm auras of you. Tomorrow I have to walk in and teach, knowing I'll never hear your heels in the corridors again, that well-known click, approaching my room, your face in the centre pane of glass, framed by the door. That smile.

I used to believe I had a separate inner life. Now (I tell myself) I know that I was wrong, and that human identity is invested in relationships. So much of me was invested in her for all those years, and now that she is dead I feel my own identity obliterated. When she died, I died too, the real me, the essential self. There is no bringing either of us back, the pain will never go away. Normality from now on will always be the abnormal. Even work is no escape – the old toad is going to let me down, I can tell. I come home each afternoon to this hellishly empty house, its lonely floors, its appalling walls.

School lurched to its half term – with a list of things on my desk to drive me insane before Friday. And all for paying a few bills. Sickening, poisonous and out of proportion, yes, but I got there, stumbled into bed on the Friday night and looked at the same page of the book I'd opened on all the preceding nights, falling asleep, wakening again in the morning and staring at the same unread page, propped up on my chest. I must have slept still as a stone all night long. Once, instead of a book, it was a glass of rum. Often enough I'd wake up in the morning to find my chest sticky with sugar cane and me feeling like a dead man. The other morning I blinked my eyes open to see the glass still sitting on my breastbone, the measure of rum undrunk, unspoilt. A measure of my exhaustion. Fifteen men could have been sitting on my chest, survivors of drink and the devil. Robert Louis Stevenson drifted into my mind and drifted out again. I heard the sound of a train's wheels rumbling in the dawn and thought of Shakespeare. I had decided to take the children down to Stratford for their half-term break.

It was hard setting off on our first holiday without mum. We took the sleeper down to London and as we rocketed through the darkness, lying supine in our narrow bunks, I felt like a Pharaoh, the shell of a dead man, travelling through time. Why were we going? In the belief that somehow things would be better at Frinton, or Venice? – as an old shag said. A dead old shag – who once said too that nothing, like something, happens anywhere. So why not Stratford? We had planned to go in the past but the Grim-Reaping Granny had got in the way as ever. Orkney had been possible only because it had been presented as a business trip of sorts, having some connection with my writing. I felt we were owed Stratford at last. And as we'd never made it together, I wanted at least to take our children. They were all that was left now of their mum. So we arrived, saw the sights, attended plays, *The Tempest*, *King Lear*, witnessed the great wheel of the Shakespeare industry turning out the tourists, turning a dead dramatist into a commercial cult. Somehow the art survived, though I saw it as a mere spectator, never feeling the involvement that I'd always imagined. The heart had grown too cold for that. And loneliness no longer clarified as it was supposed to.

A holiday then, with a dash of culture slapped in. A necessary break for the kids and a far cry from Portobello. But it wasn't Stratford itself that remained with me long after we'd come back home – it was Adlestrop. We hired a car and drove around the Cotswolds without a plan, and it was on this unexpected autumn afternoon of aimless driving that I happened to glance at the map and saw the name: Adlestrop, also the title of the poem by Edward Thomas. He'd made the place name famous in English poetry by writing that fine piece about how his train had stopped there and how he took in the quiet pastoral atmosphere of the obscure spot, breathless and beautiful in its timeless anonymity.

So we stopped at Adlestrop. And we stood and stared at where the little station would have been, part of a vanished English culture. Stood listening to silence, imagining meadow-sweet and willow-herb in June, the heat and hiss of steam, and the birds, two counties' worth, churning out birdsong, and the stopped train, and the haycocks, and the grass – and how it was. Exactly how it was. My head was full of how it might have been had *she* been there. Instead I registered again that she was *dead* (the brutally ugly monosyllable kept echoing in my mind) and I continued standing there for what seemed like hours – the Cotswolds all before us, a world without sound. It might have been the moon for silence, a landscape of the heart, laid bare. The trees were all on fire with change, gilding decay. A cold October sun was pouring out its wine that day, ignored. Somewhere beyond the blue sky the stars were burning to waste. And on the vast air, so I noted, not a single bird was singing, in all of Oxfordshire and Gloucestershire. That's how I remembered Adlestrop.

The experience sent me straight to my poetry notebooks for the rest of the holiday, in search of strength for the second half of the autumn term, still believing, I suppose, that literature could be a substitute for life, or, if not a substitute, then at least a counsellor, a consoler.

> *Tonight I can write the saddest lines.*
> *Through nights like this one I held her in my arms,*
> *I kissed her again and again under the endless sky.*
> *Tonight I can write the saddest lines.*
> *To think that I do not have her. To feel that I have lost her.*
>
> *What does it matter that my love could not keep her?*
> *The night is shattered and she is not with me.*
> *Because through nights like this one I held her in my arms*
> *My soul is not satisfied that it has lost her.*

Nobody could throw language so easily over experience like Pablo Neruda. But his verses tore me apart.

> *Love is so short . . . forgetting is so long.*

I wake at three, gulp down coffee and roam deeper through the notebooks, looking again at the philosophies that I used to admire when I was an adolescent – though I lost faith in them over the years. Maybe they spoke truer than I knew. Let's see.

Marcus Aurelius at three in the morning. Delude yourself no longer, you will never reread these notebooks, or that special selection of texts you've put by for your old age. Press on then to the end, rid yourself of futile dreams and desires. Yesterday you were a drop of semen, tomorrow you will be a scattering of ashes. So what difference does a long life make? It's all a waste of time. There's no new thing under the sun, all is as trite as it is transitory: brief, banal, sordid and unchanging from generation to generation. The play is always the same, it's only the actors who alter, all enduring only for a day, all now long since dead and rotten. Some forgotten as soon as gone, some passed into myth, some faded even out of myth itself. Where are all the great ones now? Vapour, ashes, earth, a tale – perhaps not even a tale. Just nothing. What's death, after all? A release from the senses, from stirrings of appetite, from journeys of the mind, and from slavery to the flesh. A release from everything and an entry into nothing, absolutely nothing. So, why make such a song and dance about this business of dying?

Ah, but the Marcus Aurelius argument is flawed, as Larkin pointed out. This is the specious stuff that says that no rational being can fear a thing it will not feel – ignoring the fact that this is precisely what we fear: extinction. No sight, no sound, no touch, or taste or smell. *Sans* teeth, *sans* eyes, *sans* taste, *sans* everything. The anaesthetic from which none come round. Nothing more terrible. Nothing more true. So we're back to that again. But that's because it *is* so true. Being brave lets no one off the grave. Death is no different whined at than withstood. Marcus didn't go down too well in Hull.

Or, in Edinburgh either, at four in the morning now, with Bertrand Russell telling me that intellectually the Emperor Aurelius was actually a rather pathetic figure. The English philosopher is optimistic, in spite of his atheism, keeping the big questions open, not closing life down like the reviled Roman. What's it all about then? Is man merely what he appears to be to the astronomer, a puny piece of impure carbon and water, an impotent insect inhabiting an insignificant planet? Or is he what he appears to Hamlet: noble in reason, infinite in faculty, in form and moving how express and admirable, in action how like an angel, in apprehension how like a god, the beauty of the world, the paragon of animals? Or is he both? Is there really a way of life that is noble and another that is vile, or are all ways of living merely futile? And must what is good also be eternal in order to be considered worthwhile, or is it worth striving for even if the universe is expanding inexorably towards its own extinction?

Whatever you come up with, so Russell assures me, you have to answer as an individual facing what he calls the terror of cosmic loneliness, and especially you must avoid the traps set by science and religion. Science tells you what you can actually know, but what you do know is limited, and if you ignore these limitations, forget how much you can never know, you become insensitive to the big issues. Theology, on the other hand, induces dogma, the belief that you actually know the truth about something, whereas the real truth is that you know nothing, and so theology generates a kind of impertinent insolence towards the universe. Between the two lies the no man's land of philosophy. And the philosopher's uncertainty, though painful, has to be endured if you want to live without the support of comforting fairy tales. So this is the answer. To teach you how to live without certainty and yet without being stricken by doubt, by Hamlet's intellectual hesitation, this is what philosophy can do for you if you care to study it.

Thank you, Bertrand, for your proud words of paraphrased philosophical wisdom, scribbled down in my teens from your *History of Western Philosophy*, words devoid of any real insights. Now I know that I know nothing, and somehow I'm supposed to feel noble in my ignorance. I don't know if this is any less pathetic than Marcus Aurelius. What I do know is that the holiday is at an end. After Stratford and unexpected Adlestrop, the warm bath of poetry and the cold plunge into philosophy. That's it. That was the October break. Over.

It didn't help. I set off for school again like somebody travelling to his execution. In the small hours of Monday morning I was wakened by breathlessness in the chest – panic, untriggered, unbidden, suffocating; a tightness and a pressurizing pain that made me think heart attack. And even through the panic there was this little thrill of expectation. Come quickly, then, you bastard, and take me to her! You don't frighten me, you come as a friend! Then I cursed myself even more foully for deserting my poor children, even in thought. But thought is the worst betrayer of all. Thought's the slave of life, and life time's fool. Don't think, then – just get up, and get on with the day, the term, the rest of your life. This converted itself into the desperately enforced vocal glee with which I'd become accustomed to rouse the kids for school. *Up! Up! The sun doth gild our armour! Therefore, to horse! And let us not be dainty of leave-taking but shift away!* Mad dad rides again. Maybe they're right.

The October clocks go back. An added hour. Always I used to take great pleasure from that moment in the year, the illusion of being able not only to stop the stream of time but also to make it flow backwards, and snatch that extra hour like a flower from the flood. Not today, even though it's Sunday, pre-dawn. What's another hour to a man merely marking time? What art thou, Faustus, but a man condemned to die? In the middle of the fun and frolics he suddenly stopped and saw it and just for a second got it whole too, speaking for us all. We're all waiting to die. It's when something presses the pause button and the fun stops that you remember what you're waiting for. Most of the time most of us try to ignore that fact. Which is both logical and sensible, since there's nothing you can do about it. Right now I feel neither logic nor common sense. But I'm sobered for a moment in the pre-dawn darkness, waking to find my daughter standing by the bedside in her nightdress, peering at me palely. She's feeling my pulse, poor lamb, checking to see that I am still alive. Sleepwalking? Her eyes are open. *Aye, but their sense is shut*, I hear a voice murmur from *Macbeth*. I lead her gently back to bed, make coffee, go back to bed myself and lie thinking.

About the children. How are they really coping? Jonathan has stored it away, deep inside himself, to deal with later, when he has the maturity. It's a thing that boys do, perhaps, a sensible defence mechanism which allows him to function, to survive. But there are nights I think I hear him crying in his sleep – when the guard is down, consciousness lies drugged, and pain slides past, slips its insidious stiletto into the mind.

Catriona's struggle is carried on out in the open, and the bruises are there for all to see. Literally. She leaves the house some nights and comes back late, her knuckles scarred and bleeding, as if she's been in a fight. She has. With stone walls, trees, anything she can hit herself against, any mute surface that can soak up her pain. Talking doesn't help – it's much too early.

So here we are, the three of us, lying trapped in our separate rooms, linked only by our common loss. And our wretched grief. Not an admirable example of unity, but possibly truer than a false attempt. John Donne was wrong. Every man is an island. And there are certain seas that can't be crossed. A murky morning invades the room. And I keep on thinking.

55

About Sunday. There are letters to answer, shopping to be done, clothes to wash and iron – and to buy. Kids keep growing, though they've lost their mum, and dads aren't so good at this sort of thing, but they've got to bloody learn. There are also lessons to be planned – new lessons for that other brave new world of what used to be called English teaching and is now something else, and will be something else again next year. My novel, *Last Lesson of the Afternoon*, satirizing all this, lies in the attic, gathering cobwebs and erudite mice. The publishers want it seen to. I can't go on mourning forever. Can I?

> *Thou know'st 'tis common; all that live must die,*
> *Passing through nature to eternity.*

Shopping then. It sounds less awful than going back to the book I was writing when she was dying. So I lie and consider the Sunday shopping instead, contemplating the trolley I'll soon be pushing around Sainsbury's, a trolley loaded with abominations of food. A calf is born by lamplight in a winter shed to produce something that someone will consume in a railway station somewhere between Oxford and Hull: an awful pie. 'Twere to consider too curiously to consider so? It won't get the shopping in, that's for sure. And the shopping will be followed by the cooking, the hoovering, the marking, the mail. And miles to go before I sleep. That's enough of that, the other voice insists, the iron voice that despises self-pity. Think of your kids, think of the women who do it every day of their lives. Think of the holocaust. And get a bloody grip! Get real. Get a life.

I try. But all the same it was a dead man who did the laundry. A corpse that cooked the dinner. A deaf ear that took the telephone. And a ventriloquist's dummy that answered through gritted teeth: 'Yes, of course, of course I'll come.' What else is there to say when the lights come on at four at the end of another year? And a dead hand records the dates in the diary.

Still on a Friday night, though, I pour out two glasses of wine, one for my life's cup-companion. I can't drink alone. When she was here we'd sometimes pour a third glass 'for absent friends'. Now it's down to two. The extra glass stays undrunk on the mantelpiece all night, like the one the kids used to leave out for Santa Claus, together with the apple for the reindeer. In the morning I pour it away into the earth among the flowers of the back garden, a libation to the lips that drink no more, as old Omar used to say. *Ah! make the most of what we yet may spend – before we too into the dust descend.* Wine no longer tastes the same in any case. Nor does teaching. Or writing. Or living. I want to self-destruct, decompose, disappear into that serene slot where all past years are. Colleagues now start to tell me that they think the kids and I need counselling. Crap, I tell them. Larkin and Lear are my counsellors – that feelingly persuade me what I am. I *need* the pain, don't want it to stop. When the time comes oblivion will work the trick, the ultimate anodyne. Meanwhile I want to *mourn*, if you don't mind. And *I'll* look after the kids. What are dads for?

Ah, but what if I were to come downstairs one Saturday morning in a magical dawn, to discover that glass of wine drained to the dregs, a smear of lipstick round the rim? Then maybe I'd have gone mad at last. But if so I'd be glad enough to be mad, and mad enough to be happy again. I used to go to bed and picture that glass downstairs, mysterious on the mantelpiece. But when I came down in the morning the glass still stood undrunk under her portrait, above the ashes of the cold fire. No, she hadn't stolen into the house during the night. There is only a glass of old wine to empty into the garden, that's all. So the days drift by, the nights so quiet I can hear the frost fall; the evenings so empty I talk aloud to her and strain my ears waiting for her answer; the mornings so cold and dark and sleepless I drink slow coffees in bed long before dawn, waiting for day to storm the house and force me to get on with things. I hear of wars. I understand that there will be budgets, conferences, severe gales, interest cuts, rate rises, that it will be minus three in Warsaw, minus ten in Moscow.

So what? Staring at my half-shaved face I let slip the heavy jar of soap. It cracks open the bathroom sink and the water floods over my bare feet. Yellow Pages. And acres of plumbers, eager to oblige, apparently. Until you call them. The sink stays shattered for weeks. The other day the police fined me for driving around seemingly in a dream – without a seat belt. Didn't I know it could be a matter of life or death? I burst out laughing at that, sitting like a criminal in the back of their panda car, was breathalysed and pronounced sober. More mad laughter. They asked me if I had a reason for my behaviour. I could have taken them through a wilderness of reasons. 'No' seemed the easiest answer. Well, it's a busy road, sir, we'd better see you safely off. And they handed me back my car keys and waited for me to go. As I was pulling out from the kerb I heard this furious honking of a horn behind me. Looking over my shoulder I saw the two officers waving at me furiously. I wasn't wearing my seat belt! More mad giggles wanted to break out but I suppressed them, feeing I'd tried the men's patience sufficiently. At the same time I felt assaulted – and was twenty pounds the poorer.

Ice in the ditches now, mirroring winter. Dawn. Just below

the skyline the soundless foundry is busy, churning out light for another day. Sunrise arrives, as always, turning the windows to oblongs of gold. A Siberian sunlight, the roofs and grasses caught in an arctic calm, a breathless and cruel beauty. Death lies on her like an untimely frost upon the sweetest flower of all the field. This is the leafless hour. The trees stand like stanchions, ringing the city, the branches snarled like barbed wire, etched on the sky. A blackbird lands in the tangle, hangs there like a fat black grenade, ready to burst into song. *Ye'll break my heart, ye warbling bird.* Don't explode, I beg you. *That wantons through the flowering thorn.* Don't give me the Banks and Braes number, not this morning. *Ye minds me o' departed joys, Departed never to return.* But nature is a beast without a heart. I close my eyes.

And I see again the dead white face on that dead white form, lying six feet beneath the white frost – and the clasped hands, professionally arranged in the knot of peace, the way hands are. When the heart stops its pumping the hands lie there on the breast, giving it this cold cuddle. There is nothing else left for them to do. But I never went to see her coffined, preferring the image of the newly dead, the tired bride, fallen asleep. She came to me in white and she left me in white. A man doesn't think, when he kisses his new bride, that one day cancer will kiss her with white lips. I left her before she'd had time to settle into the death pose, the grim fixity of stiffening and nullity. Left her simply looking tired.

I'm tired too. Nobody unbereft knows how exhausting bereavement can be, and the sheer stress of mourning. I never felt so tired. Tired of shaving, of getting dressed and undressed. Tired of my fingernails and hands and feet, tired of my shadow and my hair. Of being alive.

And now come the first sheets of snow, rumpling the

streets, the goosey mornings, the brass-monkey weather, the grouchy breakfasts, the shrouded cars, the bleary shaves, the dim-lit early morning classrooms, and all that noisy, unreflecting, hopeful, hormone-driven youth that simply will not go away.

My forty-ninth birthday arrives. Washing my face this morning I watch the basin turn red with bright lashings of blood. Only a nose-bleed, a sign of tension. Even so, fear would normally have clutched at the bowels. Not this morning. Instead a curious detachment. Even a grim whiff of interest. The dread of death no longer flashes afresh to hold and horrify. Not any more. The King of Terrors has become nothing more than a friendly tour-guide to the next world. I go on living. I go on waking.

Waking in the early November dawns, still drinking coffees, still picturing the first fingers of light, Homer's rose-fingered east again, picking out the lettering on her slab, reflecting that golden fire over the city that is setting her name alight, gold touching gold. Oh, not another beautiful fucking day! Days are for the young, who think, like the bees, that warm days will never cease. Days are for men with wives, not for zombies and the undead, scribbling in the white solitary confinement of their diaries. And yet, where can we live but days? So the days pass, night closes its shutters on their deceptions, the illusions and the lies. God obviously saw that when he was busy writing the Bible. *Day unto day uttereth speech and night unto night sheweth knowledge.* So much for days – the broken dreams that reflect the sunlight, the thousand and one excuses that keep us going. Only at night, when the last guests have stepped into the windy street and gone and the listeners throng the shadows, do I begin to talk sense to myself. I start up conversations with the moon, lozenge of love, and with the vanished Larkin, now one of the Dead Poets' Society, to remind me of the poignancy of the past. And to acknowledge that it is precisely because it is past and will never come again, that it lacerates, simply by being over – that's what makes life so sweet.

And so bitter. Could I be cracking up? Pursued by the wolves of memory, that's all. They'll tear you apart, this pack of lies. Running from them, I get caught in friendly fire – colleagues aiming their advice at me from all quarters, the yapping faces and clattering syllables assuring me that I'm wrong to reject counselling. 'Come to dinner and we'll talk about it.' Another evening filled with forks and faces, rather than repaid under a lamp, hearing the sound of the wind, or facing up to the other things, the failure and remorse that stand just beyond the lamplight. I hear Larkin backing me up. The counselling still gets the thumbs down.

So does education. I managed somehow, in the middle of all this, to get the manuscript of *Last Lesson of the Afternoon* to the publishers. It was a mess. I was in pieces as a writer as well as a man, though an intelligent editor did for the book what all the king's horses and all the king's grief counsellors couldn't have done for its author. Put it together again. I didn't believe anything could put me together again. Ever. The management revolution in education wasn't helping. By systematically dismantling everything I had believed in and worked for as a schoolmaster for the last twenty-five years, the bureaucrats were busy knocking away one of my last remaining crutches. The English which I used to love to teach was becoming barely recognizable as a subject.

The only lifelines were the kids, without whom I'd have taken my own life, and the domestic routines that offered at least their short-term challenges. Two soaked duvets, one in Coca-Cola, the other in cat-piss – there's something to concentrate the energies for five minutes, that's yet another lifebelt thrown. But life can end up throwing too many: exam correction, pupils' reports, exemplars, ironing, lunch packs, letters, bills, the proofs of the novel suddenly needing to be read, the kids' homework, the car breaking down on cue as December approaches, Jonathan with a bad chest, Catriona coughing like a consumptive – and Granny Graveclothes on the blower again, huffing and puffing and uttering curses: soul-blenching, sanguinary, oriental things. I harden my heart like old Pharaoh in Egypt's land. But how long can this go on? How many slices of bread precisely stand between me and death? How many lunches, Saturdays, periods of poetry? The trips to Sainsbury's, the meetings endured, shoes polished, shirts ironed, curtains drawn and undrawn, exams compiled, graded, moderated, recorded? Tomorrow and tomorrow and tomorrow. To the last syllable of recorded time. To the last syllable of my breath. Just how many breaths do I have left before I'm out of it all? Someone must know. It's all predetermined.

That's what the cancer specialist said to me. The biology of this illness was written from the start. Even from before it began. A free gift in the genes, a clutch of cancer cells, a non-smoker's special prize. What does it all add up to, the love-looks and laughter, the house building, the furnishing, the planting? Down their carved names the raindrop ploughs. O, what made fatuous sunbeams toil to break earth's sleep at all?

This is the stuff of madness. The diary is still my safe-house, my sanity-chamber, my breathing time of day, my iron lung, my oxygen tent, my secret garden, my island full of noises, my sea-cell beneath the whelming water. Till human voices wake me. And I drown –

In the smart new air-conditioned theatre of education, in which the briskly efficient young ladies (or not so young) trot out their conference lines in grating metallic voices, exterminating all the mumbling middle-aged men. Lines written for them by the Dalkeith Daleks in the Ironmills district of Edinburgh. Worlds away from the Palace of Green Porcelain where the books now moulder.

It doesn't matter. The books have failed in any case. Art isn't the healer I thought it was. Nor is nature, as I've already discovered, nor the ideal cottage by the sea, everybody's dream.

December came in with storm-winds and lashings of rain. From my classroom window I watched the hills taking the hammering. Oh to be up there now, to be lying flat out on the ridge feeling the rains driving through me like nails! And then feeling nothing at all. But here come the dim Fives, wanting to be taught, or at least to be entertained. Oh yes, I can do that for you, though my heart is breaking, what does that matter? *Vesti la giubba.* Be bright and jovial among our guests, my lord, sleek o'er your rugged looks, it's time to make our faces vizards to our hearts, disguising what they are. No problem. I have become a master of disguise these past few months. Only the diary knows how I lose my mind, hearing what I think, what I whisper to the white paper.

Except for last night, when I lost it altogether. The kids fought again and I snapped. No shouts or screams or swear words or knife-throwing. It was worse than that. I just turned and walked out on them without a word, drove off in the dark and sat in the car and smouldered. For a full two hours. It didn't really take me that long to calm down but I wanted to enforce the point. I came back to find Jonathan searching around for me in the back garden, with a torch, poor little bugger. He apologized so decently I felt rotten and cried a bit in secret. Next day Paloma broke her hind leg and had to be taken to the vet's. When I brought her back home the leg was in plaster and Pushkin went berserk, spitting and snarling and going for her with talons bared. So now the bloody cats had to be kept apart, on top of which she couldn't use her litter tray and I came down next morning to find her floundering in her own faeces and making pathetic attempts to bury the mess. I cleaned her up, arranged separate trays, feeding bowls and rooms incommunicado, made the packed lunches, the breakfast, shot out to the corner shop (God bless Pakistan!), got the kids up, went through the timetable and schoolbag drill, executed a swift vicious drive to school and arrived shouting *Fie upon this quiet life, I want work!*

Advent arrived unregarded in the midst of hell – the time of cards and candles, goodwill, and peace on earth, and long black clouds brushing the whalebacks of the hills as they sailed over Edinburgh on their journey east. Always travelling east, it seems, passing my classroom window, out across the firth and over to Fife. Where I was friends with perished people, as Housman's poem has it. *And there lie they*. And there lies she. Unblurred by tiredness and time. December also brought an added tiredness to the general exhaustion – a tiredness with the power to change tenses, a tiredness which loads down the limbs and loads up the head till I feel it start to wobble, unbalancing me. I find myself actually touching my head with one hand to check that it's not about to fall off. When I notice the pupils imitating this action I realize I must have been doing it for some time. Another sign of incipient madness?

In the small hours of the fourth day of the month thieves

tried to steal the car and the alarm system gave the entire street ample warning of World War Three. I had a battle on another front that needed urgent action. After glancing at the smashed window and buckled door, I came inside to ring the police and found Jonathan doubled up over the toilet, puking violently and clutching his abdomen on the right side. I put him in the back of the car and drove off to the hospital in the rain with a gaping window, a door that wouldn't close, and sitting in a heap of broken glass.

They whipped out Jonathan's appendix and that was him fixed. But what can fix my head, I wonder? It still keeps lolling about like a poppy-turned-turnip on its stalk. What kind of doctor can cure this curious condition? The question is as rhetorical as Macbeth's to the physician.

> *Can't thou not minister to a mind diseased,*
> *Pluck from the memory a rooted sorrow,*
> *Raze out the written troubles of the brain,*
> *And with some sweet oblivious antidote*
> *Cleanse the stuff'd bosom of that perilous stuff*
> *Which weighs upon the heart?*

The words of a man close to despair, I tell the Fourth Form. He doesn't know it yet but he's going to get even closer. He's about to lose his wife.

I sit at my school desk desperately trying to stay awake and equally desperately wanting to sleep. By evening I'm glad to be able to lay my head on a couch or cushion to ease the conscious burden of keeping it upright on my shoulders. How can I go to the doctor and say that I think my head's coming off? I lie crushed in bed, haul myself up from a stormy sea of sleep and it's morning again and I'm back in the classroom staring out at the hills. The white hand has dusted them during the night but already the veils of rain are drifting up from the south. Two minutes later the first drops batter the window panes. Down on the muddied rugby pitches the landlocked gulls are pegging about like ancient sailors mooching in bars, ungainly on spindly legs. They're waiting for morning break, when the kids will chuck away their crusts, ignoring the litter rules. A class is working silently in front of me, working at something they don't care about and neither do I. I don't give a shit if they can spell, punctuate, comprehend syntax, construct sentences, paragraphs, essays, analyse and evaluate literary masterpieces, write them themselves, reach beyond the words, beyond the ideas, emotions and aesthetics to become supremely aware of themselves, their neighbours, their world, their universe – all of that which used to be the precious object of my trade. Not any more. Someone else is wearing my clothes and inhabiting my classroom. This old wizard has lost interest in the trick of teaching. The magic has gone. And Prospero prepares to break his staff. And drown his book.

The rainclouds scatter and now I can't bear the fierce white sunlight. I close the blinds and the class moans. I fire Milton at them. My secret weapon. Hide me from day's garish eye.

> *And when the sun begins to fling*
> *His glaring beams, me goddess bring*
> *To archèd walks of twilight groves*
> *And shadows brown that Sylvan loves.*

There. It'll help you to concentrate. Much better for the brain. What Milton calls 'a dim religious light', *Il Penseroso*, don't you know?

Of course they don't.

We head towards Christmas and once more the Pentlands turn to white whales, stranded in a sea of Prussian blue. The cards start to arrive, the first snowflakes – qualified greetings this year, hinting at awkwardness, incongruity. Merry Christmas? Merry hellfire. I hear on the radio that the Bishop of Durham has just pronounced the non-existence of hell. What a lovely Christmas present for all of us! No hell? He hasn't spent seventy-seven days without her. Hell is absence, hell is loss, remember? There could be plenty of that in the next world, if there's a next world. He didn't mention what he thought of heaven.

The year ended at midnight, as years do. Church bells, explosions, shouting and songs – rockets fizzing out among the cold constellations. And there, straddling the skies and glittering through rime, was Orion, under which we'd courted, by the skirts of the winter firth, and I'd slipped my lover's hand under *her* skirt and felt that secret warmth. God, the love we made after that! The wild nights. Many moons ago. On some other planet – also moonlit: a reminder of the strength and pain of being young, that it can't come again, but is for others undiminished somewhere. And now Orion was sparkling on her stone, lonely up there in the cemetery, not far from another stone that commemorated someone's beloved son of nine days old. And all those other stones. Yours in the ranks of death, my love. The minstrel boy to the war is gone.

And now it's 1994 and my literary diary tells me that Stevenson, that other marvellous minstrel and my hero, died a hundred years ago – his wild harp slung behind him. The thought made me take a much longer run than usual, through the gathering light up to the Pentlands, past the shrouded cars and the cats on windowsills. I passed a train trundling northward through the half dark, a clattering caterpillar of light, a thin line of gold threading the city. By sunrise I was up among Stevenson's old snows and looking back on Edinburgh still rumpled under its bedsheet.

She wasn't there to greet me when I got back from the traditional New Year's Day run, but that didn't surprise me. We're getting used to three of us in the house now, not four. There's one thing I still can't get used to, though – her bracelets and bangles, still stacked, hoopla style, on one of the slender supporting columns of the dressing-chest mirror. Still where she left them. Still looking as if she might come in at any moment and choose one from the stack. Which one shall I wear tonight? Do you think this one goes? Is there a flower that suits?

I go to Mortonhall and place red carnations like drops of blood on her grave, remembering again the single drop that splashed her nightdress the night she died. Flowers now for the first day of the year, and there's just myself and an old widow up there, a withered thing whispering something to her husband's stone. What am I doing here, a man in his forties, standing around among all these vanished lives along with one solitary old woman? A poor, weak, palsy-stricken, churchyard thing. Angela among the ashes. Well, I'm safe here, anyway, away from the whinings of the Grim Granny, the eternal enemy of optimism. At least I keep my own bellyaching quiet. Only the white page soaks it up. Today it's literal, though. My stomach feels as if it's skewered to my spine and there are pains in the chest. Did I overdo it on the Pentlands run? I come back home and gulp down tablets to combat acidity.

And I open up the diary again, putting more offerings into the ill-shaped urn of words. The rain starts up, dribbling down the panes, the only other sound the lick of a flame in the chimney. The day ticks by. Happy New Year.

Next morning I lay and drank coffees from five till seven. Drink enough of them, Rush, and you may even kill yourself – a protracted version of Tchaikovsky's cup of cholera. Failing that, you could fake an accident on Arthur's Seat. I drank on, safe inside the black envelope, the blanket of the dark. Till dawn shredded it, slowly at first and then with great stabs and slashes, the bloody bond of day. The second day of the year. Soon the useless holidays will be over and I'll be back to the mindless grind: cooking the mince, paying the bills, turning up for work, correcting the spelling, grinning like an ape, swilling back the coffee in the mornings, the solitary glass by night. And all for what? A loaf of bread beneath the bough. And thou beside me . . .

Ah, but now the telephone blasts, and guess who is ringing from hell? Your mother's voice. Mother. Sometimes I don't believe it. You had nothing of her in you, thank God. You didn't even look like her. That selfish, brainless, narrow-nosed old neurotic gave you absolutely nothing of her from the crazy jigsaw of genes. And the bellyaching old bitch has now sent Meals on Wheels packing. *Think I'm going to pay good gin money for that inedible garbage, do you? Think again, sonny boy, I'm your responsibility now, it's what your wife would have expected of you, so I'm relying on you . . .*

Relying on me. But I am seriously beginning to think that I am no longer reliable, that I am actually going under.

Under the sea of troubles – the worn carpet, the burst couch, the empty fridge, the sinkful of dishes, the vases of dead flowers, the mother-in-law that needs the needle, the mother of all ironings, the hours in the night when the blood creeps and the nerves prick and tingle. What else? A wardrobe of empty dresses, a jumble of unworn jewellery, a telephone that terrifies, a future I don't believe in, a pair of shoes I dread to step into each morning. And those three huge oxygen cylinders still standing there by the bed like scabby black bombs. Why doesn't the hospital ask for them? Doesn't somebody else need to breathe? Why don't I return them? It's been five months now. Do I still believe she's going to come back and ask for a breath of air? To try again?

It was in the thick of all this that the washing-machine broke down. A Sunday afternoon, snow falling, and a jumble of sodden schoolwear shut fast behind the bolts and shackles of technology, and me a DIY dunce. This was the last straw – the hatchet in the back, more like. I walked straight out of the house and stood in the middle of the street, among the swirling flakes. I'm not sure why. Maybe to show myself more openly to God and to beg for mercy or a miracle – how to get the kids to school in the morning without clothes. Maybe just to help me decide whether to scream or cry. Or laugh hysterically. God had an alternative idea. Round the corner swung a tiny bicycle, and riding it was an equally diminutive cyclist who looked just like Lenin. He was wearing a Russian hat. Problems? His accent was crude and heavy. I doubted whether he would understand me but I said it all the same. Washing-machine. His eyes sparkled. I fix. After fixing it in five minutes his slanted eyes roamed the house hungrily. Did I have anything else that needed fixing? CD player? VCR? Television? He spoke the third suggestion softly, after a dramatic pause, and in a manner that made it sound like nirvana.

Viktor turned out to be a medical research scientist from Moscow, with a passion for tinkering. His field was cancer. With a bottle of vodka between us in the back room and the snowflakes whirling outside the French windows, I spoke a bit about cancer from another perspective. He shrugged. Travel, my friend. You need to travel. Get it out of your system. I explained to him my long-held view: that the most interesting people I'd ever met were those who had never travelled but had stayed in one place, and by coming to understand it had come to understand the universe; that this was because travel narrows the mind and is for those who constantly require external stimuli, lacking sufficient inner resources of their own. Travel, in a word, is for people who have nothing better to do. The slanted eyes on the other side of the vodka bottle narrowed. It seems to me, my friend, that you *have* nothing better to do.

The Little Russian became a friend and as familiar to me as Tchaikovsky's symphony of that name. The seed he sowed fell straight into the snow and disappeared. I suppose it took root in secret, though I soon lapsed into lassitude again and lay for sleepless unproductive hours watching the dawns, great long carriages of clouds, thundering eastwards in the long slow surge where the skies bled red and the trees took fire with the sun.

And here come the long columns of rains, stalking over the hills, turning the grey old huddle into a congregation of ghosts. I hear the cry of gulls, keening across the crumpling graveyards of the waves, up from the firth. Here come the droplets, pattering on the panes. I pad barefoot through the house to the library window, past the ranks of fine bindings, bathed in the bleak reluctant light. The hills have collected pockets of snow that the rain still can't empty. The trees bend their heads. I picture her dead head under the scything sleet.

February opened with gales and rain, her streaming stone facing the black sky, unread. In the afternoon the wind dropped and the sun came slanting through the sodden world. But by evening the trees were roaring again with seas of wind crashing through their bare branches. I went to bed listening to the gusts rumbling in the lums in this house of six chimneys and seeing the raindrops latticing the window-panes, a silvery net in the lamplight from the streets. But I couldn't sleep and got up to read by the embers downstairs. I woke at half past four with the candles burnt and guttering and staggered back upstairs for another hour of sleep. The alarm clock is an effective aggressor at 5.30 a.m. I made a coffee and stared at the windows, flecked by spindrift stars. Night after night they come, like a soundless white tide, breaking over her head. Night after night.

So morning breaks yet again and off comes the coffin lid. Even February has to be lived through. Soon enough March will be drying up the earth, April will green it, May embroider it, June thump it with sunshine. Another brash summer will have to be endured, and another searing September, before we get back to the bone, the black and white of winter and the skeleton that spreads its structure just under all the shams and flams. No way of getting off early, is there? Off this treadmill of time's trivia, nature's funwheel, the artful deceits of the calendar, the charades of seasons. No way. So let's get the kids up and get the bloody show on the road and get out there to work.

A surge of adrenalin and some arsing around sees me safely through the first lesson. They file out and I sit down hard in my chair, realizing how much it took out of me, to do what I just did. They who are the masters now want us to be instruments, not teachers, and surgically remove all non-conformist spontaneity from our teaching style. I can't do it like that. It's performance – or it's nothing. But I'll have to do it again next week. And the next and the next, and the next, to the end of term. Then next term. Then next year. And the next and the next and the next to the last fucking syllable . . . It's impossible, I can't do it and I need out. Better disengage.

No chance. She's on the phone again, that gin-drenched gibbering old bag of sticks, Grim Granny, down to an ugly little stump of life, stuttering and guttering and cursing and gaunt – but still bloody refusing to go out. No brief candle, that one, and plenty of sound and fury, prophesying war. I put the phone down less than two minutes ago and she's on again, the whining bundle of nonsense and nerves and crushing futility that you carried on your back all your days, my darling, hag-ridden by the devil's dam. She was your millstone, your black dog, your ball and chain, your cross, your *via dolorosa*, your bed of nails, your plague sore, your path of burning coals. And she murdered sleep – for all the house. This afternoon I brought her up for dinner and she ladled into herself a pint of hot soup and a steak and kidney pie and potatoes, followed by ice-cream and apple crumble and an entire box of chocolates, well washed down with gin *during* and brandy *afterwards* and a fistful of cigarettes. Then she had the decency to cry a bit and say that her days were done. But what horrified me was the enormous relish with which she packed it all away. She actually *enjoys* eating and wants to go on living. That's what she said – *I have so much still to live for*. What the fuck is there to live for? Darkness is our only friend.

The window lightens: six squares of faint blue sky, my share of eternity at seven in the morning. Eternity. Thou hast it now. All of it. And I want more than my six squares. I'm hungry for death. That's the breakfast I really

73

want. But I ram some toast into myself and the kids and get us into work. Where I hear colleagues talking about her. About *her*. She, her, hers. And I find myself thinking again how strangely inappropriate the pronouns are now, to specify one who has slipped the bonds of gender. As of time. As of place. And I'm not alone. Shortly after murdering Desdemona Othello hears the word 'wife' and the enormity of it just hits him in the face. *Wife? What wife?*

Alas, I have no wife.

I'm teaching this to a Sixth Form class and have to leave the room in a hurry, cracking up. They stare into their desks when I return, my face washed, composed. So the old cock blubbed again.

Sunrise arrives. Showers on the city barbaric pearl and gold. Almost Miltonic. Is it Saturday? I shut my eyes tight in my terror. No, not the Granny run, surely, not today? I can't do it. No, it's Monday, thank God, you can blink again. I open up for business and the day runs down the plughole. What are days for?

It's past midnight again, with freezing flakes of snow falling like iron filings on a thin bitter wind. My nose is running, my head pounding, a common or garden cold, nothing more. Even so I can't get to sleep. Can't get used to the unrumpled side of the bed. *Her* side. I miss little things: her slender wrists with the distant blue veins, like rivers seen from a height, winding into invisibility along her arms. I miss her shoulders, her ankles and eyebrows. It's not just about breasts and thighs. It never was. I miss her back, which I stroked and fingered like a cellist, as if her vertebrae were notes in a secret score which we'd keep on returning to night after night, playing our night music. Not tonight. I lie and watch three seasons of stars constellate the windows, passing pane by pane.

Kill or cure was the morning decision taken on the cold virus. I pulled on my running gear and made straight for Arthur's Seat. Up the flank of the lion couchant, on to his spine, and so on up to the head, on gradients of more than seventy degrees. No problem. But high winds were streaming over the summit. It was like being suddenly hit by a freezing river, turning the skull to iron and the lungs to an ice-bucket. I came home on fire. The telephone was shrilling. The monstrous regiment of moans trumpeting down the line, blasting me to hell. *My feet are blue, the circulation's stopped, I'm freezing, I've lost all my money, I can't find my brandy and I'm needing more gin! When will you be down? The dog's not well. You'll have to take him to the vet, and me to the Post Office. I can't wait till you have a bath, I need you down here now, I need looking after! You can start by finding my false teeth . . .*

The weather shifted briefly, bringing cruel blue skies, then the grey veils of rain again, drifting down from the hills, then snowflakes on cheekbones and eyes, stinging like white bees. The Portobello neighbours of the Mad Gran called me to an emergency meeting. They wanted a doctor's opinion of the state of her mind and body. I arranged to approach her GP, caring for her only as duty demanded. Completely heartless now? Not quite. But I strike it and it turns to stone. Othello has taught me that much at least.

But the Granny File is yet another problem to soak up time and sanity, what's left of either. There are too many desks to sit at – teacher's, administrator's, author's, dad's. Catriona has begun staying away from home at nights, suffering from attacks of anger and depression. She comes home next day with more bruises on the backs of her hands, where she has begun again in earnest to smash herself against solid surfaces in the fury of her bewilderment and hurt. It had to happen and now it's here, the real suffering, the black anger, following the black dogs of depression and despair, and the cessation of numbness and shock. Lacking the energy to deal with this, I tell her to snap out of it. That's a laugh, coming from me, but I come out with all the clichés.

So do the weathermen. March will go out like a lion, they say – wild, wet and roaring. The sun comes out briefly, a flickering storm-lantern, lighting up the bare waving trees, the pewter streets. The first buds nose through like green bullets. Spring will be a killer this year. Morning is a windowful of raindrops on fire.

Our wedding anniversary comes round. What to do with it? I go out for a run round the hill and taste dust on my tongue. A sure sign of spring. On the same day comes news from the hospital where the Grim Granny has finally submitted to tests. The results are through. There are shadows on the lungs. There is talk of cancer. Can it be true? If so, it comes too late. Cancer has already done its worst. I drag myself along to see her in the Geriatric ward, peopled by all those who'd sloped arms some September. Made love, made children, made castles in the air, made lives on sand, in water. Now life has run away from them. Now they are the old fools, not knowing how, not hearing who, the power of choosing gone, sitting through days of thin continuous dreaming with lighted rooms inside their heads – rooms without mirrors, fortunately. They can't see what's happened to them: ash hair, toad hands, prune face. This is the view from just beneath extinction's alp.

April is the cruellest month, they say, echoing another poet of pessimism. And it's here.

Cruel? It's an invention of the devil. The news comes

from the hospital that the grim witch is fine, she doesn't have cancer after all. I've got to get the kids away. Plots must be laid. For Easter I place her in the hands of the iron angels of Home Care, an agency of last resort. It costs £300 a week. But it's seven days of liberty. We'll go to Fife for a week and when we come back we won't answer the phone till the holiday is over. We'll pretend we're still away. We'll have a fortnight's freedom. Hallelujah after all!

Easter Sunday, 3 April. The phone rang early. It was Home Care. They'd been sent packing. Best-laid plans of mice and men. Gone to ploughlands every one. I went out immediately and bought an answer phone, installed it and left a fiction of a message that we'd all gone abroad on a school trip. Abroad. That was a laugh. We'd never been abroad in our lives. It had always proved impossible to leave her. There had never been anyone else to look after her. As a matter of fact we'd never been further than the fifty miles to Fife, and never a day passed without reporting into barracks by telephone, sometimes twice a day. Now that she was almost eighty, the iron umbilical she'd forged and kept a tight grip on all these years, playing her daughter like a wounded fish, pulling her in pitilessly – well, I'd cut it, hadn't I? We'd been to Stratford and now we'd gone to hell. And cut the lines behind us.

Pleasure and action make the hours seem short. Next Saturday suddenly loomed and I felt like the *Titanic* looking for an iceberg. Let's go north like the Ninth Legion and let history swallow us up.

But before the imagined axe falls, I learn that she has been picked up by the police. Her mind in revolt, she has been found wandering the streets barefoot in her night-clothes, her front door wide open, all the gas fires turned on unlit, and smouldering scraps of paper strewn across

77

the carpet in some crazy bid to light cigarettes without matches. The neighbours panicked at the thought of gas explosions and she is to be sectioned under the Mental Health Act and detained in the Royal Edinburgh Hospital from which I am assured she cannot discharge herself. I go mad with joy, like Basil Fawlty with a kipper up his jumper. 'Oh, joy! I'm so happy! Oh, thank you, God!' Complete with imitation of mad Cleese goosestepping up and down the garden, oblivious to the neighbours. An appalling state to get into. Maybe I'm the one who should be sectioned, but I could have kissed the shoes of the doctor who told me. Her feet were beautiful, like the feet of those that bring the gospel of good news. So the Grim Granny has been weighed in the balance and found wanting. Her days are numbered. Sectioning. It has the pleasant sound to me of vivisectioning. I'm tempted to ask the doctor, 'Will it hurt?' Mr Fawlty Hyde is in control. I hardly know myself. The mad mask grins at me from the mirror.

When I returned home I nearly collapsed with shock. A string of curses came shrieking out of the answer phone. But she'd left them there the previous day, before the sectioning. I played them over again, the second time for hysteria and hilarity and again was shocked by the face from the other side of the mirror. Who was that wild-eyed monster?

The first day in the year arrived on which you could say, yes: I remember summer. Girls wearing shorts, showing off their white winter legs, people playing with frisbees in the parks, couples lying in the meadows – dry grass at last. And an unbroken sun pouring out real heat. I didn't hear the cuckoo but I did hear the sound of the first lawnmower. I went home and lay in the hammock among nine months of weeds. After five minutes the book slipped from my hand into the long grass. I made instead for the hill, its flanks now sparked by the first whinflowers, dazzling droplets of gold. Things looked almost hopeful. Almost. But hopeful of what, precisely? No answer to that one.

Nature tyrannizes yet again, the garden straggling violently out of control. The coiling brambles make it look more like a neglected section of the Western Front. The roses trail in their rotting strings, hanging off the walls, and the grass will soon be knee-high, the green world strangely depressing where it's meant instead to comfort with its illusions of eternal cycles and rebirth.

Tomorrow is her birthday. The clematis and bluebells I used to cram into vases for her are growing to waste. I'm tired, tense, steam-rollered and spent; my legs are trembling, even my fingers feel weak and can barely hold a pen. I'm dealing now with all the old witch's affairs: home insurance, Council Tax, gas, electric, British Telecom, Home Care, bank, lawyer and vet, all in a shambles, in addition to our own affairs and the educational dump that teachers now inhabit like maggots in a midden, some of them thinking that this is actually it – that they have arrived!

There is no let-up. June turns the hills to golden waterfalls of whinflower, cascading above the city. Evenings glide in like sharks. She's got to be visited. I do so armed with everything I can think of, Black Magic in my hands and arsenic in my heart. She sits in her web as ever and weaves her spells of despair. She is the corrupter, the death-force, the bringer-forth of blowflies. She is the killer that sucked out my wife's soul and left me the husk to bury. Now she is sucking the mental marrow from my mind – what's left of it.

What *is* left of me? All those people I used to be. The fresh schoolboy, the wild student, the teacher, the poser, that young man standing with his arm around his bride, the young man in the photograph, the star-struck husband – and the new father striding down to the sea between those banks of barley, blurred by summer mists, the toddler on his shoulders, whistling 'Greensleeves', singing a song of a lad that is gone. None of these persons exists now except on fading celluloid and in the fading grey cells of the brain. Only the husk of Rush is left. A breath could blow me at the moon. The hot June days just happen around me now. I'm hardly there. And by the fag-end of the nights I'm asleep on the couch. The kids get me to bed. Or a friend phones and the voice on the other end, sensing the situation, guides me to my feet, into the bedroom and under the duvet, like the Control Tower talking me down. I've forgotten how to navigate, it seems, the days, the nights. The machine is a mystery to me. I'm a headache on legs, a stomach ready to throw up, a back beaten and sore, a dead weight. The essential me has emigrated somewhere. An alien sits scribbling in my place, in command of my desk. I can just make out his hand, holding the pen. I can see the words on the page. But their sense eludes me and the sentences start to swim . . .

And then the thunderbolt. The old bird is to be let out of her cage, which she has fouled most abominably. She is a bird of very little brain but she is not mad and a reassessment has determined that she is no longer suitable to be placed in a ward of ladies with no minds left at all. What they don't realize is that she is a bird of prey, a vulture who will rip out our hearts and eat us alive down to our very nails and teeth. It makes no difference. Soon she is back at the dinner-table, complaining that the food is impossible for her false teeth. Has to be taken to the dentist's. Has to be driven to restaurants, where she gives the waitresses hell and sends us out between courses, cringing with shame. And will have to be taken on holiday.

On holiday? Christ, no! The boredom and bitterness of life are bad enough without this hellish substitute for the woman I loved and lost. Chaos has come again, the skin stretched tight across the skull, the soul stretched tight across the sky, like a silent scream, my beaten shoulders, my crushed back, my jellied knees, my shaking fingers losing the pen, my mind losing the place, while the desks are adrift with letters and the vestibule awash with bills, dusty clusters of nettles choking the garden that she once kept so well. The cut grass lies frail, exuding the brief fresh breath of mortality but dying the long death in the white hours of long-leafed June. Things are tougher than we are. They don't go away. But I need to call the electrician, book the sweep, write reports, change the beds, take the cats to the vet, hoover the rooms, edit the school magazine, mark the exams, interview parents, see to the usual rounds of shopping and washing and ironing, get myself a pair of shoes that don't leak. If only it didn't rain! But it does – and though I can't sing in it, I think I need to stand in it instead, to stand in it and scream, long and loud and hard, world without end. I've come to the end of this particular world, it seems, and I have to find another. I crawl off to bed while it's midsummer and still light. The birds are singing, copper beeches are staining the clouds and the lime trees are licking the sky.

PART TWO

Between Two Lives

ONLY CONNECT. I forget who said it – F.M. Forster, perhaps. Does it matter? In the year following my wife's death nothing much seemed to matter any more, even literature. Only connect. It had something to do with how one should write literature. The art of writing is not much different from the art of living, in this respect. If you are out of connection for too long you will start to perform badly – as an artist, as a human being. When my wife died I lost the ability to connect. In both senses. And if I am not writing I am not living. In the decade before 1993 I'd written ten books and a screenplay. It would be another ten years till I managed to break the silence – with the present book. The language of the first part, forced on me by experience and hewn from my diaries, reflects the nightmare of breakdown, loss of connection: what follows reveals the return to authorial normality after a decade, where happiness is always threatening to 'write white' but not ever getting there. I hope not, anyway. Happy people don't write real books. So much for literature.

Not that I'd have personally survived such a state of disconnection for anything like ten years. One year was frightful enough. I had to connect. And quickly. When the school session in 1994 thundered to a close I hit the buffers, was thrown out on to the streets of Edinburgh without a timetable, and, exiled from hell, panicked in the bitter heaven of the summer holidays.

Everywhere I went, she died – as Norman MacCaig said in his memorial for his wife. No sunrise, no city square, but has her death in it. She can't *stop* dying. She makes me her elegy. I am her sad music. Writers don't necessarily connect – but all of us connect through death, and I remember a deliberate daily quest to find my way back to the rest of humanity.

I went down to the sea again, to the call of the running

tide, over in Fife. The truth was that were was no call – and no response. When I arrived the water was at low ebb and the rocks stood like broken tombs in a cemetery. What is the secret of this stone, I asked myself – the one that I am holding in my hand? What absurd era does it belong to? Then or Now? All eras are absurd. But I envy it its unequivocal existence, its preposterous aplomb: such thereness, such fixity, such joylessness and calm. I give it back to the beach, placing it carefully against the strewn stillness of the strand, the dumb drift of shingle – groping instead for consolation in echoes of half-remembered lines of Sorley Maclean, the poetry of shores. *And if I were with you, for who my care is always new ...* Was that how it went? I would stand beside the sea, renewing love in my spirit, while the ocean was filling Talisker Bay eternally. I would stand there, on the bareness of the shore, would stay there till doomsday, measuring sand, grain by grain, would wait there for ever, in front of the wide loneliness, till the sea was drained, drop by drop. The sequence of words eluded me but the scene evoked the austerity of the island shores where the great Gaelic poet vowed to his love that he would never cease to wait for her ... till the joyless surge dragged the boulders and threw them over them.

Looking up from the pebbled beach I saw a ship on the skyline. 'When our boat comes in,' she used to say. And it did. Only it wasn't the one we'd awaited and expected from the sparkling armada of promises, flagged, its figure-head resplendent with golden breasts. One breast was blackened, matching the sail. It was the black-sailed unfa-miliar that finally arrived, towing at her stern that huge and birdless silence. In her wake no waters bred or broke. Back in the cottage the silence probed like a surgeon, dissecting the darkness, and then the wind started to howl again – a beast caught in the chimney.

Back in Edinburgh I wandered the city streets in the early mornings when the kids were still asleep – partly for lack of anything to do, anything that I really wanted to do, that is; partly to escape the awful Granny, whom I wished dead in the fury of my heart, and who ripened my thoughts for murder. As it happened I didn't have to break the Sixth Commandment. Another sudden deterioration in behaviour brought her back into care, from which she never re-emerged, eventually entering the slow coma that leads only one way.

In a mad sort of way I missed her. Missed the all too easy target for my grieving anger. It was the one thing I had believed in. Now I just didn't believe. Full stop. Didn't believe in the useless dawns that found me in deserted corners of the city, having outlived the night, still practising the sounds that went to make up *her* name, still turning them over in the streaked darkness, telling them to the few stray dogs and to the few stray stars of the dawn.

I found myself standing outside No. 17 Heriot Row, Robert Louis Stevenson's old house. As I stared at this New Town literary shrine I started to speak to myself very deliberately, telling myself that I had to connect up my life and my writing once again. I recalled some words about there being no essential difference between the man who suffers and the poet who creates. I remembered Viktor, the Little Russian. I reflected that Stevenson's best book had been his own life. Death at forty-four – even younger than my wife – had simply cut short a masterpiece. And I remembered something else. It was a childhood reverie.

And it went something like this.

A young man, an aspiring writer in his late twenties, left Victorian Edinburgh from this very house and started to travel. He had certain things on his mind, a sadness in his soul, and Black Dog on his back. Eventually he found himself in southern France, where he bought a donkey, and with no fixed map in his mind, he began to wander through the mountains. The following year his account of this journey, written up from his journals, was published under the title *Travels with a Donkey in the Cévennes*.

It was his most accomplished publication so far. Until then he'd appeared mainly in periodicals, though this brought little satisfaction to his parents, Thomas Stevenson and Maggie Balfour. The sanguine Balfours were church people, the melancholic Stevensons engineers, builders of lighthouses. Little difference really. Lighthouses were stars for seamen in an age which read metaphors literally. *Thy word is a light unto my feet and a lamp unto my path.* Jovial joyless divided Thomas Stevenson, himself the victim of a stern patriarch, married nineteen-year-old Maggie, the daughter of a terrifying religious martinet, the Reverend Lewis Balfour, who inhabited the Colinton village manse, five miles from the heart of Edinburgh. The white-haired maniac with the bloodshot eyes had been brought up under the rod and passed on the same treatment to his own children, as well as the pulmonary weakness which Maggie transferred to young Louis, named after his grandfather with a Bohemian change of spelling.

They fuck you up, your mum and dad. But they were fucked up in their turn. Man hands on misery to man. It wasn't hard for me, looking at Heriot Row exactly a hundred years after Stevenson's death, to imagine the draughty eighteenth-century barns that these houses once were, and to picture the plump, curly-haired child of 1854 moving into No. 17 three years later, soon to melt away into the spidery specimen of all the later photographs. A child's garden of viruses grew readily in the echoing interiors, and in those biblical pressure-cooker times bricks and mortar could combine with the genes and play their part in paving the road out of Edinburgh. Out of anywhere. To somewhere else. *I should like to rise and go where the golden apples grow*. It was a sick man who went to the Cévennes. But he was a man empty of self-pity and determined to make the best of things. A man to emulate.

With this in mind I drifted down to Colinton, where his grandfather's church and manse still stand. So do the tall roaring trees lining the dark brown river where he'd sailed paper boats, later to form themselves into a famous children's poem about journeys and landfalls, about going away, about escaping the present and coming back home, changed in some mysterious way.

I began to draw parallels. Before I was three years old I'd had the fear of death and damnation put into me by a stern old great-aunt, Epp, who had a fundamentalist view of hell which, she assured me, was just beneath the floor-boards, with Satan himself sitting on our chimneys. I was trapped, to put it mildly – not that she ever did. I'd written about her in an earlier memoir, *A Twelvemonth and a Day*. Epp was to me what a woman called Cummy was to the young Louis. When he was two Alison Cunningham became his nurse, and however much she doted on him, she proceeded to fill his nights with terror. Her bedtime stories saw to that. As well as the bloodcurdling stories from the Old Testament, she fed him tales of destiny and damnation, of resurrection and resurrectionists, revenants, infanticides, hangings and stabbings and poisonings and unquiet graves. Just like the stories I'd heard round the fire in the forties in the house of my fisherman grandfather on the eastern edge of Fife: drownings and exhumations, ghosts and ghouls, monsters of the deep and terrors of the dark. For good measure Cummy took little Louis round the Edinburgh cemeteries and showed him the graves of

Protestant martyrs, reviving for him their gruesome ends by fire and rope and sword. Nurse Cunningham was another religious maniac and every inch a bigot and yet Maggie Stevenson allowed her a free hand with her son. It was a hand that in one sense pointed out the road to the Cévennes and ultimately beyond the Cévennes to Samoa, as far away from the past as he could possibly get.

But you can never escape your past entirely. Cummy's Covenanting ancestors had filled the Pentland hills south of Edinburgh with their bloody and fanatical history and when, in Louis's seventeenth year, his father leased a cottage up at Swanston on the edge of those hills, he found an Eden to escape to. In the long summer light I took a run up to the Pentlands and stood on the whale-backs, imagining Louis reliving those religious killing times in his historical imagination. Near the end of his life in Samoa he was still remembering the Pentlands and praying that he would see them again in dying.

What exactly he did see as he slipped into the coma brought on by a cerebral haemorrhage on 3 December 1894 is a question beyond scholarship. But high places and faraway places were central to his writer's vision and it was no accident that when the restless spindle-shanks made for the High Cévennes, he was homing in on a piece of French Protestant history every bit as bloody as what had happened in the Scottish religious struggle: a curious commitment on the part of the Bohemian whose self-declared atheism caused rifts and storms in Heriot Row. Fathers in his fiction do not come off well – a son's revenge, perhaps. I'd drowned my own father deep in my mind in *Twelvemonth*: another literary reprisal. And another parallel, so I thought. Standing on those hills, which had been the backdrop to my recent miseries and the worst experience of my life, and looking down on Swanston and

Colinton and on Edinburgh itself, I followed RLS further into his life and inside his skin.

Two years after the religious storm broke in Heriot Row, and having already turned his back on engineering and the law, Louis went to the forest of Fontainbleau to visit the artists' colony at the Hôtel Siron at Barbizon. Returning the following year, in the summer of 1876 he went along to the Chevillon hotel at Grez-sur-Loing to look into a report that the opposite sex had been allowed entry to the male Bohemian Elysium. He arrived just as dinner was being served, vaulted through the open window, according to the mythos, and looked into the dark eyes of a woman ten years older than himself but mannishly handsome: Fanny Vandegrift Osbourne. The bearer of three children, one of whom had died, she was a mother figure in other ways. A horsewoman, she shot from the hip, she cooked beef in fifteen different ways and she smoked her own rolled cigarettes – a free spirit, a strong protectress and a force to be reckoned with. Also a woman who aspired to art and to Bohemia. In short a perfect companion for the fragile Scotsman. Within two years they were lovers in every sense and regarded themselves as man and wife.

Louis wrote about her passionately, romantically. She was a golden girl, a gypsy, a flowing shadow. And she bloomed like a tiger lily in the snowdrifts of the bed. The image says it all. The social reality was quite different. She was a married woman and a mother, living with another man. The times were the times and Louis's parents could hardly be expected to be encouraging. Into the bitter wound of religion was rubbed their son's intensely salty love-life. A powerful undercurrent of tension and unhappiness was now running darkly through Louis's days and this suddenly surfaced in June 1878 when Fanny's money ran out and her husband summoned her back to America. She squirmed but had little option. Louis couldn't support her, and had she refused to obey it would have been an open admission that she and Louis were lovers.

In August of that year she packed her luggage in London and Louis went with her to the boat-train. It was a desperate parting, a species of bereavement. Her unhappy partner did not even wait for the train to pull away. Pale and speechless with grief, he wrapped himself up in his coat and his torment and strode off down the platform without once glancing back – not unlike an angry child turning its back on its mother and refusing to look or speak. No John Donne demonstration, no valedictory lesson forbidding mourning could have comforted the young writer at that moment. As far as he was concerned his woman, the woman he regarded as his wife, was going halfway round the world to return to another man. He had no way of knowing if she would ever come back to him. Nothing made that prospect seem at all likely. His tragedy, as he saw it, was complete. Uneasy with his parents and robbed of his chosen companion, he followed the injunction of the 121st psalm, as sung to him by Cummy: *I to the hills will lift mine eyes, from whence doth come mine aid.* A month later he was in the Cévennes, exploring Le Monastier.

He was reconnecting with himself.

At what point in the nightmare I actually decided to reconnect by doing the same, to take a donkey across the French Highlands in the footsteps of the master, I can't say. Probably there was no single moment of truth. But many things go back to childhood and, though they may seem to die, they often stand and wait, biding their time until they can be of service. I remember how, as quite a young schoolboy in the fifties, I was intoxicated by reading Stevenson's account of his night among the pines on Mont Lozère, sleeping *à la belle étoile* while Modestine munched her black bread and he drank ice-cold water, smoked a rolled cigarette and thought of the woman he loved. Beyond the pine tops the Milky Way was a faint silvery vapour above his head and the only sound was the quiet talk of the stream over the stones. I thought at the time what an incredibly liberating and exhilarating experience it must have been. And undoubtedly this fired my early imagination. Exactly how early I'm not entirely sure. I seem to remember I was still in short trousers. But I must have been on the doorsill of adolescence, because Stevenson was not the only fascination. There was another book in what was an extremely primitive school library at that time and it was entitled *The Complete Poetic Works of Geoffrey Chaucer*, printed in the original fourteenth-century English. It was, of course, largely beyond our linguistic grasp. Nonetheless young boys have a nose for anything faintly anatomical and someone had lit on the passage in 'The Miller's Tale' where the raunchy young Alyson sticks her naked backside out of the window in the pitch dark so that the lovesick parish clerk, Absolom, can kiss it. He thinks he is about to plant a kiss in the conventional place and the joke is on him when his lips are confronted by an apparently bearded Alyson. Something rough and hairy had appeared – such is Chaucer's crude way of putting it. The tone is light and farcical. Naturally, however, we didn't read it that way. It gave us post-war innocents the most wicked thrills imaginable and the page containing this particular passage had been thumbed practically out of print by generations of juveniles.

The same was not true of the book containing the passage from Stevenson. It was a School Reader, an anthology of poems interspersed with prose extracts, and it advertised little in the way of forbidden excitements between its business-like covers. There was no jostling for that particular book. We were allowed one period per week during which we could simply read for pleasure. The books in one of the sections were for reference only and for some reason both the anthology and the Chaucer belonged to the non-borrowing section. Anyone wanting to re-live Alyson's night of sexual adventure or Stevenson's night among the pines had to do so during that single period. And live on the memories for another week till the period came round again. Probably I was shouldered out of the way by bigger boys with more demanding hormones, though I like to think that Stevenson's night of innocent communion with nature attracted me more strongly than Alyson's nocturnal romps. At any rate I did go to the trouble of tracking down a copy of Stevenson's *Travels with a Donkey*, and it was one of the first complete books I read in my early schooldays, along with classics such as *Robinson Crusoe*, *Kidnapped* and *The Coral Island*. As for *Treasure Island* I had devoured it whole when I was about seven, I reckon, and its sights and sounds haunted me then and still do, decades later: Black Dog saved from the cutlass by the signboard of the Admiral Benbow; Billy Bones struck dead by the Black Spot; Blind Pew trampled by thundering hooves; Israel Hands lying dead beneath clear sea-water, nibbled by the quick fishes; the lone seaman's skeleton pointing the way to the treasure; the song of the rum-raddled Captain Flint and the shrieks of Silver's parrot, named for him. And above all the sound of the surf booming about the island coasts.

These were the central and shaping images in a largely bookless upbringing. My fishing-village family on Scotland's east coast were the inheritors of a tradition of language that was still mainly oral and though I was well taught, my own childhood was literate rather than literary. Fishermen tend to be both superstitious and religious, because fishing is an act of faith – at least it was largely so in those days. Consequently there was one book that had a megalithic impact on me and that was the King James Bible. Other than that it was stories round the fire and stories on gravestones that whetted my appetite for adventure – adventure that was still safely confined to the village boundaries, or to the porous borders of the imagination across which a child reader can easily run back home if the excitement becomes too real.

Travels with a Donkey was in a different category. I had believed implicitly in the events of *Treasure Island* and had I encountered any of its characters on the bouldered beaches or in the cobbled closes of my childhood I should not have thought it strange. They were more alive to me than real people and I can recall a dawning sadness when the knowledge of their purely fictitious nature began to be borne in upon me. This marked the end of the age of innocence. Stevenson's *Travels* I understood to be about the author's real-life experiences and although it lacked the drama and sensationalism of swashbuckling novels, it gave me inklings of a different kind of adventure – of the sort I might conceivably take part in myself. One day.

Except that I went on from there to live a life philosophically opposed to travel. I had meant what I said when I told Viktor, the Little Russian, that travel narrows the mind. I embraced fully the Yeatsian credo that you can only attain to universalism through what is near to you and what is meaningful to you: your nation, your village, the cobwebs on your wall, the hailstone that is the journeyman of God, the grass-blade that carries the universe on its point. I had quoted Yeats many a time during debates about travel. 'One can only reach out to the universe with a gloved hand – that glove is one's nation, the only thing one knows even a little of.' Seeing the sights of other countries might well provide you with a lifetime of superficial experience but it would have very little to do with a person's real self, considered on the deepest human level. My supreme example of that was the poet Robert Burns, whose work, steeped in the consciousness of his own country and culture, was essentially universal and had won over the whole world. And Burns did this without travelling. Another hero, a contemporary one, was George Mackay Brown, who had succeeded in universalizing the local without ever moving out of Orkney.

But our opinions, emotions and habits are a mass of contradictions. For example, it never struck me at the time, but the fact is that even my very limited childhood reading was all to do with travel. Granted, this was on the level of mere adventure, though it could have been argued that this constituted no contradiction, simply underlining my view that the best travelling is carried out in the mind. But Stevenson was in a different class. I could scarcely hold him up for admiration as the icon of the non-travelling reader. He was forever leaving places and he left his own country with alacrity, happy to shake the dust of Edinburgh from his boots. Stevenson was a force to be reckoned with in the travel debate. And there were another two factors to be taken into consideration. One was that during the whole of my married life travelling had been virtually out of the question. The Grounding Granny had seen to that. The other was that I had a fear of flying. Not so much a fear, perhaps, as a rational objection. I was philosophically opposed – so I contended – to *all* control being taken out of my hands, which is exactly what happens when you board an aircraft. It does not happen to nearly the same degree when you get into a car or embark on a ship. But if you are serious about travelling the world then generally speaking you have to be prepared to fly. 'I am not prepared to do it,' I said. 'I shall never travel – and I shall most certainly never fly.'

Never say never. After cancer had taken the one I loved I took to the mountains of France to reclaim my sanity. The decision was made early that summer of '94. I knew I couldn't go on living in my diary, a scribbling schizophrenic. I craved calm waters. A port in a storm. A new journal. And a new journey. Different words, different writer, new experience, new man. I set my sights on the Cévennes. Of course I knew that it had all been done before, especially since 1978, when the centenary of Stevenson's journey had drawn hundreds to the Cévennes, but I also knew that this would in no way invalidate my own personal journey. On the contrary, a man who holds such absurdly snobbish views about travel is likely to be egotistic enough to feel that he has more right than most to make the journey. What I felt primarily was that I *needed* to make it – and it was a deep personal need that had to be satisfied and that I reckoned would either kill or cure.

Stevenson set off for the Cévennes in the late summer of 1878 when he was not quite twenty-eight and was suddenly bereft of the woman he loved. We both knew about long goodbyes. Death is the ultimate parting. She had left him to return to her husband, but that was six thousand miles away and he had no idea when he would see her again, if ever, or in what circumstances. As good as dead, then. His personal life was in ruins. 'A miserable widower', as he described himself at this point, he went to France for mountain air, consolation and escape. Also for exploration: of a region of France which interested him but about which he knew next to nothing; of his own feelings and identity; and of the possibility of writing a book about his travels. In the event these travels were transformed for himself and posterity by his reluctant travelling companion. Modestine, so named because of her size (not much bigger than a Newfoundland dog) was the donkey who carried all his luggage but became in turn an abominable encumbrance, in spite of having cost him an outrageous sixty-five francs and a glass of brandy. All the same, this 'self-acting bedstead on four castors' shouldered a joint of cold mutton, a bottle of Beaujolais, tins of Bologna sausage, books, blocks of chocolate, loaves of bread, changes of clothing, and an eccentric assortment of other items including an egg whisk, a brandy flask, a spirit-lamp and pan, a lantern, a jack-knife, tobacco and papers, a blue-lined schoolboy's exercise book, some candles and a revolver. Central to the image of the bedstead was a sleeping-bag made of green waterproof cloth on the outside and blue sheep's fur within, which Stevenson called 'the sack'.

Modestine carried these belongings but the writer carried his own burdens. He was depressed and confused, on the rebound not just from his girl but also from his God – the fearsome middle-class God of No. 17 Heriot Row, where Cummy and his parents held sway. After the stormy scenes in this establishment fortress Louis needed to break out. The loss of his woman was the trigger. But these in themselves were just two of the forces that impelled him to light out from rainy Edinburgh (in his mind) and sunny Paris (in geographical fact) in order to cross the rough and solitary French Highlands. The Cévennes was a multiple-choice test, self-administered, of endurance, independence, introspection, decision and truth.

Did it work? Later he was to write to a friend, 'For the first time in a year I feel something like peace.' If it was an initiation he had completed his rite of passage. If it was a pilgrimage he had reached his shrine. If it was a quest he had found his holy grail. For Stevenson the therapy had worked. It seemed to me to possess all the ingredients of a kill-or-cure medicine. For a man who had never been abroad in his life and had proclaimed his intention never to travel, it would be an experience out of which he would not emerge unchanged.

The fact that so many had already followed in the footsteps of the trail-blazing Louis was of no relevance. Death had wound me up and set me going – not so much like a fat gold watch as like a grenade, primed to go off. Death seldom strikes one as a good idea at any time, but when a mother and wife is still young and strong and lovely, death arrives on the doorstep as a particularly brutal irrelevance, and there is a human longing to make it relevant, to make it mean something.

All that apart, I knew that there were very few people who had done the real Stevenson thing – and this still holds true today. Enthusiasts turn up in different parts of the Cévennes and take out a donkey for an afternoon, or perhaps a day, usually in summer. They fly back home and say they've done RLS in France. Next year they'll follow him to California, or even to Samoa, and take the planned cable-car to the summit of Mount Vaea, where he lies, the ocean beneath him. Or a journalist pops across the Channel for a nice rustic meal at an inn where Louis is known to have dined, interviews a couple of garlicky locals, and writes it up with a few literary references. Some hardy souls do attack the entire route, but usually as summer back-packers, and they do it in their own time, perhaps extending but more often compressing the experience according to the weather and other variables. Not everyone elects to go alone, *avec un âne*, through what is still one of the most depopulated regions of France. Bikers, hikers, coach-travellers, motorists, donkey-for-the-day folk, all are guided down to a sane hotel each night, or to a tourist centre where Stevensoniana will be on sale, complete with plastic donkeys.

I knew all this. Or at least I thought I knew. Even Richard Holmes, the literary biographer, and easily in my estimation the most genuine and gifted of Stevenson's followers, didn't take a donkey. But I was fragile enough emotionally and pompous enough intellectually to consider my own motives as being closer than anyone's to Stevenson's. I had passed well beyond the romantic notions of childhood and the idealism of adolescence, and now, a miserable widower like Louis, thought myself the saddest and fittest if not the wisest of men for the journey. In spite of my fisherfolk lineage my sense of direction was notoriously deplorable. It was a family joke that I had once got lost in St Andrews. I had never used maps or a compass in my life. Nevertheless my plan formulated itself with iron exactitude. I intended to imitate Stevenson's exact itinerary and timetable, leaving the same places on the same dates and at the same times and arriving at the same destinations on schedule, camping out where he had bivouacked, booking in where he had lunched or slept, even to the extent of staying the night with the monks of Notre Dame des Neiges and attending Compline in the monastery chapel. Our Lady of the Snows was still there, I was told, but I had absolutely no notion of what else might still stand. There was only one way to find out. I packed a rucksack, boarded a plane for the first time in my life, and headed for Le Monastier, where it all began.

Where it all began.

How easy it is to say so. But where does a journey really begin? My own road to the Cévennes began not with my wife's death from cancer but way back in my schooldays, with *Treasure Island* and the *Travels*. The road echoed with the ghostly footfalls of pirates and the little hooves of a recalcitrant donkey. It boomed with surf and glinted with scattered coins – and the scent of cognac and tobacco was on the air, mingling with the pines. Stevenson's first footsteps on that road were also taken in early childhood.

Even earlier, in actual fact. Most journeys begin long before we are even born. They begin with weather, with stocks and stones, with a jumble of genes. Some believe they begin with stars. The last is impossible to prove and as fruitless as the moon to contemplate, but it is not difficult to assess the role played by climate in pointing Louis's laced-up boots towards the Cévennes and away from Edinburgh. Writing about the city of his birth in *Picturesque Notes* he says that 'Edinburgh pays cruelly for her high seat in one of the vilest climates under heaven. She is liable to be beaten upon by all the winds that blow, to be drenched with rain, to be buried in cold sea-fogs out of the east, and powdered with snow as it comes flying southward from the Highland hills. The weather is raw and boisterous in winter, shifty and ungenial in summer, and a downright meteorological purgatory in the spring.' He goes on to picture himself leaning over the windy Waverley Bridge and watching the trains smoking out beneath him, vanishing into the tunnel on a voyage to brighter skies – and he envies the passengers who have shaken off the dusty city and heard for the last time the howling of the east wind among its chimney-tops. It is easy, he said, to 'aspire angrily after that Somewhere-else of the imagination where all troubles are supposed to end'.

I often thought about that comment during those long sleepless nights as a beginner widower when I lay listening to the Edinburgh gales shrieking round the gable-end of a house as well-built and windy as Stevenson's. Somewhere else. In all his life and in all his writing he is constantly dreaming of that somewhere else. Samoa is somewhere else. So are the Cévennes. In *Ordered South* he still can't forget the grim wintry streets of home. Even in the Mediterranean the images of Edinburgh continue to haunt him, occasioned by the merest drop in temperature: 'the hopeless, huddled attitude of tramps in doorways; the flinching gait of barefoot children on the icy pavement; the sheen of the rainy streets towards afternoon; the meagre anatomy of the poor defined by the clinging of wet garments; the high canorous note of the North-easter on days when the very houses seem to stiffen with cold'.

A human being is just another seed drifting on the wind. It was an Edinburgh east wind that carried Stevenson to the mountains of southern France.

It was not quite as Louis left it when I arrived in Le Monastier in the summer of 1994 to investigate the region as a preliminary to planning my journey, but my first impression was that change happened here at a distinctly bucolic pace. Nobody seemed in any hurry to get anywhere or to do anything in particular. I recalled that in Stevenson's time the men of the district had a reputation for bibulousness, though it may have been pure untypical chance that I was welcomed in the street by strangers with the question: *Vous avez soif?* Cassis glasses clinked and the chattering started. If they were drunks they were convivial ones. They lived in crooked bulging houses with blistered shutters, elaborately carved doorways and intricate iron balconies, bright with laundry and potted geraniums.

Their windows were still snow-white with lace, though a century on the women who had made the place a people of lacemakers were long gone. Stevenson watched them sitting in the streets in groups of half a dozen, the whirl of their bobbins and their chatter passing from one group to another. Only the silent patterns remained, decorating the ghostly white windows. The cassis drinkers on the other hand were very much alive and vocal and seemed determined to confirm Stevenson's earlier observations that they were fond of the bottle.

They also appeared to be subject to sudden surges of religion as they stood up, drained their glasses noisily and made for the big church, L'Eglise d'Abbatiale in the Place du Couvent. Here God was being processed in typical Catholic fashion, which my herring-and-brimstone hangover from an evangelical St Monans of the mad forties and morbid fifties could never allow me to embrace: doors left wide open, doors slamming, people strolling in late, people leaving early, a cattle auction happening just behind the church – where my recent drinking cronies had really been headed for, and where the gendarmes presided lightly over an amiable pandemonium, encouraging recalcitrant calves into the backs of straw-strewn Citroëns. As I stared at the scene through a haze of cassis it seemed to freeze into the leaf-fringed legend that decorated Keats's 'Grecian Urn', a scene of ageless pastoral innocence:

> *Who are these coming to the sacrifice?*
> *To what green altar, O mysterious priest,*
> *Lead'st thou that heifer lowing at the skies,*
> *And all her silken flanks with garlands drest?*
> *What little town by river or sea-shore,*
> *Or mountain-built with peaceful citadel,*
> *Is emptied of its folk this pious morn?*

Easy for time to stop and turn Greek when you've been quaffing cassis under an early morning blue sky. My old Presbyterian mentors raged from their graves. But the farmers washed their hands and faces in the pure ice-cold fountains that refreshed the town and then came inside the church to take a good cold guzzle of God before going back to work. They had fierce cheekbones and noses, shaggy moustaches, jawbones you could plough fields with – features sculpted by history and weather. All the modern gear they were wearing, cosmopolitan and brash, couldn't hide the insistence of heritage. They looked every inch of this world and bored by the merest intimations of the next. They made religion look like brushing your teeth – something you really ought to do before getting on with the business of the day. I didn't see many sparkling teeth as a matter of fact, though there were plenty of tobacco-stained grins that kept the atmosphere affable and attractive.

But I did see the château with the Salle de Stevenson, the Esplanade Stevenson, with its superb view over the valley of the Gazeille to high pastures and wooded hillsides, the Place de la Poste from where he set off. And so on down to the river, my eye keenly seeking out the start of the trail. And there it was – a tiny track disappearing among green leaves and leading up into the hills. I felt all the excitement I had been searching for. This was where it had all started, as a matter of geography at least, this was where he had begun, after leaving the village. And this was the start of a new journey for me. I had no idea of what I would find on that journey. I had even less idea what I was actually looking for, what I was expecting to find. As I'd risen into the air over Edinburgh for the first time in my life, I'd looked down in horror on the Pentlands. Under that cold clump of green hills all that I'd loved lay dead in a box, lapped in a black fathom of clay. Mortonhall was still in my mind – and the image of that most precious oblong of earth in the world, from which I was flying farther and farther. For what? The only way to find out was to take that little footpath leading into the trees on the west bank of the river Gazeille.

First, though, I had to buy a donkey. I made inquiries and was directed to St Martin-de-Fugères, five miles away. In superb weather I walked to this tiny hamlet in search of Monsieur du Lac, who kept and hired donkeys. I asked an ancient apparition in blue dungarees if he could tell me the way to the house. He stared at me as if I'd asked him the route to the Chapel Perilous. In any case he wanted some conversation first before he would even dream of giving out such information. He studied me from his impressive fortress of a face. A face flagged by white moustaches and darkened by race and four-score years of sun. Why was I here? Where had I come from? Where was I going? Stevenson had been amused by the very same questions that could have been fired at you from anywhere in Scotland. Scotland? No, the old man had never even heard of Scotland. He'd been to Austria, had been a prisoner of the Russians (it was not clear why) but Scotland was a new one on him and he'd certainly never heard of Robert Louis Stevenson. Great Britain then? Astonishingly, that rang no bells either in the fortress, at least none that he admitted to. But he did finally admit that Monsieur du Lac lived in that big house over there and that he even kept some donkeys. It would have been difficult to deny. There were a dozen or so donkeys cantering about in a nearby field.

I rang the bell and André du Lac appeared and ushered me into the dim solidity and stillness of his walled fifteenth-century farmhouse with its huge fireplaces and ancient wallpapers. We sat down in the dusty vaulted kitchen. It was cool and quiet, a welcome sanctuary from the soaring temperatures out in the fields. Over the fireplace hung the portrait of an illustrious ancestor, a former mayor of Le Puy, who had opened the city gates to Henri IV and had been hanged for treachery by his own citizens. I expressed respect for such a lineage. (My school French hammered into me in Fife by Herbert Soutar by the sweat of his brow and the strength of his formidable right arm was coming back into play.) Oh, that's nothing, Monsieur du Lac assured me. Some of his family had been known to write their name as one word – Dulac – so as not to scare people off with notions of their nobility, making the name sound rather like a well-known brand of paint. In fact, he said, the du Lacs have been here for centuries, ever since Lancelot – of the Lake. Monsieur du Lac's eyes were twinkling, but all the same the vaulted roof looked ancient enough to have spanned that era, and the furniture appropriate to the age of the great Arthurian icon. Much of it seemed to have been just dumped down randomly and forgotten. I wondered if I were sitting in an armchair at all or whether I was suspended in myth.

A conversation about donkeys started up, prolonged by the apéritifs brought in by Madame du Lac. I promised to bring an English version of Stevenson's *Travels* when I returned in the autumn to cross the Cévennes with one of his donkeys. And you must meet me with it, I insisted, in the Place de la Poste, Le Monastier, on 22 September, at nine o'clock in the morning precisely. Madame du Lac fell about laughing, which made me realize how absurdly British this pedantic obsession with punctuality must appear. But it seemed to convince her that I was all right and the pastis gave way to wine. 'Don't get too stuck on time,' she said. 'French time is different from your time – even from Steamson time.' I recalled how Stevenson had found no living creature, not one, able to pronounce his name in the region. We drank to Steamson and to the French concept of time. Then we toasted one another's countries, the success of the journey, Arthurian heroes and asses. In a half-drunken dream I lurched out into the sunlight, into a field of daisies and donkeys. Old Father Time, French style, in blue dungarees, was still standing nearby, looking over the fence. Monsieur du Lac and I began to discuss the best type of donkey for my purpose. Stevenson had never really understood donkeys, that was his trouble. It takes a wise man to understand a donkey. Stevenson was wise about many things, of course, but not about this. In the first place a male would have been better for his journey than the female he chose. A castrated male would have been even more manageable but a male with all the usual equipment intact, though less docile, would have been the better promenader – if and only if you let him know from the very first step of the journey who was in charge.

Monsieur du Lac appraised me keenly as he spoke and I felt he could see through me all too easily. Clearly I was going to be walked all over by this donkey, whatever its sex or absence of sex – or indeed size. Stevenson had allowed himself to be beguiled by the dainty dimensions of the donkey he bought from Father Adam. From the very start he overloaded her and his troubles began there. 'Modestine was the sort of donkey that was ideally suited to pulling a little cart,' explained Monsieur du Lac, 'and that's exactly what this Father Adam used her for. He wasn't a priest at all, as some people have imagined, but a local pedlar. They say he was a bit crazy but he saw Stevenson coming, all right. Sixty-five francs in those days was robbery. And he must have known very well that this donkey of his was unsuitable for scaling the High Cévennes. I would never have given your compatriot such a donkey!' Monsieur du Lac had not only read the French edition of Stevenson's *Travels* many times but was thoroughly conversant with the previous and future life of little Modestine. She survived the *voyage*, he said, and was subsequently bought by a retired military man called Eugène Dumas, who had the sense to return her to her original employment, pulling a tiny cart. After this old army officer died she was bought by a chap called Volpelière from St Jean-du-Gard. 'When you come to the end of your journey you can still see her hitching-ring displayed close to the entrance of his old house at 125 Grand-Rue.'

Donkeys seemed to survive their owners at an alarming rate. I began to feel inadequate to the task ahead. 'Don't worry,' said Monsieur du Lac. 'You've heard of the Ten Commandments, I suppose?' I started to quote them at machine-gun speed, fruits of the evangelical erudition instilled into me in the Braehead Kirk, St Monans, four decades earlier. Monsieur du Lac beamed. '*Très bon!* Now, if you can know your donkey like you know your Bible, you will be his god on the journey and he will obey you. If not, then he will be your devil and you will be in hell!' And he took me through the Ten Commandments for donkey drivers. Don't beat him, don't leave him on his own or allow him to wander or to roll in the dirt, and don't ask him to carry more than forty kilos, twenty kilos to each pannier – the two sides must be perfectly balanced or there will be trouble. Above all remember that the donkey is an intelligent animal. It is the inexperienced donkey-driver who stands in need of education! I listened with mounting alarm as it became clear that the donkey detests, among other things, bridges, water and heights in the form of sudden drops and yawning spaces. What, I wondered, had led Stevenson to a donkey as his choice of travelling companion through the mountains? I worried about provender and was assured that the grass that grew by the wayside was terribly convenient, if also an ever-present threat to progress. He'd give me a bag of barley and farmers would be happy to provide me with sacks of hay.

'But', he grinned, 'here is the master touch.' He stripped a small bough from a nearby tree and shook it in my face. 'Ash leaves,' he explained. 'The donkey adores them. And after he's eaten them and stripped the bough bare, you can use it to beat him with *s'il est méchant*. So it's better than a carrot. It's the carrot and the stick in one – a goad in both senses, *n'est-ce-pas*?' He sighed, and as if against his better judgement agreed to let this complete novice have his best beast, the prince of donkeys. His name was Anatole. 'And the price is nothing like three months' salary, which is what Monsieur Stevenson's sixty-five francs amounted to.' We settled on it and parted. 'And don't worry, ' he shouted after me, 'there are thousands of ash trees between Le Monastier and St Jean-du-Gard. And you won't even have to identify them – the donkey will see to that part of it. He's much cleverer than you!'

The relic of the *ancien régime* arrested me with a gnarled hand as I left the field. Why wasn't I taking the donkey away? Had Monsieur du Lac demanded too high a price? I explained that I was returning in the autumn. To follow Stevenson through the mountains. But how long ago did my fellow countryman set off? I told him: 1878. 'You'll never catch him,' he said gravely, 'he's got more than a head start on you. He'll be well ahead by now.' I studied the impregnable face for a hint of humour but there was not a twinkle in his eye. And in any case it was entirely the wrong time of year to travel, he assured me. Too cold, too wet, too solitary. A particularly rainy autumn ahead of us in addition, he assured me. He could feel it in his bones.

The knotted hand rested lightly on my shoulder and I stood like the wedding guest, staring into the glittering eye. 'Take my advice, my friend – give the whole thing up. You'll not find your friend. And you'll never return.' When I looked back five minutes later I could see him still standing there staring after me, as though looking his last on the stranger from the unheard-of country. Death in dungarees. I dreamed of him more than once after that.

I returned to Edinburgh with many anxieties and reservations, asking myself just what I thought I was really doing. The question sharpened itself as the summer wore on, putting an edge on my nerves. I kept thinking about what the old apparition had said as he'd held me like the ancient mariner. *You'll never find your friend.* Maybe he was right in the essential sense. Which of the Robert Louis Stevensons was I expecting to find out there, if any? Poet, puritan, rebel, romancer, Covenanter? Intrepid adventurer, lachrymose invalid, louche Bohemian? Hard-nosed Scotsman, globetrotting gypsy, cowboy, mummy's boy, big white chief, loner, landowner, storyteller? The more I looked at him the more the Victorian chameleon changed shape with Proteus and disappeared like a will-o'-the-wisp into the French hills. A stork, a scarecrow, a spider, a skeleton, he was no fixed star to follow anywhere. And anyway, what did I care? What exactly was Robert Louis Stevenson to me and why was I about to follow this phantom? For a childhood dream, a death, a mid-life crisis of a kind? An identity crisis? Stevenson was always an insidious sort of mirror into which people looked, like Hamlet, and saw themselves. I saw someone brought up, like myself, on the Bible, porridge and the Covenanters. I saw someone whose childhood had been similarly filled with nightmares induced by storytelling and religion, someone to whom

travel was an escape from the continuing, confining claus-
trophobia of that childhood and from a feeling of present
exile. We were asking ourselves the same question. What
am I doing here? What am I fleeing from? What am I jour-
neying towards? The answer was unclear but the impulse
was all the stronger simply to go, to make the personal
voyage, to find respite and escape, to clear the head and
calm the nerves and settle the heart. I felt myself filled,
like Stevenson, with a nervous energy that would surely
take me there in spite of my recent exhaustion. I knew I
was no athlete and that Stevenson had been an ill man but
I reckoned that my years spent running around Arthur's
Seat would equip me physically at least for the demands of
the journey. What I really knew nothing about, however,
was the Cévennes.

Few people did, either then or now, and Stevenson
was no exception. Only the area's bloody religious
history explained his interest and decision to travel there.
Before leaving he borrowed from the Advocate's Library
in Edinburgh a large number of books relating to the
Cévennes. I tried to carry out a similar programme of
reading but found it daunting. After a month all I really
knew was that the Cévennes were a series of mountain
ranges forming the south-eastern part of the Massif Central
and that they were not unlike the Scottish Highlands,
especially in their mountain rivers, the Cévennes being
the source of some of the great French rivers, the Loire,
the Allier, the Lot and the Tarn. The old drove roads, I
learned, were still a distinctive feature of the landscape and
it was apparently easy to get lost following their unfurling
labyrinths of white ribbons over the mountain sides.
'Adders', I read with consternation, 'constitute a threat to
the traveller.' I reached the stage where I began to talk
myself out of going at all, of dropping the whole quixotic

idea, born of death and desperation and likely to result in who knew what?

Meanwhile the next academic session resumed and I had to go back to work for a month, waiting for that day in late September to come round again, the day so close to her death, the day Louis began his journey. The school had agreed to grant me sabbatical leave for the duration of the trip and a day or two on either side. Everything started up again just as before. I looked up to the towering Pentlands, knowing how tame they were compared to the looming Cévennes. The slow drift of clouds went on, the windy city beneath them seeming to me as immaterial as ever, as old and remote as the Roman and his trouble.

Back in the classroom I found myself again having to think really hard before I articulated a question or evaluated an answer. I heard myself putting the words cumbrously together, arranging them like boulders, heard them tumble from my mouth and fall clattering like lumps of rubble, their shape lost. The very sound of my own syllables practically deafened me. It was all starting up again, the high-pitched whine of nerves on edge, just underneath my skin, accompanying the shrill bleeping from that mouldering old bag of bones, still in care but not yet entered the rest of silence. The nightmares came back, which summer had kept at bay. I dreamed of racing along the country roads of Fife. I ran for miles, all the way to St Monans, the village where I had been born, arriving eventually at the pewter sea, to find the little town silent and soulless. I stood on a promontory, stared down into the waves and threw into the depths a text I had been carrying. My plan for the Cévennes? *Travels with a Donkey*? Prospero was drowning his book again.

Then there was the enormous question of the children.

112

They'd come through hell, like me, but they didn't have the exit strategy that I'd dreamed up for myself. Surely they were more vulnerable and would be left helpless without me, in spite of the colleagues and friends who had rallied round and agreed to help by coming to stay with them in my absence. Was I being selfish?

And very nearly I didn't go. Terror and confusion almost had their way, even up to a couple of days before I was due to depart, and even though both Catriona and Jonathan had urged me to go ahead and do whatever I had to do to make myself whole again. No, I thought, this is a literary man's dream, it has absolutely nothing to do with real life. It will achieve nothing. But leafing through my notebooks I came across a sentence I'd noted down years previously from the retiral speech of a former colleague who'd left a job in finance to come into teaching. He'd said, quite simply, 'Don't be afraid of change if you are ever in a position that imprisons the spirit.' Some years later I'd met him at a dinner and told him how I'd admired his philosophy and how he'd put it into practice. He added to his advice, something to the effect that even if the change you sought was only temporary, it might well produce a lasting effect. I read this little note and decided to go ahead with my plan.

My unconscious mind wasn't quite done with me, though. Before leaving again for France I had two dreams about graves. In the first I was struggling to bury my wife properly, but there were no cords attached to the coffin and I was standing quite alone in Mortonhall. The assemblage of undertakers and mourners had vanished. I had to go down into the grave myself with the coffin and try to arrange things correctly, with her face to the east, so that she would be facing the right way for Jerusalem when she stood up on Judgement Day – a legacy of literal

113

Bible-teaching in Sunday School. The coffin was incredibly heavy and I woke up from that dream with an excruciatingly painful back which I took with me to France. I don't know if the pulled muscles had sparked off the dream or had been caused by it. Either way I must have been writhing about in bed. In the second dream I was standing looking down at my own body – which was in the shape of an open coffin, filled with earth, from which flowers were sprouting. Apart from the obvious and ultimate fear, and also the need to lay my wife to rest at last, the dream seemed to betray my disquietude about direction. At school I had loved history and loathed geography. On 20 September I left Edinburgh, without a compass, on a plane bound for Lyon.

PART THREE

In the Cévennes

B Y SIX O'CLOCK that evening I had reached Le
Monastier and the Hôtel de l'Abbaye, a Dickensian
warren on four floors which seemed to contain no
one, not even a caretaker, though it was easy to imagine
life-forms of one sort or another eking out their existence
in secret behind its dark doors: failed lawyers, disgraced
doctors, divorced drunkards, deadbeat Scottish authors,
widowers, necrophiliacs. When Madame Fayole finally
did appear, a gaunt shadow, she put a key into my hand
and requested my presence in the eating-room in two
hours' time. My room was on the top floor, which struck
me as wildly absurd, as I was the hotel's solitary guest. I
noticed, though, that she guarded her granddaughter with
flashing eyes. Maybe she thought that writers were not
to be trusted. Perhaps she'd been plagued by a long line
of Bohemians stretching back to 1878. She seemed sufficiently sibylline to fetch back that far. Maybe I just looked
mad to her. After all what kind of men take donkeys over
mountains? Men with women on their minds. She was
not to know that my love affair was with a lost wife. Later
I learned that she'd had a run-in with Monsieur du Lac. I
began my ascent of her eyrie.

The flights grew progressively narrower and darker with
no stair lights to guide me at this twilight hour, so that I
ended up tapping my way like Blind Pew, while remembering David Balfour's near-death experience in the tower
at the House of Shaws in *Kidnapped* – the murderous
staircase with the missing steps. When I reached the top
storey my hands told me that there were three doors.
The first two keyholes refused the key. Inside the third
room there was a light bulb and a bed and not much
else but it hardly mattered. I opened the shutters to let
in the last of the evening light and found myself looking
out across the valley of the Gazeille through a drifting

haze of woodsmoke from the chimneys opposite, and a shuttle of swallows and sparrows. On the crows' nests of the dormers across the street the roof tiles dipped precariously into space, some of them held down by boulders borrowed from the garden rockeries four floors down. It didn't bear thinking about what might happen should just one of these tiles or boulders chance to slip, though at this point the totally deserted streets took the edge off any idea of danger.

But my eye was drawn by the valley and the river, green and blue and peaceful. This was the view that greeted Stevenson when he looked out of the rear window of the building opposite, which at that time was his hotel, run by Irma Morel in the Place de la Fromagerie. One of his own drawings shows that his room looked out south-west over the valley, down to the spot which became his favourite place.

A place to hear birds singing; a place for lovers to frequent. The name of the river was perhaps suggested by the sound of its passage over the stones, for it is a great warbler, and at night, after I was in bed at Monastier, I could hear it go singing down the valley till I fell asleep.

This was how Stevenson described the most agreeable scenery to be found in Le Monastier, where the Gazeille waters the village common and flows on downwards to join the Loire. Madame Morel remembered him as an early riser who was adamant about making his own breakfast of eggs, milk and rum beaten up with a whisk. He spent the whole day tramping around the countryside, had his meals in the evenings in the company of local government officials, sitting with them at the head table, then did a bit of writing in the dining-room, after which

118

he bedded down early to lie and listen to the sound of the river. I strained my ears to hear it, wondering what the kids were hearing right now. I'd said goodbye to them only this morning, but it felt like a century ago. I could still feel the strong curve of Catriona's arm around my neck and her cheek against mine. *Take care, Dad. Come back safe. I love you.* And down in the street, stepping into the airport taxi with my two rucksacks, I'd looked back up at the front bedroom window and watched Jonathan's white dawn face gazing palely down at me, seeing his sad slow wave.

My reverie was splintered by a screeching from the ground floor. Madame Fayole's vocal cords were her dinner gong. I came back down through the gloom and into the light, where the youngest grandchildren were playing on the floor of the bar and the juke-box had been switched on for my imagined entertainment. It was couched incongruously in one of the low medieval arches, and its throbbing must have quickly exorcised the lingering ghosts of any monks who were still mad enough to try to whet their whistles here, even in spirit. The Hôtel de l'Abbaye was so named because of its monastic origin and it still looked uncomfortable enough to mortify the flesh. This turned out to be an illusion. I dined on *charcuterie* and tomatoes, steak and green beans, and a barrage of cheeses, washed down with a thick, dark, strong red wine, unbelievably big. I'd asked for *rouge ordinaire* to keep things cheap, but Madame was not organized. This was late September and there were no tourists. No one comes here now till next summer, she told me. There was relief in her voice. Afterwards I found out why the hotel had been deserted when I arrived. She'd been out shopping at the last minute for the portion of steak that formed my evening meal. With no *vin ordinaire* in stock, she'd plundered the Abbaye cellars and come up out of the cobwebs with a wine that would have brought a dead man back to life. It might have been a leftover bottle missed by the monks, according to the story it told the palate. I'd never tasted anything approaching its eloquence and power. At any rate she poured this 'ordinary' *particulier* into a cheap carafe and served it without comment, as if the container could have disguised the sheer quality of the nectar presented at the price of plonk. My bill read: *une bouteille de vin ordinaire*. Two hours later I reeled back up to my blacked-out eyrie and fell into a cold bed, which I quickly filled with heat. My head was singing with the Cévennes. And through the sound of the singing I could hear that other sound that had so charmed the ear of Stevenson: the sound of the Gazeille gurgling over the stones of the river bed as it went warbling down the valley to meet the Loire.

Next morning Madame Fayole brought me hot black coffee, much needed, and the information that there was in Le Monastier a certain *garagiste* who was a Stevenson enthusiast. He was called Monsieur Pradier and was an important civic official, though everyone knew him simply as Jeannot. He had heard on the grapevine – always luxuriant in France – of my arrival, and was keen to meet me. If I liked she would ring his garage and I could call on him. I called and it soon became clear that merely to come in the name of Stevenson was enough to win the heart and soul of Monsieur Pradier. When I entered the garage at the end of the village I saw a knot of men in boiler suits bent over in an oily huddle, peering like Druids into the entrails of a car. Monsieur Pradier? I inquired politely. One of the men unbent slowly, turned around, and looked at me. He knew who I was. And I knew at once that I was looking into the face of a man for whom the word 'fanatic' would be a pale apology for the truth. There was a kind of mad joy in his eye: the sort of expression characteristically worn by Anthony Wedgwood Benn and Enoch Powell and which made Kingsley Amis famously explain the reason why neither of these gifted men ever became Prime Minister: 'Both of them look absolutely barmy!' Monsieur Pradier looked charmingly barmy.

Eagerly but with great politeness he asked if I might be the *écrivain écossais* who wanted to talk about Stevenson. I confirmed that I'd come to follow in my fellow-writer's dead footsteps and that I'd be delighted to speak to him at his convenience – not right now obviously, as he was so deep in work. The mechanics looked at each other smilingly and Monsieur Pradier looked at his blackened hands which were dripping oil over his shoes. No, no, now was the convenient time, *bien sûr*, he wished to speak straightaway. And as for the footsteps – he smiled – they were far from dead. 'After all, *monsieur*, the footsteps of a ghost, they never die, you can always hear them walking!' The mechanics shrugged and stared back into the bowels of their patient – abandoned with such alacrity by the chief clairvoyant of Citroëns.

The hands were quickly washed, the wet handshake performed, and Monsieur Pradier led me out of the garage, past a rusting pile of more abandoned cars, through the garden and into his stately home, with its château-thick walls, its stone sarcophagi, elegant furniture and -- the *pièce de résistance* – a door within the great arch of the fireplace which actually led into the study, a library laden with treasures, old tomes and archives, parchments dating back to the fourteenth century. My head reeled. It was a bibliophile's paradise, an Aladdin's cave of Academe. 'I have family wills from 1538,' crooned my host, 'but there have been Pradiers around here from long before. Since

1317 as a matter of fact. Of course when the Revolution happened my ancestors lost everything and had to leave – with just a bag on their backs. In some cases not even that. The revolutionaries left them their heads on their shoulders, that was all. It was enough, though. In time some of them were able to start building up again, and here I am today, I suppose – the inheritor of what was left of their legacy.'

Monsieur Pradier then confided to me his grand plan. He intended to *bake* the story of his entire genealogy on to tiles and build the family tree into a great wall right here in his garden – The Great Wall of Pradier! It was at that precise point that I could feel stupid tears coming to my eyes, tears of relief. I knew just what was happening. I remembered something that the journalist Bernard Levin had once said in a passage about cities. He'd been in Moscow for several weeks back in the grim old Soviet days, made grimmer by winter. He'd seen enough misery and cruelty and poverty and general ugliness to last him a lifetime but in the end it was a simple incident that brought him to the edge of despair. The traffic guard-rails round Bolshoi Square were being painted by an army of old women, working mostly without coats in temperatures that had plunged to minus twenty degrees centigrade. Each woman held a paint pot in one hand and a brush in the other, but the paintbrushes barely existed – they were just bits of wood with a few worn bristles sticking from the ends – and with these pitiful objects the old ladies were smearing the rails as best they could. They were hunched up against the bitter winds as they worked on in this way, and on their faces Levin saw an expression of exhaustion, hopelessness, pain and pointless suffering pointlessly endured such as he hoped never to see again on any human face.

When he left Moscow he flew straight to Copenhagen and at lunch next day ordered something called 'Ice-Cream Surprise'. It came with a ring of sparklers stuck in the vanilla ice and a metal rod sticking from the top. The sparklers were lit, blazed, fizzled and died. Just as they completed their display there was a click and a tiny Danish flag appeared from the igloo of ice-cream and ran up the metal flagpole to flutter proudly at the top. At this point, Levin says, the last remaining trace of his nervous crisis flared up and he burst into tears, tears of innocent happiness. He realized then that what he had been missing most in the Soviet Union was just such purpose-less absurdity, the true mark of civilization. It is not to be found in cities that have lost their sense of laughter. Or in whole countries that have forgotten about laughter and innocence and enthusiasm. As for me, I knew I'd been living in a country of the dead for the past year, similar to Levin's Moscow, and that innocence and absurdity and enthusiasm were what had been missing from the experience. Monsieur Pradier was the original enthusiast, and as I listened to him talking about his plans I could hear laughter again, and relief flooded over me like a sea. I came back to my senses to hear my host telling me that the house we were sitting in now had originally been up in the hills fifteen miles away, but he'd had it brought down, stone by numbered stone, all 600 tons of them, and rebuilt just where he wanted it, here in Le Monastier. As for the garage, the business of earning daily bread was obviously little more than an irritating constriction to Monsieur Pradier, at best a hobby. His heart was in the French Highlands, busy chasing other deer.

There was a sudden burst of activity. He leapt up from the table and rang his secretary. Drop everything and come round here at once. Marie-Rose came round and whisked me off to the *mairie* to see a Stevenson exhibition. A journalist was contacted and he interviewed me about my trip. Articles about Stevenson were found and copied for me. Then we drove to the Hôtel de l'Abbaye and drank apéritifs. Madame Fayole was flustered by the sudden flurry of custom. 'You can see the place is pretty run down,' my new friends murmured apologetically. 'Gone to the dogs since her husband died.' I assured them everything was idyllic and exactly as I would have wanted it to be.

After the apéritifs there was a *cuisine familiale* of sausage, bread, chips, cheeses of the region – and a Stevenson cake. You can buy these at the patisseries in Le Monastier, with Stevenson's name iced around the rim. Following this there was a lunch at the *maison de campagne* of Monsieur's secretary, and then it was off to their town house to drink champagne and watch Monsieur Pradier and Marie-Rose on television, being interviewed about guess who? You couldn't be secretary to Monsieur Pradier without becoming an RLS connoisseur. Dinner was back at Monsieur Pradier's, where I noticed that all the bottles brought up out of his cellars were without labels. Good wine needs no bush and each bottle could have been pasted proudly with the wine stanza from Keats's 'Ode to a Nightingale', tasting of Flora and the country green, dance and Provençal song, and sunburnt mirth. And so, with beaded bubbles winking at the brim, and purple-stainèd mouth I listened to all this French talk of Monsieur Stevenson.

He dined well, as I had, before setting off. In Le Puy, not far from Le Monastier, he'd indulged in a gargantuan meal: a big slice of melon, some ham and jelly, a fillet, a helping of gudgeons, the breast and leg of a partridge, some green peas, eight crayfish, some Mont d'Or cheese, a peach, and a handful of biscuits, macaroons and things ... all for three francs.

He had a girl, naturally, in Le Monastier. She had a child after he had gone, and naturally again this family had inherited his pulmonary disorders, all of them dying off young in spectacular ways from chest-related illnesses. The girl in the local legend had been an expert in the art of *dentellerie* – not to be confused with *bordellerie*. I was shown a letter from an RLS aficionado who had written to Monsieur Pradier asking for a picture of the local women who practised *bordellerie*. There is a subtle difference between those who make lace and those who make love. The Stevenson devotee had to be advised that in this innocent little French town the *dentellerie* had long since died out and the *bordellerie* had never even begun – fortunately, or regrettably, depending on your point of view.

It occurred to me at that moment that if Louis had really become worried about the potentially interesting condition in which he might have left a local girl, his choice of transport hardly offered him the world's fastest getaway vehicle. Modestine would always have kept him within easy range of a shotgun. So why the donkey? There were various practical explanations but above all the Monastrians felt it was an original choice and a touch eccentric. At any rate the method of going mattered less than the fact of being on the go. Travel was the eternal antidote to sadness, confusion and doubt, and a bereft and depressed Scotsman, with the power of the Pied Piper, had set the pattern for others to follow in his footsteps in their own ways and for their own reasons.

'I have them all here,' said Monsieur Pradier, producing a typed list, 'and exactly when they came.'

The first was a Mr Skinner from Edinburgh in 1926,

125

but he did it in a motor-car and therefore didn't count, according to Pradier, the purist. You can't do Stevenson in a car any more than you can do the marathon on a bicycle. You have to be on foot. So no one made it on to Monsieur Pradier's list until 1948. That was when a certain Miss Singer came. She was the first person known to have made the journey complete with donkey, though she got lost on Mont Lozère and the fire brigade had to come to the rescue. She was followed by Mr White in 1950; Mr and Mrs Richardson, the first couple, in 1955 and Mrs Gladstone and her two daughters, Roberta and Carola, in 1963. Mrs Gladstone was the first American and it was she who paid for the plinth in the Place de la Poste. After that came Mr Holmes in 1964, and in that same year Mrs Jane Tarr, who came back the following year with her husband and did it again. A couple of Oxford students also did it in 1965, and another married couple, the Plancks, in 1967, followed that same year by Mr Clifford Fowkes. A journalist with *Le Figaro* appeared in 1968, after which things went quiet, till in 1978, the centenary of Stevenson's voyage, there was quite an influx of enthusiasts, *avec âne ou sans âne*. Then it went quiet again.

'And now you have come,' Monsieur Pradier smiled, 'and it's good that you have decided to do so. A writer following a writer. It's best that way. You will understand him more.'

And he went on to unveil his great plan to have an actual statue of Stevenson erected in the Place de la Poste.

'It will happen one day, you'll see. When a writer follows a writer it's a sure sign that things are happening.'

By that time I was agreeing with everything. The talk turned to a grand plan of my own, drunkenly shared with Alastair Reid, the *New Yorker* journalist, poet, and translator of Pablo Neruda – to have a statue of Stevenson created by stealth in an Edinburgh that never saw fit to honour him in this way. The scheme had to be carried out in the dead of night so that in the morning the city would rub its eyes and find its doyen of respectability, Sir Walter Scott, removed from office, and RLS sitting in his place, enthroned on the famous monument. An alcoholic fantasy. Still, I assured Monsieur Pradier that if I ever made any real money out of writing I'd like to fulfil his dream of a Stevenson statue in Le Monastier. And in place of Sir Walter Scott's dog there would of course be a little donkey.

I floated back to the Abbaye on a wine-dark sea and levitated to the top floor. As I crashed out I was vaguely aware that some big adventure was getting under way at nine the next morning, and that I was worried about something connected with this. What was it? In a broken sleep it came to me. Monsieur du Lac had not answered his telephone all day and I hadn't seen him since July. Had he remembered about the donkey?

The question was answered at eight a.m. precisely by a stentorian braying that sounded as if it might have come from the House of Commons on a bad day but was in fact issuing from the street far below. I staggered to the shutters, peered blearily out of the eyrie and saw Anatole's muzzle pointing up at me as though directing me to rise, take up my sleeping-bag and start walking. I hadn't fallen over till four, was short on sleep and strong on a sore throat and a thick head. The sprained back muscles from the last Edinburgh nightmare were still paining me. It was raining hard and I couldn't see across the valley for mist. This was the moment of truth. When the quaint notion of taking a donkey over the mountains of southern France is suddenly converted into four hundred pounds of donkeyflesh honking at your hotel door – delivered complete with bag of barley, and saddle to be fitted around the steaming back and belly, and seen not through a glass of cognac but a dim cocktail of *le brouillard et la pluie*, bottled in Castle Reality – the romance dies on the spot. I dragged my two rucksacks down the dark flights of steps, said goodbye to Madame Fayole, and emerged into the downpour. My bright new walking boots, purchased from Tiso's in Edinburgh, changed colour in seconds and I felt the huge wet drops bouncing off the back of my neck and sliding down my spine underneath the waterproofs. The hat I'd bought was obviously no match for rain of this ferocity.

The next problem was that my rucksacks had to be emptied out and the contents evenly distributed between the two panniers, forty pounds on each side, as Monsieur du Lac had advised. A couples of pounds more or less on either side would result in discomfort for the donkey and run the risk of saddle sores early in the journey. This was the sort of thing that could spell the end of the adventure and had to be got right before I even started. Anyone who hasn't tried to make up two evenly weighted piles of travel gear and pack them into panniers in the pouring rain to see how they will hang on a stamping little donkey, simply hasn't lived. There was a lot of trial and error, in the course of which the contents of the saddlebags received an early baptism. How do you decide between the relative weight in pounds of a sleeping-bag, a tent, bottles of wine, books, notebooks, a camping-stove, spirit containers, tin plates, cutlery, changes of clothing and all the smaller paraphernalia of travel? Not to mention my military writing-box, an antique Regency contraption which unfolded to provide a man on the road or on a battlefield with a sort of mini desk-top. In addition to which I had gone to some unnecessary trouble to reproduce Stevenson's kit as far as possible, taking along a bottle of brandy, a leg of cooked meat, a hip flask, an egg-beater, black bread and white, purchased in Le Monastier, tobacco and cigarette papers, a jack-knife, and even a quantity of Bologna sausage, bought from Valvona & Crolla in Edinburgh the week before I left for France.

'Does it *have* to be Bologna sausage, sir?'

'Exactly – and in tins, if possible.'

'In tins. May I . . . ?'

'Don't!'

I also carried two bibles. One was a copy of Stevenson's *Travels with a Donkey*; the other was *Footsteps* by Richard Holmes, the first chapter of which describes his 1964 journey, thirty years before mine, made without a donkey but accompanied by the most intelligent observations I had ever read.

Oh, and some maps. All of which were sodden before the packing was complete.

It was mere consolation in misery for me to remember that Stevenson too experienced an ignominious beginning. Monastrians of all shades of thought in politics nevertheless achieved unanimity in assuring him of death in many possible forms: cold on the heights, robbers, wolves, nocturnal surprises. But they left out, he says, the main danger – the pack and saddle.

On the day of my departure I was up a little after five; by six we began to load the donkey; and ten minutes after, my hopes were in the dust. The pad would not stay on Modestine's back for half a moment. I returned it to its maker, with whom I had so contumelious a passage that the street outside was crowded from wall to wall with gossips looking on and listening. The pad changed hands with much

129

vivacity; perhaps it would be more descriptive to say that we threw it at each other's heads; and at any rate, we were very warm and unfriendly, and spoke with a deal of freedom.

I had a common donkey pack-saddle – a *barde*, as they call it – fitted upon Modestine; and once more loaded her with my effects. The doubled sack, my pilot coat, a great bar of black bread, and an open basket containing the white bread, the mutton and the bottles, were all corded together in a very elaborate system of knots, and I looked on the result with fatuous content. In such a monstrous deck-cargo, all poised above the donkey's shoulders, with nothing below to balance, on a brand-new pack saddle that had not been worn to fit the animal, and fastened with brand-new girths that might be expected to stretch and slacken by the way, even a very careless traveller should have seen disaster brewing. That elaborate system of knots, again, was the work of too many sympathisers to be very artfully designed. It is true they tightened the cord with a will; as many as three at a time would have a foot against Modestine's quarter, and be hauling with clenched teeth; but I learned afterwards that one thoughtful person, without any exercise of force, can make a more solid job than half a dozen heated and enthusiastic grooms. I was then but a novice; even after the misadventure of the pad nothing could disturb my security, and I went forth from the stable-door as an ox goeth to the slaughter.

My Anatole was fitted with exactly the same pack-saddle as Modestine. The *barde*, as Stevenson refers to it, came, Monsieur du Lac assured me, from the old Occitan *barda*, the word for the wooden frame that we were now strapping on to Anatole's back. Anatole was used to this whereas Modestine, accustomed to pulling Father Adam's little cart, must have objected to this unusual load on top and consequently refused to adopt any pace at all to begin with.

'But you, my friend, should have no such difficulties.'

Monsieur du Lac beamed and wiped rain from his eyes. Rivers of water were cascading from the brim of his hat.

'Your only problem right now is the weather. Try to forget about it and have a pleasant first day.'

By the time I was ready to go and Anatole was properly saddled up and the panniers balanced correctly, the rain had increased and was pelting down the plinth in the Place de la Poste which told me that this was the starting point. *D'ici partit le 22 septembre 1878 Robert Louis Stevenson pour son voyage à travers les Cévennes avec un âne.* Yes, this was it. In spite of the expert help I had just received in saddling up, I felt not unlike my fellow-writer as he set out like an ox to the slaughter. It was an abysmal beginning. Still, the dismal little crowd that had gathered for my departure gave a brave cheer as I headed down into the mist-hung valley. And though I'd risen three hours later than Stevenson I had caught up and was leaving on time. For Stevenson it was a Sunday and he left to the pealing of church bells. This was a Thursday and there were no bells, only the sound of water, the rain from above and the Gazeille in mad spate down in the valley. I could hear a bell in my head, though, and it made me miss my children desperately. It was the first period bell in faraway George Watson's College, Edinburgh, summoning my Fifth Form English class to be taught by my replacement. The world had opened up for another day's business. It was nine o'clock precisely.

131

Of course it's a magic moment, whatever the weather. You know for sure that on this first leg of the journey at least you are taking the exact track as it drops down to the river Gazeille and vanishes into the trees. That you are treading, quite literally, in his footsteps, and in the footsteps of others who went before you. And that if there are ghosts, his ghost is here. Of that you are certain. What you are not sure about is precisely where you will sleep tonight. You ask yourself for the hundredth time why you are going, why you are here at all. And as you turn around and see the red roofs of Le Monastier growing smaller behind you, the answers ring less convincingly in your mind with every step. Feeling the need for company, you connect with Stevenson again, assuming a similar mingling of emotions in his mind as he set out on that first September day and went over his own reasons for being here: confusion, grief, challenge; fascination with the country of the Camisards, the Protestant religious rebels, and their struggle against their Catholic oppressors. Perhaps he remembered George Sand's novel *Le Marquis de Villemer* which had first made him interested in this unknown region of France. Perhaps he had a copy in his luggage, just as I was carrying his own *Travels*, one certain reason for my presence here, zipped into one of my water-proof pockets. Above all else, perhaps, he simply had to feel the planet, new-made and unknown, underneath his feet. And as you go into a green woodland tunnel rising rockily ahead of you, you can feel on your pulses the truth and the thrill of the whole Stevenson ethic about travel. For a man who has never travelled in his life and has spent a quarter of a century as a gong-tormented Edinburgh schoolmaster, knowing precisely how each day will be governed and how it will end, who he will be talking to at any given time, it is quite something simply not to know for sure just what is going to happen next. The adrenalin flows.

And it had to flow, to meet the challenge of the steep climb on that first morning. As the rough and rocky road went steadily up through the trees, like a staircase spiralling out of the valley, it was dappled by sudden sunlight. I was all geared up for the mist and the rain, and the sweat was knocked out of me viciously by the first few miles before I had the sense to remove my waterproof jacket and leggings and stuff them into the saddlebags. I could see nothing in this chequered green night in which I was toiling at a snail's pace – nothing but sun-splashed green leaves hemming me in on either side of the path. But I could hear cow-bells tinkling from the basalt villages of the Velay three thousand feet above sea level and already well beneath my feet. They sounded idyllic, and I began to break one of the golden rules of donkey-driving – never feel sorry for the donkey – as I watched Anatole, the brave little trooper, struggling between his forty-pound panniers and stumbling as he tried to avoid low-growing branches sticking like trip-wires across the narrow road, while avoiding the sharp-edged rocks and rubble with which the path was strewn. It was a relief to emerge suddenly on to a plateau and see the valleys of the Gazeille and the Loire stunningly exhibited in the distant down-below, shimmering now in early morning sun. The steam was rising from the valleys in bright white clouds.

So far the uphill business in the sudden heat had been the only problem. My eyes were stinging with sweat and the thermal vest I was wearing clung to my back like a cold wet blanket. All the same I reckoned I was having a better start than Stevenson, who had felt so sorry for his donkey as she sweated and trembled under the load that he had allowed her to determine her own pace, with the result that for the first few miles she practically stood still. She also refused to attempt gradients, shed her load, took detours and refused to abandon them and disappeared into shops, searching out their cool interiors through the beaded doors. A peasant who happened to overtake him watched the comic advance and took pity on the ignorant Scotsman by cutting him a thorn-switch from a hedge and teaching him the Masonic signal of donkey-drivers: the word 'Proot'. By prooting and beating Stevenson achieved a pace that finally got him to St Martin-de-Fugères, where the church was so full that the congregation was spilling out on to the steps, listening to the chanting of the priest from inside. The church-goers at Costaros laughed at him as he was castigated by their fellow-villagers for his inhumane treatment of a poor dumb animal. Couldn't he see she was tired and overladen and not up to the task in the first place? '*Elle est petite – il ne faut pas trop la presser.*'

Exasperated by their decision to side with the French donkey against the foreign driver (normally they would have beaten her themselves without a shred of sentimentality) Stevenson told them to mind their own business – unless they preferred to do some transporting themselves. And he continued to belabour her with an unwearying bastinado, two blows to every step, under a blazing blue sky, all the way up the long hill from Goudet. He was sickened by the sound of his own blows, especially so as Modestine began to remind him of a lady who had once loaded him with kindness, and he was conscious too of the absurd image he presented: a gangling unathletic figure, a drawing-room being, a thread-paper, beating an ass unremittingly – Don Quixote supplanting Sancho Panza, a double caricature.

Nevertheless he carried on with the flogging. He was

anxious to reach the Lac du Bouchet before sundown and make his first camp and everyone and everything seemed to be against him. They'd laughed at him in Ussel where Modestine had caused the whole caboodle, saddle-bag and saddle itself, to swivel below her belly and bite the dust. The roads didn't help either. They were a pointless labyrinth and kept sneaking back towards Costaros or northwards somewhere else, anywhere but in the direction he wanted to go. 'The failing light, the waning colour, the naked, unhomely, stony country ... all contributed to a degree to my distress.' When he begged a mother and son for directions the son ignored him and all he got out of the mother was *fuck* and *bugger* – expressions that he wrote down in his journal but omitted from the published version of the *Travels*. He was compelled to use physical force to make this pair even stand and pay attention to him. The mother said that all he had to do was follow them but what the fuck did he want to go to the Lac du Bouchet for, at this time of night? Implication: there's fuck-all there. Complaint: I've an hour and a half's fucking slog in front of me yet myself, on the fucking road. (Had the various curses made it into the printed edition I read as a schoolboy, it might have attracted the same attention as Chaucer, but Stevenson had his reading public to consider and the Victorian publishing ethic.) He followed this amiable couple but was not impressed by the prospect.

> The view looking back was singularly wild and sad; the Mezenc and the billowy peaks beyond St Julien stood out in trenchant gloom against a cold glitter in the east; the intervening field of hills, except, here and there the outline of a wooded sugarloaf in black, here and there a white irregular patch to represent a cultivated plateau, here and there a blot where the

Loire, the Gazeille or the Lausonne wandered into a gorge, had fallen together into one broad wash of shadow, differently tinted for wood and field. I was too cold and weary to admire.

By this time he had even been reduced to jettisoning some of his cargo. The container for milk, the leg of mutton and the precious egg-beater all had to go. Even his own white bread was sacrificed to the gods of shipwreck, though to his credit he kept the black bread which Modestine loved to munch. Eventually, after his wide detour to the west from Ussel he arrived not at the intended lake but at the village of Le Bouchet-St-Nicolas where, cold, sore, dead beat, with a cut shoulder and an arm that ached like toothache from the thrashing he had given the ass, he asked for the *auberge*.

Weighing up our comparative experiences on this first day I felt grateful to Anatole for causing me no trouble. Sometimes he struggled on the steep ascents and seemed inclined to offer an opinion about this venture into which he'd been conscripted, but I couldn't bring myself to lay a finger on him and to my great relief he needed no such chastisement. I could see, however, that the main problem was not going to be the donkey but the driver. My sense of direction was far from strong and the maps seemed to bear little relevance to the landscape. Where a map showed one turning the reality was often a maze of major intersections with no signpost to the next stage of the journey. As for the locals it was impossible to determine whether they were more helpful or less than they had been to Stevenson. They simply weren't around to ask. Already the depopulated nature of this terrain was becoming alarmingly obvious. Man and donkey, big sky, fields and forests, hills and valleys, a landscape emptied of people. I sensed trouble ahead. Consequently I was glad to come through the little hamlet of St Victor, deserted except for two hens, and arrive at St Martin-de-Fugères, where Monsieur du Lac interrupted his breakfast to wave me *bon voyage* and *bon courage*. 'And remember your Ten Commandments, *monsieur* – don't break any of them, otherwise you will be punished! By the way, there's a flood warning. It's going to get wet again . . . ' The words came floating lightly on the breeze.

Stevenson lunched at Monsieur Senac's inn at Goudet, a couple of miles on from St Martin-de-Fugères. But when I inquired in St-Martin about the possibility of taking a midday meal there, the blonde-haired one-time beauty threw back her pretty head and laughed.

'Monsieur Senac? He's only been dead about a hundred years! You'll get nothing to eat in godforsaken Goudet, *monsieur!* You'd better stay here and eat with me – so long as you don't expect me to set a place for your donkey!'

The sun had brought Sidonie out on to her tiny *terrasse*, where table and chairs were planted precariously on the uneven baked earth. There were half a dozen people gathered round and I was invited to join them for what turned out to be an excellent lunch: potato omelette, marinaded rabbit with herbs, sausage, bread and cheese and pots of coffee, all washed down with cold white country wine and green plastic bottles of tap water, brought straight from the freezer to melt in minutes under the blinding sky. The sun was bright to the point of invisibility and the temperature was soaring. The condensation from the bottles dripped on to the bare wooden table. I had never tasted so awesome an omelette and I asked if it was a speciality of the region. '*Un specialité de moi!*' she said emphatically. When I begged her for the recipe she smiled and shook her head. 'My grandmother would break out of the graveyard and terrorize us all, *monsieur*, if I gave away her recipe – it's a secret.' *Désolée*. I knew all about grandmothers who terrorized and tyrannized and I failed to prevent myself from imagining one in particular, safe underground, bony wrists bolted to the pelvis to prevent her from coming back as a vampire – the way the undertakers used to deal with fearsome old witches in Sidonie's part of the world not so very long ago. But the Sidonie speciality did not encourage the lingering of angry thoughts. As I lay there like a foundered wreck she came out on to the terrace holding in her hand an enormous sausage. Sidonie, the ageing blonde, had devoured many men in her youth and many a man in his prime. I had learned about her other specialities from Monsieur du Lac. So I ventured a risqué remark about the size of the sausage. She gave me back an enormous grin. 'The important question, *monsieur*, is not how big it is, but does it *work?* Does it *satisfy* you?'

I knew someone who would have laughed at that, whose dimples would have responded. Someone who'd have loved to be here – in her element on this humble *terrasse*. I decided it was time to be on my way. According to my notes Stevenson had already lunched, two miles further on. Before leaving St-Martin I looked into the eleventh-century church that had been full and running over when he passed. It was silent and deserted and offered a sanctuary from the fierce afternoon heat. I stepped into the dim unlit coolness. The sun still filtered through, but in stained-glass sections, coloured in centuries ago. And here it was again, the tense, musty, unignorable silence and the knowledge that back in my Edinburgh classroom somebody would be teaching the next round of Larkin poems, perhaps even 'Church Going'. Would Sidonie come here some night to talk recipes with her dead grand-mother? Would someone like me forever be surprising a hunger in himself to be more serious, and gravitating with it to this ground? Catriona and Jonathan would be in their afternoon classes, only an hour behind me but intensely, infinitely unreachable, to the point of tears. I climbed up to the gallery and a narrow stone spiral took me to the bell-tower from where I could look out far across the Loire valley. There were four bells, only one of them still in use, its clapper revealing gleaming metal on either side of the struck portion. Apart from that one sonorous spot all was rust, and the clappers on the other three bells were completely rusted over. Three silent tongues glooming over the valley. The symbolism suited the church and the village, three-quarters sunk in obscurity and neglect. Where had they all gone, the numbers that Stevenson saw? Long time passing. Gone to graveyards every one. And to Paris and the towns before that, presumably. But the silvery peals of Sidonie's laughter rose muted from the distance down below. There was still plenty of life in that old clapper.

I came down to Goudet nervously because I'd been warned that Anatole would have to cross the Loire. That turned out to be a joke on the part of Monsieur du Lac. It was the Loire all right, but at that point it was a Lilli-putian trickle under a narrow bridge. Even so, an old man standing on the bridge assured me that the Loire was in great spate on account of the recent rains. 'And there will be a lot more rain to come!' he shouted after me. 'Get your oilskins ready!'

The old weather prophet was right. There is a castle above Goudet, capping a volcanic plug, and as I stopped to watch a buzzard wheel about this Wagnerian ruin, I saw the sun vanish. The clouds had regrouped. Suddenly Ussel and Costaros were hidden behind thick curtains of rain. By the time I reached Le Bouchet-St-Nicolas – some houses clustered round a church spire – I was freezing and exhausted, well aware of just how tough a traveller Stevenson must have been. The first layer of the romance – the schoolboy layer, all those poetic images of strolling the nut-strewn roads, stubbly with goodness, under the southern sun, cigarette in mouth, brandy-flask in pocket and open book in hand – had been stripped away by one day's travelling. It had been a walk of about sixteen miles and over ten hours. Light was almost gone. Stevenson found an inn and some comfort. I managed to get myself to a *gîte d'étape* and stood there in the dark, shivering.

Getting into bed without her. I'd grown used to it at home, practising for a year, night after night, entering the arctic sheets and lying there in the dark, imagining how it would be if I could just break through the walls of flesh and bone that held me in, the bolts and shackles of mortality, if I could simply pick the locks and be free, undo the intrinsicate knot of life and make my invisible escape to Mortonhall, lie down with her there and be wheeling around for ever in the slow cosmic spin of things, till the sun above us was a white dwarf and the earth a spinning graveyard, a cold cinder in space. But back in Edinburgh, with my children lying near me, it was easier to return from the death-wish brink. Here in France, in a strange bed, I dreamt that I was Heathcliff, dreaming within the dream that I was sleeping the last sleep with that sleeper, with my heart stopped and my cheek frozen against hers.

I slept badly that first night. Later I dreamt of Sidonie and sausages but there was a violent thunderstorm and the shutters of the *gîte* kept flapping all night long. Then I dreamt there were two of me – another self sharing the sleeping-bag, lying beside me, and we kept arguing about who was to get up and close the shutters. Neither of us did – and we were the sole occupants of the *gîte*, just as we had been at Madame Fayole's. It seemed as though I was destined to pursue a solitary voyage, wandering through France like a ghost, and splitting myself up in my sleep for company. In the morning an aged caretaker came to see to the shutters – there was a fierce gale blowing and he begged me to assist him. I had to lean far out and seize the heavy wooden sails that were still swinging wildly in the freezing wind. We went from window to window. They were twenty feet above the ground and I almost fell out of the last one when the shutter came off one of its hinges. I snatched at it and the old man grabbed me by the seat of my trousers and my belt, sitting astride me till I'd slotted the thing back on to its rusted old hooks, by which time I'd added a pulled muscle in my chest to the one that was still troubling my back. These pains plagued me for days to come.

Stevenson left Le Bouchet early, having risen at five a.m., and I was behind him already. A quick bite of bread and sausage (a present from Sidonie) and the same to Anatole to supplement his grazing, and we were off: destination Langogne on the Allier, a trek of fourteen miles. I'd covered sixteen miles on the first day and this morning my joints were feeling it. The muscles had stiffened up and I could move only with the greatest difficulty and some pain, exacerbated by the vicious little stones of a Roman road. There were times when I actually had to lift one leg with both hands, just behind the knee, so as to surmount a sizeable obstacle. I felt ludicrous and was sure I looked it. Anatole, even between his panniers, seemed to need neither sympathy nor encouragement.

Modestine received additional encouragement at Le Bouchet, having already grown insensitive to her driver's cudgelling. The innkeeper made Stevenson a goad and he found that the slightest prick was worth a thousand cudgels. From that point on they devoured the miles and he blessed the anonymous inventor of goads and the landlord who had introduced him to their use. Unlike me Stevenson had company in the sleeping apartment in the form of a cooper and his young wife who occupied the other bed. *Honi soi qui mal y pense* was Stevenson's reflection for the night. But his language and tone betray an interest in the beautiful bare arms of this young woman, full, white and shapely, and in whether she slept naked beneath the covers – one of the first indications of where his thoughts were secretly straying as he wandered through the Cévennes.

Having swung west, he now turned south, headed for Langogne through Landos, Les Uffernets and Pradelles. The road was dead solitary, he says, all the way to Pradelles – on its hillside high above the Allier, where the peasants were cutting hay. It was a windy morning for him too and the gusts brought the unseasonal scents wafting across his path. But the shadows of the racing clouds, purple and sad and menacing, made him think darker thoughts in his solitariness. He decided to rest up for the remainder of the afternoon and evening at the inn at Langogne, which he reached just before the rain started to fall. Here, with Modestine stabled and himself well lunched, he settled down to frighten himself with a book of local lore – rather like Jonathan Harker arriving on the edge of Count Dracula country and reading up about vampirism. In Stevenson's case however he was entering no mere imaginary world of folklore. He was now leaving the Velay and coming down into another region altogether, wild, mountainous and uncultivated – Gévaudan, the country of the wolf.

This was the district which for three years between 1764 and 1767 was terrorized by the notorious and mysterious Beast of Gévaudan, the Napoleon Bonaparte of wolves. It pursued armed horsemen and carriages and attacked lone women and children, especially young girls and shepherdesses famous for their charms. The beast had an eye for beauty. But the beauty that attracted it to its female victims didn't save them. Their bodies were found half eaten, mutilated, drained of blood, lying in the fields where they had been tending their flocks. Sheep may safely graze, was the word at the time, but shepherdesses were marked for slaughter. The Beast operated around Langogne, Cheylard l'Evêque and Luc, even putting in appearances in the Auvergne, well north from the Vivarais. Its crimes were announced on placards and ten thousand francs were offered for its head.

The myths mushroomed. It came out in thunderstorms, on the night of the full moon, it leaped from hilltop to hilltop, it had the power of bilocation, appearing in different places at precisely the same time. Prayers went up from the churches, the dragoons were ordered into action on the greatest royal hunt of all time, and even the King himself offered a reward of six thousand *livres* to the man who could kill or capture the beast that was devastating the Gévaudan. Various wolves were killed and publicly displayed, including a massive one-hundred-and-thirty pounder which was stuffed and presented at Versailles to the astonishment of the court. But the relief was premature – the real beast struck again. And this time with increased ferocity. Two teenagers were ripped apart on the Lozère.

Once again the population panicked. Farm workers neglected their tasks, people refused to go out after dark or even to open their doors. The beast had the entire

143

country pinned down and it pursued its terrible career unchecked. Until one summer evening in June 1767 a local woodsman, Jean Chastel, put a single bullet through the brain of a wolf twenty pounds lighter than the monster of Versailles and so put an end to the Beast's bloody and terrifying orgy. In spite of the unexceptional appearance of this second wolf and its rather mangy hide, Chastel became a folk hero.

I hadn't worried much in advance about this aspect of the journey, consigned as it now was to local history. I was more worried about the real threat posed by the vipers that were said to crawl into sleeping-bags, attracted by the body heat of the unconscious occupants. I knew I had to sleep out on several occasions if I wanted to imitate the master with accuracy and I frequently imagined waking in the darkness to feel a scaly cold-blooded companion sharing my sleeping gear. It would be a long wait through the night, lying with muscles tensed and mind racing, motionless till morning. Even then what would it be best to do – unzip yourself with infinite slowness and tenderness, letting in the cold blue air of day notch by notch? But what if you just turned over in your sleep, unaware of your reptilian friend, and felt the bite in the night, the mark of the venom going in? Imagine it spreading, death coming closer, closing in on the heart, while you stumble around miles from human help, miles from anywhere, awaiting the inevitable end. That was a horror that dispelled the death-wish and kept my imagination feverishly alert. Right now, though, I had other problems to worry about – and they were far from imaginary.

It was a day of unbelievable weathers – galloping gales, thick mists, columns of rain marching across the hills, drenching the pinewoods and the dreary fields. I passed

144

plunging gorges, Gothic forests, streams in spate, river-banks ripped open, fields flooded, a brown soup drowning the track. Water was roaring in my ears, the wind kept yelling at me and glass rods of rain were splintering on my cheekbones, the angle of the onslaught creating the illusion that the raindrops were several feet long, like spears whistling down, sometimes striking me almost horizontally in the face. It was impossible to look straight ahead and I had to force myself to keep going. It's only rain, I told myself, not machine-gun fire. And I remembered the gallantry of the Newfoundlanders on the first day of the Somme, walking across No Man's Land and tucking their chins into their chests, heads down to meet the hail of bullets, just as if they were walking into a wind. The trick worked and I kept on going.

Anatole had no such nonsense in his skull (mine was the ass's head) and kept turning his rear to the gale, as if wanting to head back home. Hauling him in my wake – another golden rule of donkey-driving gone (never attempt to pull the donkey) – was a constant effort and made my chest hurt all the more. But if I kept alongside him he refused to move and I couldn't bring myself to beat him, even in extremis. The pines bent like tall ships to the storm-wind and the roads disappeared into the distance like shining grey threads. I never saw so many roads as I did in France and was seldom sure which was mine. I wanted to avoid main roads but at times Steven-son's original route lay along these, where the cars buzzed by like rare insects. Today even drivers had decided that it would have been madness to attempt any journey that wasn't absolutely necessary. In my case it was necessary. The day, the hour, the minute, the route, the weather – everything had already been mapped out for me. It was predestined. There weren't even cows or horses for company in the fields, not a solitary sheep, not a crow, nothing but roads and rain. And there was hardly a house for miles at a time, though there was always plenty of noise. The wind crashed through the trees, the telegraph wires throbbed and sobbed in the rain. I could feel my knee-joints threatening to seize up completely – I wasn't nearly as fit for this as I'd imagined, in spite of my years of running up Arthur's Seat, and I was lagging well behind my master.

Had the landscape changed much since he came this way? Down from Landos, over the last high farmlands of the Velay to Pradelles – once a shrine for medieval pilgrims but now drained and derelict, courtesy of Langogne, which had sucked its life-blood away. I splashed along the dark little cobbled streets, strewn with sodden dung, past roofless houses, saw the church containing the famous wooden Virgin, Our Lady of Pradelles, who had performed many miracles since she was brought here by the Crusaders. Weather wasn't one of these miracles, I thought sourly. She looked quite unmiraculous in fact, standing at one end of the church, clad in her stiff white wooden dress. There was little temptation to lunch with Stevenson here, and in any case I couldn't afford the time, not if I wanted to reach Langogne before dark. I passed through and left Pradelles to its Virgin and its rain. The only sign of life came from the window of what appeared to be a hospice. A curtain fluttered and a vacant face appeared staring at the rain. The head of the inmate never moved as I passed by – the eyes looked right through me, a man with a donkey, out in the worst weather in the world. I was of no interest to him. Or her. It was impossible to say. So much for Pradelles.

There were four miles left downhill to Langogne. All

around me lay old lichens like snow on the evergreens, and pine needles in huge Christmas heaps, like the ones left on the carpet on Twelfth Night when the tree has been taken down and thrown out with the refuse. I was suddenly crying without knowing it – or why. Scents are evocative and I was smelling the ghosts of Christmas past. I pictured my children's faces in happier days, the snug warm house I'd left behind in Edinburgh for this wet hell. Richard Holmes admits to inexplicable weeping fits. Maybe he too was reacting to scents. When you are far from home and on your own almost anything can trigger tears.

And I was crying for another reason. Walking through this wilderness of rain had brought back an image of the morning my mother died, only two Christmases ago. It was replaying itself in my unconscious mind as I trudged along – how a figure had appeared in the fire on Christmas Eve, just before she died. It was the endpiece of a chunk of Irish peat, sculpted by the flames, a Santa Claus figure to begin with, glowing redly in the grate and grinning with what seemed to be a broad wink, his jocularity a titter of flame. It was incredibly clear and I stared at it, mesmerized. He stayed that way for a long time, nearly an hour, though the busy fingers of flame worked on him incessantly, like waves on driftwood. But as night wore on he changed, becoming shrunken and stooped and grey. The smile fell to a frown, then to a sadness. At last he bowed suddenly and fell down, his act over. It was the ghost of Christmas yet to come and I felt it as an omen. The following day I saw my mother for Christmas dinner and I never saw her alive again. She died suddenly on Boxing Day, early in the morning.

I drove to the hospital through blinding rain, like this rainstorm. Was diverted by a kind, whispering nurse, who took me through the screens and left me there, alone with her. Oh, mum, you're not dead after all, I see. This is mere sleep – you've fallen over, that's all. That's what Jesus said, didn't he? She is not dead, she sleepeth. Kiss her on the cheek then, the forehead, still warm. Stroke her hair. Be careful that these tears, splashing on her face, don't wake her. Oh, but look, her mouth is slightly open and there is a tell-tale lack of breath. That endless chatter of hers has been stilled in her mouth, the stories of shopping and siblings and the news from abroad, from Fife. Stopped. Bend over her, then, grizzle-bearded man who is her son. Bend and weep. Forty-seven years ago she lay down in a bed like this and prepared to push me into the world. She was full of me. This morning I'm full of her, crouching in labour over her dead face. You will burgeon, mother, you will grow greater in me in the time to come, the days, the years. I will never be able to expel you, as you had to expel me.

I couldn't drive after that. Patricia took the car, told me to walk home through the rain, told me it would do me good, to feel the furious rain on my face. And that's what I did, walked two miles through the downpour, crying, feeling the big drops gratefully on my blind face, washing away the tears I sprouted as I walked home for the first time in my life without a mother. Through rain like this. And it struck me in that nowhere land somewhere between Pradelles and Langogne that somewhere along the line I'd stopped mourning for my mother. That my wife's death had not only stopped all joy in me, it had stopped all other grief as well – necessary grief that should have been allowed to continue its course. Life and death have to go on, both of them.

This, and the wailing wires in the rain overhead, brought the flashbacks into play. Father, mother, wife – all within four years. Or was it three? I still had no sense of time. As the white waterfall came flooding through the letterbox, the tributes to a dead wife, they were accompanied by the endless telephone calls. From the south, from the north, from round the corner. From the bottom of the world. I pictured the heart-rending sentences travelling out into space, her passing processed by the dark recording angels of technology. All day long a throbbing of wires, broken sentences and lopped columns of words left standing – monuments to a vanished chapter. A black bouquet of words comes out of Australia and already an uncle is on his way. Twelve thousand miles to kiss a wax doll in a shroud, to speak the cold valedictions of the funeral parlour.

Weeping wires. It seemed to go on all day. In France. In Scotland. Making those first calls the morning she died – that was the hardest part. Physically impossible almost every time, even to get out the first word, never mind sentence. A strangulated cry, truncated, protracted, the noise an animal might make in terror, and the sound of alarm at the other end, the unfortunates hauled from their pillows in the grey dawn, unsure what was going on, working it out, wondering what to say. What could they say? *Give sorrow words*, says Malcolm to the stricken Macduff who has just heard that his wife is dead and who cannot manage to speak, not a single syllable. Give sorrow words – the grief that does not speak whispers the o'er-fraught heart, and bids it break.

Cry, some folk said. Go on, let it out. And I cried. But not for long on the road to Langogne. The tears were washed away by the French rains. And suddenly I felt glad of the physical discomfort. As I did that day my mother died.

All the same I was seriously thinking of giving it all up

as I limped into Langogne, dead beat in the dark, only to discover that there was no hotel that anyone knew about on the near side of the town. To make matters worse the river Allier was now bursting its banks and I was given loud local assurances of a drowned donkey in the morning if I were foolhardy enough to camp out on the only green area in sight that this ugly industrial swamp of a place appeared to offer. Nobody gave much for the chances of the donkey-driver either. My best plan would be to cross the bridge and make my way to the other side of the town where there was a comfortable enough hotel. My donkey would just have to join the line of cars. The four castors were about to become four wheels.

It was a big busy bridge, lunatic with traffic to a degree only the French know how to achieve. Anatole didn't like it and his recalcitrance was intensified by his antipathy to water and the noise of tons of the stuff roaring underneath his feet and past his ears. He stalled right in the middle of the bridge, holding up the traffic both ways, and no form of persuasion could dislodge him. A double-massed queue of drivers stared at me in amazement from their windows: a wet, staggering Scotsman tugging and pleading and swearing at a stationary mound of donkeyflesh. I'd lost my ash stick and picked up a broken branch that lay in the gutter but it had too many leaves on it and acted more like a brush than a cudgel – Fawlty beating up his stalled car. Somehow I forgot to laugh. The laughter came from a few of the drivers, but most of them just kept on staring at me in disbelief. I must say they remained remarkably patient, for the ding-dong battle of wills in the middle of the bridge was now seriously impeding the progress of traffic. At last the cavalry came to the rescue – the *pompiers* who were busy trying to stop the river from flooding its banks, and who may have considered the donkey as a form of light relief from the Battle of the Allier. Three of the firemen took the strain and dragged Anatole off the bridge, after which he reverted at once to magical amenability. By the time I reached the hotel I might as well have crossed the river at the point where Stevenson had crossed, I was so soaked.

The old bridge was long gone, broken down and washed away. This depressed and daunted the eighteen-year-old Holmes, making him reflect later that you can't always follow writers exactly as you would wish, in the pages of your mind. Life itself does not stand still for you like an obedient model, and you can't connect neatly with the past through the role-playing of literary pilgrimages. The broken bridge at Langogne is still a striking symbol for the truth of the matter, that you have to make your own connections.

Not that I had any such thoughts at the time as I slogged through Langogne which offers nothing to any traveller, wet or dry. Everything I possessed was sodden, all my changes of clothes, the spare pair of dry boots, the precious sleeping-bag. I threw it all on the floor of the hotel room, crawled frozen and shivering and supperless to bed, too tired to eat, and lay in a miserable huddle until the merciful Morpheus administered a quick injection. The last thing I was conscious of were the pains in my chest and back and the sound of the rain – still pissing down. Anatole was parked at the back of the hotel between two Citroëns, to one of which he was tied. I prayed that I would wake up before the owner arrived in the morning to find this outrageous attachment to his bumper.

There was another reason why I particularly wanted to get going early. Stevenson had not left the inn at Langogne till two o'clock in the afternoon. This gave him time to get his journal written up and his knapsack repaired, but the delay cost him dear. He had a bad day on the hills on this third day as he set out for Cheylard l'Evêque on the edge of the Forest of Mercoire and ended up benighted and notoriously lost. Although I wanted to be faithful to the master I had no desire to imitate his errors. He estimated an imagined four hours, allowing for Modestine, having been advised over-optimistically in any case that a man without a she-ass could do it in an hour and a half.

Landscape and weather worked against him.

All the way up the long hill from Langogne it rained and hailed alternately: plentiful, hurrying clouds, some dragging veils of straight rain showers, others massed and luminous as though promising snow, careered out of the north and followed me along my path ... moor, heathery marsh, tracks of rock and pines, little woods of birch, jewelled with the autumn yellow, here and there a few naked cottages and bleak fields, these were the characters of the country. Hill and valley followed valley and hill; the little green and stony cart-tracks wandered in and out of one another, split into three or four, died away in marshy places, began again sporadically on a hillside and above all on the borders of a wood.

It took him less than two hours to cover the five miles to Sagne-Rousse and he had every reason to feel confident of reaching Cheylard l'Evêque in another two at most, but he came out of a firwood where he'd been wandering to find not the desired destination but a rough and tumble of hills. He asked directions of various peasants, all of whom were deliberately unhelpful. One old devil barricaded his door, another misdirected him and calmly watched him going astray, while two little hussies giggled and taunted him. One stuck her tongue out, the other told him to follow the cows and see where that took him. The Beast of Gévaudan ate about a hundred children of this district and Stevenson began to warm to him. Left to fend for himself he finally found the hamlet of Fouzillic – three houses on a hill. Three lighted windows. Here a delightful old man put him on the right road and the situation was saved.

Only for a short time. As I found out to my own cost, the roads in this region bifurcate many times, the bifurcations bifurcate, and the ramifications are as endless as they are infuriating. Within two or three steps Stevenson found himself in this predicament. Meanwhile night fell at a single swoop, never blacker, and he couldn't even make out his own hand at arm's length. Soaked by rain, he retraced what he thought were his footsteps to find Fouzillic again and that nice old man. By this time the wind had freshened into a gale and more heavy rain had come flying up out of the north. In the roaring blackness he wandered around pathetically, hemmed in by stone walls insurmountable by Modestine, till eventually he saw the red glow of the windows again. But this time there were more than three of them and they were differently disposed. He'd found not Fouzillic but Fouzil*lac*, a hamlet light years away in spirit from its nearby sister hamlet that had housed the helpful old man. Fouzillac turned out to be the world's worst centre for tourist information. Nobody would help, and though he offered one man ten francs just for guidance the man remained adamant that he was not going to cross the doorstep, not even to take him to another house, not even for one moment. '*Je ne sortirai pas de la porte!*' Stevenson called him a coward. It had no effect. '*C'est que, voyez-vous, il fait noir.*' They were all afraid of the dark. And of the Beast of Gévaudan, implies Stevenson, though he himself must have cut quite an unprepossessing figure by now. He'd waded through bogs, wandered through woods, looked offbeat and *outré* at the best of times and was an alien with a weird accent in a region which had quite conceivably never seen a single foreigner in its entire existence. Hardly surprising that no one wanted to step out with him into the pitch blackness of a stormy night or even risk lending him a lantern. They were all quite obviously terrified. But to Stevenson these were the true beasts of Gévaudan. After knocking at the other houses, all of which remained black and silent to his entreaties, he gave up Fouzillac with a curse and in groping around in the dark to find Modestine, fell into a bog.

In the circumstances the resilient and resourceful Scotsman made a virtue of necessity. He took shelter in a wood, which it took him nearly an hour to find, lit the spirit lamp, tethered the drenched and despondent Modestine and fed her a supper of black bread, changed into long dry woollen stockings, strapped himself like a *bambino* into the warm woolly sleeping-bag, using his knapsack as a pillow, broke open a case of Bologna sausage and a cake of chocolate, ate well, washed down 'this obscene mixture' with neat cognac and finally smoked one of the best cigarettes in the world. The wind was roaring among the trees and the lamplight doubled the darkness on the edge of his cave of leaves, cutting him off from the rest of the universe. The wind in the trees was his lullaby and the subtle glue leapt between his eyelids as soon as they touched. He fell asleep contentedly among the woods of the Gévaudan, perfectly at home in this alien wilderness.

At home. Waking up in Langogne in a dim dawn, I felt in a strange sort of way more at home than I'd been for a long time in my own sadly altered version of home, even

154

a year on from her death – especially in the first filterings of daylight, when there was no sleepy voice on the other pillow, no loving murmurs in the streaky quietness, urging me to stroke her back and belly, to nibble her nipples and suck her tongue. God, how I missed all that! Missed drinking in that maddeningly adorable drowsiness of hers in the dark, hearing that sigh of pleasure when she tasted the first sip of coffee I brought up to bed, feeling her suddenly aroused and abandoning herself to sex before the blue light poured in and came between us. As death the bastard did.

Does. As death does, I thought – not did. Her death isn't something that happened, it goes on happening, every day. Death is the continuing absence, the daily bread. It is eating alone, sleeping alone, waking alone. There's nothing romantic about that, in spite of Shelley. *Music when soft voices die vibrates in the memory.* So he said. *Odours when sweet violets sicken live within the sense they quicken.* Alternatively you're simply left with silence and the scent of decay. And yet here in Langogne, in a hotel room I'd never see again, I experienced a fleeting sense of being at home with my morning thoughts of her, felt for the first time that I could confront my memories with something approaching fondness and warmth.

I left Langogne early, determined to avoid Stevenson's ordeals but admiring in recollection his positive ability to make the best of things, to keep cheerful in adversity – which was a feature not just of his journey across the Cévennes but of his whole life. All the same, I thought, if he'd woken up in Langogne this morning instead of over a century ago, he'd not have stayed long beyond breakfast. I abandoned it at once, after hot rolls and coffee, spurred on by the image of the donkey-clamped Citroën. Anatole forgave me this indignity when I brought him some fresh white rolls filched from the hotel kitchen. Once again there was almost nobody around. Leaving Langogne, however, doesn't bring any sense of fresh woods and pastures new. You are leaving the old Velay and passing into the Gévaudan of Stevenson's worst nightmare, where the landscape becomes like its old inhabitants, belligerent, blank, unbeckoning, and the road rises and spirals uncomfortably into infinity. Increasingly anxious on account of my forerunner's rough experiences in these hills – the bad weather, the bewildering landscape, the bogs and forests, the unsociable inhabitants of Fouzillac, the necessity of camping out for the first time – I quickened my pace, expecting trouble.

It came at once. It was a long steep winding road out of Langogne, with the rain that fell on that same road a hundred and sixteen years ago to the day now giving me a broadside pounding. A wrong turn that ended in a quarry, another that brought me right up against barbed-wire barriers, unknown to Stevenson, and finally the right road which, after a mile, turned out to be as pointless as the others. A farmworker told me that the way ahead was blocked by fallen trees, negotiable by man but not by donkey. I had lost a full hour and was forced to leave Stevenson's route for four miles and come to St Flour-de-Mercoire by the main road.

I was greatly struck by its church. Nine gravestones laid flat formed a pathway up to the front door, so that those below were continually trampled by the passing feet of the generations that came to worship there: a curious form of doormatting. In the Middle Ages this was a favourite method of penitentialism chosen by the proud aristocrats who, far from humble in their lives, tried it on with God in the next life, impressing him, so they hoped, with this first and final gesture of humility.

By contrast the graveyard was a tawdry souvenir shop, redolent of Rome: pottery roses, paper lilies, gold-sprayed Christs, china bibles with gilt-edged pages, tacky *pietàs* loud with passion and lurid with blood spouting from hands, feet, side; cherubs, angels, harps and lambs, bric-à-brac from Lourdes that ran the alphabet of clichés – geese soaring against setting suns, swans dying against rising moons, nothing left to the plastic imagination. Many of the marble tombs bore not merely the names of the deceased but the names, addresses and telephone numbers of the memorial sculptors who had provided them. In one case even a fax number on the stone. Just in case anyone needed to make a sudden call – following a sudden call.

One of the older monuments had been erected by a man whose wife had died young, and the universal query was engraved on the marble: why did you leave me? Absurdly the French connection made something flash into my mind. I recalled a television newscaster called Reginald Bosanquet who'd also died prematurely. Somebody had composed a jocular song about him. *Oh Bosanquet, why did you go away?* The question we all address to our loved ones. A question not so much rhetorical as unanswerable.

My thoughts were interrupted by something I hadn't seen for a long time, not since my teens, when I left my fishing village home in Fife. An old-fashioned funeral procession was approaching, a cortège of black statues, inching its way to the cemetery with slow and solemn tread. No hearse – just the sound of shoes crunching quietly on the country path, and all heads bowed, except those of the pall-bearers at the head of the column. Eyes down. That was why Hamlet remembered the shoes his mother wore at his father's funeral. Because when you're in a funeral march, with your head dutifully lowered, all you see are the feet of the person in front of you in the file – in Hamlet's case those of his mother, the chief mourner. Shakespeare had clearly recalled this detail from his own mourning duties, and so life went into literature again, as it does.

And back again – as I now recalled that day nearly a year ago when we'd driven to Mortonhall. I remembered how, as we neared the cemetery, two old men out for their constitutional in the fine autumn weather stopped at the pavement's edge, removed their hats, clapped them to their chests and bowed their heads, one white, one bald. They remained like that for the few seconds it took us to pass. Remnants from another era, they revived childhood memories of the Fife funerals where, out in the streets, little knots of men waited at corners to join the cortège as it passed along the route to the little graveyard – just as a few old Frenchmen were doing right now, up in St Flour-de-Mercoire, as the cortège approached the gates where they stood waiting. When the hearse reached them the old Fife fishermen would bow their heads and take off their hats in a single communal gesture of respect, clapping them theatrically to their chests like actors in an old melodrama. Exactly as the two old men did outside Mortonhall.

It was a weird experience, standing there on the edge of that silent gathering of ghosts, with France and Fife and Edinburgh and even Hamlet's Denmark all fused and caught in a time-warp that had the sudden effect of making me look at life and death together and see them steadily and see them whole as one process and experience. We're all dead, I told myself. We are the dead. Or, conversely, there's no such thing as death. In this reflective mood I left the dead to bury their dead and climbed to the top of the village.

Very different was the memorial here to the local men – mostly boys – who gave their lives in the Great War. Even a forgotten place like this had to give up its youth, its contribution. Every little helps. This hamlet's 'little' probably constituted most of its young men, their minds on young girls as they went off to war; or on other matters, their mothers, their brothers and sisters, their farms – not on glory. The sepia photographs were like silent bells for those who died as cattle. This was a far cry from the commercialization of bereavement displayed in the village churchyard. No mockeries for them, I thought, except the mockery of war itself, the monstrous anger of the guns, and at home here the pallor of girls' brows to be their pall, and the bugles calling for them from these French fields – foreign fields to me, naturally, but the equivalent for them of the sad shires of home. I looked at this memorial for a long time, and as I looked it was Sassoon rather than Owen who kept coming into my mind.

> I knew a simple soldier boy
> Who grinned at life in empty joy,
> Slept soundly through the lonesome dark,
> And whistled early with the lark.

Sassoon's simple soldier boy came from places like St Flour-de-Mercoire. As for the hell where youth and laughter go, that was the trenches, according to the poem. But here was the other hell – a lonely memorial in a depopulated village.

I thought of Housman too.

> Here dead we lie because we did not choose
> To live and shame the land from which we sprung.
> Life, to be sure, is nothing much to lose:
> But young men think it is – and we were young.

159

Only forty years after Stevenson passed by here, the butchers and bunglers had done their work. The slaughter was complete.

Twenty years after it ended it started up again and the young men went to soldiers, and to graveyards, and to flowers. And to sea-blooms. Every one. My wife's father among them. Had he survived I'd not have been standing here now, that much was certain. She'd have lived a different life. But they never saw one another. She was one year old when he was killed in battle. Standing there by that memorial I recalled how she had begun to talk a lot about her father during her illness and – it came back to me now – during the months of my ignorance, when she knew what was growing inside her. When you know you are going to have to say goodbye to your loved ones, your mind turns more and more to your dead. It has to be that way for sanity's sake. Easier to think about reunions than partings.

The rain that had given brief respite now resumed colder still. My hands froze. Looking down on the cemetery I saw myself again going up to Mortonhall to erase the page of blank snow from her memorial, to return it to its graven script. My hands were freezing as I turned out the old flowers and replenished the vase with water before plugging in the dim green lamps of unbudded daffodils, still in their shades. All around me a drizzling silence and my footprints filling up with brown rainwater in the slush of her grave. So this is what it comes down to: a man stumbling around in the rain, wiping the wetness from a line of words about his dead wife.

It felt cold enough to turn to hail. I stood there one April, in Mortonhall, when a hailstorm came down from the north and sowed the cemetery with sterile white stones, the cornseed of a blighted spring. I stayed on under the assault and battery, watching the bullets rattling off all those memorials that concealed a thousand cancers – cancers that killed themselves in the end. When the body stops the disease dies. A useless enough thought. But Mortonhall was the stopped heart round which the useless city revolved. I could never tear myself away from it, drawn like a moth to the cold flame of her name on that grave, flickering in the rain.

La pluie, la pluie, la pluie.

Should I have cremated her, as one friend suggested, foreseeing the outcome? Burial allows the persistence of the metaphor that death is a sleep, going on beneath the sweet green grass, the earth's bedcover. Burning is a pure and ruthless recognition that all states and affairs of the body are over. And you won't be caught in the rain in some deserted graveyard, getting wetter and wetter.

Leaving St Flour the road to Fouzillac went through the forest and was as remote as it was possible to be, climbing all the time, under endless cavalry charges of clouds and slamming gales. Then into flat gloomy water-logged woodland where the track finally disappeared and the forest floor went underwater. Sharp stones and slimy boulders lay hidden beneath the green soup. There was nothing for it but to wade through with Anatole and with freezing feet and hope that the precious panniers, newly dried out in overnight Langogne, would somehow survive: if the donkey stumbled they would end up in the soup and so would I. A wet sleeping-bag would be the worst possible disaster because I knew I had to camp out tonight, a reluctant pilgrim, sticking sedulously to the schedule of the reluctant mentor. In his master's steps he trod. St Louis he may have been to some followers but heat was not in the sod which the saint had printed. The wet cold in my feet seeped right up to my brain. I was already at a low ebb and hating every second of it.

And a weird place it was, this forest land, sprouting toadstools like mad phalluses and eastern pagodas, reviving in me childhood tales of goblins and wood sprites and more recent images of the insane root that takes the reason prisoner. This was one of the areas in which the Beast of Gévaudan went on its killing sprees until Jean Chastel ended its career, and so the forest came complete with wicked wolf. But the only killing being done around here now was by two-legged beasts. From time to time there were rifle-cracks and the boom of shotguns and I came across the occasional Renault, one of them stuck up to its doorsills in mud – and in the back seat the empty cartridge cases and the packets of Gauloise, awaiting the hunter's return.

A mile further on from this I spotted another apparently stranded Renault. I would have passed it by but for the fact that in the universal silence of the forest it struck me that I could hear sounds coming from it. I stopped and stared. It was moving, shaking, perhaps even sinking slowly, who knows, into the mushroom soup of this soggy woodland floor. There were people in it, perhaps trying to get out, somehow trapped. I didn't dare leave Anatole unattended with the panniers, not knowing what mischief he might get up to, so I waded with him carefully through the mush until I could see into the car. I realized my mistake at once but it was too late. A bare white female backside was imparting its thrusting motion to the vehicle while her supine partner was invisible underneath her on the back seat. She was still wearing her stockings. It was at that point that Anatole, not at all given to much braying on the journey so far, gave one of his best.

162

There was no method of beating a quick retreat and in any case it was too late. The owner of the backside stopped what she was doing and looked at me over her shoulder. She was curly-haired, auburn and pretty. She also had a wide, friendly grin, expressing delighted surprise. *Oh, regardes le petit âne!* She regarded Anatole for a few seconds and gave me a wink before, to my amazement, resuming her activity. I led the retreat as speedily as I could in the circumstances, afraid that her companion might come armed with a shotgun after the *voyeur avec un âne* – and wondering why two people wanting sex had any need to retreat into the waterlogged obscurity of this forest land. The whole of Gévaudan seemed so empty they could have lain down in the middle of a main road and there would have been nobody around to know or care. Then I asked myself, main road? What was I talking about? You'd be more likely to find a main road on the moon than in this deserted landscape. Even these recent signs of humanity, hardly welcoming, petered out again into total desolation and a frightening quietness. I'd no idea where I was and began to wish I'd asked the auburn-haired girl in stockings for directions. But it never occurred to me at the time and on reflection would have been quite bizarre. Had I done a Stevenson after all?

It was with huge relief that quite accidentally I saw the track again. It led with surprising suddenness out of the woods and into Fouzillac – which turned out to be more a geographical expression than a real place: a mere memory of where a place had once been. Fouzillic was a mere five hundred yards away. These two place-names were recorded on the very edge of existence, representing dereliction and depopulation defined and on display. It was an unforgiving landscape, offering nothing to anyone who did stay except toil and sweat. But the hostility

Stevenson had met with here was more than made up for in my case by the friendly Fouzillac farmer who *had* stayed, and who offered me a choice of fields if camping was really on my mind – though a nice snug barn was available. I chose the field with the best view – over the forests I'd just come up and through – and the farmer strode back to his house, his two dogs on either side of him nuzzling his huge dangling hands. He reappeared ten minutes later and shouted to me to come in for a beer. He had been asking his wife's permission, I suspect. She seemed less sure of me. But when I explained why I was here and that I had two children back in Scotland she brought out bread and cheese and laid them on the rough table. She and her husband also had children – they were now away at university and were unlikely to return, except for holidays.

I took advantage of this convivial moment to ask the friendly farmer if he knew anything about the Beast of Gévaudan. To my surprise he turned out to be knowledge-able on the subject and even had his own theories, though later I read much the same ones in various sources. The real beast had never been found, he was sure of that. A mere wolf could never have subjected an entire region of France to such a reign of terror, that much was certain, and the specimens that were killed and presented as trophies were incapable of achieving what this beast had done. Furthermore it was important to note, he said, that the attacks were not random. This beast had a passion for the young, the beautiful and especially the female of the human species. This argued an intelligence and a motive beyond the bestial. Vampirism was a possibility, though he personally didn't go along with such superstitions, or with the theory that Jean Chastel himself was the killer, a deeply disturbed psychopath with lycanthropic tendencies, who'd dressed himself up in wolfskins and done a Jack the Ripper job, terrorizing an entire community. It struck me, though, that the creator of Jekyll and Hyde would have been interested in this theory, rejected by the farmer as too fanciful. He favoured the theory that a local aristocrat, known to be a sadist, took pleasure in terrorizing his tenants with a whole pack of wolves, specially trained to kill. He rummaged in a cupboard and showed me a book on the subject, inviting me to flip through it and hand it back in the morning. Then he came to the door and shone a torch for me as I made my way to the field where Anatole was tethered.

'I still wouldn't camp if I were you!' he shouted from the doorway.

'Why?' I shouted back. 'Because of the Beast of Gévaudan?'

'No!' he roared, his words captured by the rising wind. 'Because you might have to use your sleeping-bag as a parachute!'

I thought about this as I gave Anatole some extra grain for supper, had a quiet corned-beef hash and one of the farmer's beers, and zipped myself in for the night to read a little more about the myths surrounding the Beast. Holmes's favourite theory possesses a sinister simplicity.

> It proposed, as a strict zoological possibility, a rogue family of *three* wolves (like the Three Bears) who, ostracised from the main pack, had tasted the delights of human flesh, and thereafter attacked in combination. Hence the inexplicable ferocity of the Beast, and also its ability to be in two places at once. The theory had the great attraction of leaving one wolf still unaccounted for. I liked this very much.

As for me I didn't like this theory at all as I extinguished my lamp, lay down in the darkness of the open field and, in spite of the Third Beast, fell asleep at once.

Sleep is when you are most vulnerable, whether in a good bed in south Edinburgh or in some corner of a foreign field. It wasn't the Beast of Gévaudan that invaded my sleep – it was the demons from the old life, the life that had begun to seem so far away after only a few days. I dreamt that she was leaving me, that she loved someone else and wanted a divorce so that she could marry again. I woke in terror in the roaring blackness, realizing as soon as I felt and smelt the earth beneath me and heard the sea of wind streaming through the trees, that it had only been a bad dream. Relieved I reached out for her across the bed, looking for the luminous green numbers on the radio clock, still not wholly awake. The crazy brain taunting me, that old sadistic trickster. Then I remembered that she'd gone, she'd left me already nearly a year ago, left me to marry a bastard. Death. That was the bastard she went off with. But she didn't go willingly. I wasn't jilted, I was robbed. It was rape, that's what it was. Rape.

Wide awake now, I reached for the brandy flask. And lay remembering a night like this a year ago, when I'd driven over to the Fife cottage in gales and rain, King Lear in a Cortina, ready for Act Three. Something like that. I switched on the angle-poise lamp and sat down at the desk by the streaming panes, confronted by my own reflection staring back at me from the world outside the house. I saw a man framed by blackness – a wet wild blackness in which the writer, the replica of myself, looked strangely dry. Then it started to snow – wet snow, driven on the wind – and the writer disappeared in the river of sleety flakes sliding down the panes. I was glad to see him vanish and retreated to the couch, to be wakened an hour later by a plague of

166

hailstones falling like Egyptian boils. By the time I got up, drink in hand, to open the cottage door and yell encouragement to the elements, it was over. Mad Lear had missed his chance. The skies cleared, the stars appeared, and suddenly I heard strings of night-geese passing overhead. I checked my watch. It was midnight. I could barely see them, just the soaring silhouettes, but their cries seemed to be coming out of the steadfast constellations, as if the stars had voices, Aldebaran, Arcturus, making themselves heard. Then it quickly clouded over again and through the scudding drifts the rainy Hyades vexed the dim sea, to Tennysonian order, and the voices drained southward, ebbing towards Edinburgh, and were gone.

When I looked out the following morning the fences stood like staves, strung with raindrop notes. I supposed there was a bleak beauty in this silent prelude, playing on the wires, but I went down instead to visit that grey old slut, the sea, slavering along the edges of the world. So this had been the great dream – to retire here and listen daily to this geriatric old washerwoman, scouring the stones of the shores. Down on the beach the rollers came crashing up the sands, sending the spindrift flying in wet clouds over foreshore and fields.

The gales blew harder than ever during the night. I dreamt that the entire field in which I lay camped had been lifted like a magic carpet and was floating over the forests, with Anatole standing like a little wingless Pegasus at my side. In reality the groundsheet was being lifted by the wind, snaking underneath me. I woke up for a few seconds to settle this matter in my mind and assure myself that we were not flying. Anatole was quietly munching. Don't donkeys *ever* sleep? And then it came again, the terrible dream that my wife was sleeping beside me and that I'd had a dream-within-the-dream, telling me that she'd died. I couldn't choose between real and unreal and this time couldn't wake up to settle the matter. Like a drowning man, I panicked my way up painfully to the meniscus of consciousness to escape the smothering horror of the dream – only to wake and find myself high up in France, a widower and a donkey-driver.

Anatole was braying hard for breakfast, the high winds had fallen away to a stiff bright breeze, and the sun was pouring over the forest tops and into my eyes. I could see in silhouette the farmer of Fouzillac strolling over the field, his dogs lolloping around him. He was carrying a sack of hay for the donkey and a pan of hot black coffee for the driver. At first I thought he was telling me I'd drunk too much wine during the night and couldn't understand what made him think this. But it takes time to attune your ear to the local accent. *Beaucoup de vent* sounds very like *beaucoup de vin* and the twang gets more nasal the further south you go.

The morning was a replica of Stevenson's and as I looked around there was absolutely nothing in the landscape to argue that he couldn't emerge right this minute from the trees and pass the time of day with me. I felt the spirit of the thing very closely and jotted down in my journal his own words which exactly described the scene – the sky full of strings and shreds of vapour, flying, waltzing clouds, turning like tumblers about an invisible axis as the winds hounded them through heaven. The forest we had both come through last night was far beneath my feet. I felt quite literally on top of the world and my spirits lifted, taking on some of my companion's positive attack on misfortune and despair.

Ulysses left on Ithaca and with a mind unsettled by the goddess was not more pleasantly astray. I have

168

been after such an adventure all my life, a pure dispassionate adventure, such as befell early and heroic voyagers; and thus to be found by morning in a random woodside nook in Gévaudan – not knowing north from south, as strange to my surroundings as the first man upon the earth, an inland castaway – was to find a fraction of my daydreams realised.

I didn't feel particularly heroic but there was a pristine purity about the place and the time that entered into me and made me feel a flush of optimism I hadn't felt in over a year. My sedentary wanderlust in Edinburgh had paid off for the moment, like Stevenson's. Travel suddenly felt good, though I wondered if there was a Freudian slip in his erroneous allusion to Ithaca, Ulysses' actual homeland, when what he had in mind was the land of the enchantress, Circe. Was he unconsciously torn between following his own *femme fatale* and returning to the emotional safety of the land and passion of his mother, the roots and hearth-ease of 17 Heriot Row? Hungry for skylines, suckling his blood, he homed yet for Ithaca in his unconscious longings, while putting out like the great Homeric figure to settle something by exploration. Settling and exploring, they appear to be opposed but they are processes which can pull one way. This made me think about the double-sided nature of travel, which is both an escape and a pursuit: in both my own case and Stevenson's a simultaneous pursuit and escape, of and from, both home and a woman. Holmes too had an insight at this point in the journey – that real travel is to do with disorientation rather than mere distance, that it is by losing yourself that you find yourself again. Which is what happens in the great Shakespearean dramas. Which is what happens in religion. Which is what ought to happen in life itself.

After drinking all the coffee I saddled Anatole and set off for Luc by way of Cheylard l'Evêque. The first mile or so was a beguilingly easy woodland walk and I came to Cheylard in no time at all. Stevenson again found an inn where he wrote in his journal, drank chocolate, ate an omelette and scorched his legs in front of a blazing fire. At the ghost of a café an old woman offered me coffee on the house. She seemed glad of someone to talk to, even a stranger with a donkey. I asked her what the young people did around here, for employment and entertainment. She stared into the sunlight with wrinkled old eyes that were remarkably clear. 'There *are* no young people here,' she said. 'The Germans shot them all. They were members of the Maquis, you see. They shot them just over there.' She seemed to be living half a century ago as she pointed in the direction of a nearby farm. I was on the point of asking her if she'd lost a son perhaps, but thought better of it. I thanked her for the coffee and left Cheylard. There was no memorial here. None except the old woman herself, a remembering mouth by the wayside, more moving than stone, a testimony to the futility and pity of war. *And some there be which have no memorial and are vanished as though they had never been.* So it has been said. But there are always memorials, to soldiers and fighters for freedom, even in the middle of nowhere, and their flowers are the tenderness of patient minds. Like that of the old woman of Cheylard l'Evêque. Finding it had been a real struggle for Stevenson, and he reflected candidly that it scarcely seemed worth the search.

A few broken ends of village, with no particular street but a succession of open bare places, heaped with logs and firewood, a couple of tilted crosses, a shrine to Our Lady of All Graces on the summit of a little hill.

But even this little place had played its part in a big conflict.

After Cheylard things reverted to what I'd come to expect by now: a series of steep climbs and descents through forests of conifers. At times I found myself looking down on trees that only an hour earlier had towered over me. Now they seemed like miniscule mushrooms sprinkling the floor of the world. As I pushed on through monotonous miles of pines the world turned surreal. Long scars opened up in the forest – huge tracts of trees had been bitten out to make way for pylons that stood like Martian war machines among the timeless trees. At the miniature end of the spectrum the toadstools had mated and gone mad again, producing a race of phalluses and lobsters with orange octopus eyes. Scores of golden onion domes made me feel like a giant, looking down on Moscow.

'Bonjour, monsieur.'

The sudden sound of a human voice gave me a shock. I looked up from the cities of fungi at my feet and found myself staring at a man with a shotgun. That it was a shotgun at least, that much was clear. As to whether he was a man, that was more debatable. He could have been left over from Stevenson's time and might have been my predecessor's prototype for Ben Gunn. I half expected him to ask me if I might have on me such a thing as a piece of cheese. He was caked in mud from his pulpy black boots to his long filthy white hair, in which leaves and bits of twig were entangled. He was leaning against a tree and steaming gently and foully, a sort of damp exhalation coming off his clothes, as if he'd just risen from a swamp. Other than Ben Gunn I thought of Boris Karloff and *The Curse of the Mummy*. I thought of jungle-bound Japanese soldiers living on bats and rats, ignorant of a peace that had broken out half a century ago. I could see that the shotgun was cocked.

'*Bonjour,*' I answered.

I stopped. Something about him made me decide it would be better to engage him in friendly conversation rather than simply walk on. I nodded and smiled at him. His expression of obvious suspicion and hostility didn't change.

'You were looking at them,' he said, indicating the fungi with a wave of the gun barrel that made me wince.

And before I could reply he added, 'You're not to pick them.'

I sensed helpfulness here and breathed more easily.

'Ah,' I said, 'you mean because they're not edible. Not mushrooms. Poisonous. Yes, I understand.'

He shook his head.

'No, *monsieur*, you do *not* understand. You are not to pick them because they are *mine*. I am the landowner here. I am the *patron.*'

I wasn't going to argue. I agreed smilingly.

'And what do you use them for?' I inquired politely.

He did not so much respond to my question as carry on speaking, half to himself.

'That one there – with the red spots. After I've eaten that I can tear up trees by the roots – big trees. Like that one over there.'

A huge pine was lying with its top towards us and its roots in the air like a giant frozen squid. I murmured suitable appreciation of this apparent feat and tugged at Anatole's bridle.

'*Eh bien, monsieur, au revoir – et bon appetit!*'

I retreated with tingling back, more than half expecting a shotgun blast. It didn't come.

'Just a moment, *monsieur!*'

Christ, I thought, this is it.

'Where are you travelling to, may I ask?'

172

'To Luc.'

'No you're not,' he said, quite simply. 'You are in the Forest of Mercoire, heading south-west. You need to go in the opposite direction, to Les Pradels. After that you will come to Luc.'

Lost after all. I'd had a feeling I was wandering off track but if it hadn't been for the fungophile God knows where I'd have ended up. When I looked back after a few minutes he was still standing there guarding his garden of horrors. He looked like one of the fungi come to giant human life, fertilized by the food of the gods. Afterwards I thought about the species of hallucinogenic mushrooms eaten by the Vikings to make them go berserk in battle (the insane root again) and wondered for a moment if he could possibly have torn up that tree, ripped it like a leek out of the earth. No. I told myself, don't be stupid, man, this is the *real* world.

The real world? From Langogne to Cheylard was for Stevenson 'a naked valley', the land utterly exploited. From then on the journey to Luc was so awful that he compared it to the worst of the Scottish Highlands, cold and ignoble, 'one of the most beggarly countries in the world'. Unable to think of a solitary reason why anyone would ever want to go either to Cheylard or to Luc, he came out with what is now perhaps his most famous bit of philosophy.

For my part I travel not to go anywhere but to go. I travel for travel's sake. The great affair is to move; to feel the needs and hitches of our life more nearly, to come down off this featherbed of civilisation and find the globe granite underfoot and strewn with cutting flints.

This was good enough for me in my current mood and in the surrounding wasteland. To ginger it up I began

173

shouting out whole lumps of poetry about travel, as if I were back in the classroom. Here I could really let rip and there was nobody to deafen for miles in any direction. Ulysses was top of the class this morning. How dull it is to pause, to make an end, to rust unburnished, not to shine in use, as though to breathe were life! I cannot rest from travel: I will drink life to the lees! To strive, to seek, to find and not to yield! Et cetera.

So far I'd faced no lack of cutting flints both figurative and real, but as I came down into Luc I was stunned into admiration by the view – over a great long valley with hills to the north and, topping the castle, a gigantic blue and white statue of the Virgin rising to meet me, over-looking the entire valley in an attitude of all-powerful protectiveness. So potent, in fact, that she had a lightning-conductor attached to her left shoulder. Faith and physics teaming up, just to be on the safe side. A truly monster Virgin, Our Lady of Lourdes, newly installed just before Stevenson arrived and not yet dedicated, five thousand pounds in weight of her, a colossus, like some enormous statue of Stalin in the former Soviet Union. Big Sister is watching you. Or Big Mother.

Watching over nothing at all, as it happened. Luc hadn't changed much from how it looked to Stevenson, 'a strag-gling double file of houses wedged between hill and river. It had no beauty, nor was there any notable feature.' Nothing except the old castle with its fifty donkey-loads' worth of brand-new Madonna. But he did find a decent inn, spotless and spacious, with clean checked curtains hung across the box beds, chests and ticking clocks, and the mantelpiece decorated with lanterns and religious statuettes: the very model of what a kitchen ought to be. Attended to by the landlady – a handsome old woman, though silent and black and hooded like a nun – he dined splendidly on 'capital trout, stewed hare, a famous cheese, and a palatable little wine of the Vivarais to wash all down. I would not have envied a *dîner* at Bignon's.'

Lucky Louis. Le Bignon was a Paris restaurant on the Boulevard des Italiens and a celebrated rendezvous for artists and writers in the days of the Second Empire. Unlovely Luc offered me nothing. It was a huge let-down: no hotel, restaurant, *auberge*, not even a *gîte d'étape*. Nothing. Five francs was Louis's ticket to a hot meal and a fresh bed. I'd gladly have paid fifty, a hundred. This aspect of the trip was starting to get under my skin – the complete lack of places to eat and sleep out of season where, a century ago, my precursor could eat like a king and sleep like a baby. I swore aloud for the first time, I think, on the journey. Fuck-all! Absolutely fuck-all! Unbelievable. There was nobody willing to rent a room or sell a meal and not a square inch of ground to camp on, nothing green anywhere in this godforsaken hole, a place obviously on the edge of total collapse. There was a moment of hope when a woman said her mother might be persuaded to rent me a room for the night but first would have to know my nation. What is my nation? This was an easy one, I thought. Scots are welcomed everywhere. RLS was duly mentioned – and Scotland. But when the woman returned she was shaking her head. Mother turned out to be like the old Gallic dungarees at St Martin-de-Fugères, who'd never even heard of Scotland.

'But *you've* heard of it, surely?' I pleaded.

This felt ridiculous and pathetic.

'Oh, of course, but she won't budge, I'm afraid. It's her way.'

Still, the daughter let me camp in her garden – and there I slept, using the last of my chocolate for dinner,

Anatole tethered to a whirligig of a clothes-pole decorated with all the lady's underwear, and with the river Allier coursing far below me and at nightfall an amazing display of stars. The Virgin stood towering in majestic silhouette up in the Milky Way, and it was weird to watch Anatole, also in silhouette, standing staring up at her all night long, Mary and the donkey under the stars. Maybe he carried in his ass's genes the memory of a Bethlehem story, in which somebody else failed to find a room for the night.

I took no warmth from any of this. It made me think of Christmas again, and of all past times I'd known under those same stars. Made me long for home, for the known dimensions of my rooms, for my children, for the Scotland that had never been heard of in this forgotten valley, the country of the blind. Home was not so sad tonight. And there was a nihilistic grandeur in this contemptuous sweep of stars, stunning me into a sure knowledge of my loneliness and homesickness.

I reached out for something familiar, rummaged in one of the panniers and brought out a couple of my diaries. There were photographs of the kids inserted between various pages. Photographs of *her*. Of all of us. Was Larkin right? Do these past scenes lacerate simply by *being* over? Or is there a sense in which a photograph of a past moment really starts to exist, to be, the moment the person in it dies? Our wedding albums, our kids' progress from beach buckets and spades to graduation gowns and scrolls, all those family hols, they lie unlooked at – until somebody dies. Then we go up into lofts, open up the boxes, rake in the backs of old drawers. And that's when they truly start to live. For the first time. What was I doing exactly a year ago tonight? What was I telling myself? I turned the pages to see.

25th September '93 Kept the radio switched on. Classic FM, my new nocturnal companion, surrogate

176

sleeping partner, melodic bedmate. Switched off and lay listening to the rain that can dissolve all loves except the love of death, and which, like death, can never disappoint. Her dying face haunting my dreams like the rain at night. But the rain didn't last long. Towards dawn heard the rumble of trains with their sweet nightly mirages of making journeys, of beginnings and endings – instead of this eternal present breaking out again. Didn't even have work to go to in the morning. Give me your arm, old toad – help me down Cemetery Road.

26th September '93, 1.30 a.m. Woke up on floor. At one in the morning. Television screen was a grey fizzle, the fire had fallen to a carpet of snow-white ash and my skull was buzzing. It was pressed against the fender. Looked in the mirror. On one cheekbone the perfect imprint of a bronze leaf. Staggered outside to put the car to bed and was hit by a billion stars, bitter little coffin nails glittering in a black freezing sky. The lights of an aircraft descending bleeped briefly between boughs. Up there in the twinkling darkness people were safe in their bubble world, free from gravity. Free from the gravity of this day.

Morning Oh not another beautiful fucking day! When will this bastard of a month end? Phone didn't ring in the darkness. Rang the hospital myself but no change. Roamed about house tidying things up, putting the home in order before the heart of it ceases to beat. As I know it will. My two precious bundles are asleep upstairs. The hardest thing in the world is still in front of them. How can I break their hearts? Well, it seems I don't have to do it this morning. Not yet.

Here I skipped a few pages. I couldn't bear to reread the death entry. Not in this soulless place. I'd finish this awful journey on 3 October. How did I feel last time round?

3rd October '93 Nice tidy house today, like a fucking morgue! No shoes kicked off on the floor just where she'd come in, no earrings by the telephone, no tops slung over the back of the bedroom chair, the hairbrush by the bathroom mirror, the brassière dangling from the pulley, not a trace left to show that a certain person had shared my life all these years. When she was around there used to be three hundred items in the bathroom – female things. Now my bachelor's bathroom contains about three: toothbrush, soap and razor, not much more than that. It's as if somebody is now lodging in the house. These are his things. Obviously he's travelling light, passing through, finding no continuing city, no abiding citadel. Doubt whether he's seeking one that's to come, seeing there probably isn't one to come. This is it, chaps. This is as good as it gets. Now that she's gone.

I had crossed out the word *bachelor's* and inserted *widower's* – in the interests of accuracy.

5th November '93 No fireworks. Last night was a miserable concerto of rain. It pissed on the patio, bubbling wickedly of choked gutterings and a leaky roof, nail sickness in the tiles, no doubt. I don't want to fucking know. Let it all come down. Woke at 4.45 a.m. from murky slumbers and flurries of panic and stumbled downstairs to put out the buckets in the downpour, to recycle the layer of yet another day, so that life could bed down like a time-capsule into the oblivion of past and future. Drinking coffee back in bed in the gurgling darkness, I thought of you, my love, and the frighteningly impossible future, wishing I were dead. Wishing I were dead the way I used to wish it were Friday.

I leafed through another month of the old life.

5th December '93 In school. The trees are riding at anchor, stripped masts and winter rigging. The gulls are restless, winds prowling about the buildings. Have the radio playing. Gluck came on a few minutes back and I lost control. It was the aria from *Orpheus and Eurydice*. What is life to me without thee? What is life if thou art dead? Why the fuck did it have to be that one? There will be a class along in two minutes and I'm in pieces, shaking and crying. Life without thee is but pain. Yes, I know, I fucking know. There goes the bell and here they come, screeching senselessly out there as the year wears on and the world revolves on its axis and orbits round a little star and moves on somewhere with the expanding universe, while she lies dead in Mortonhall and I can think about nothing else. Now the real trembles are coming on. Time for the old toad again. I must be idle.

Not exactly a mine of comfort, these jottings, and some of the language was blue. Back up the shaft we go then. Our anniversary.

25th March '94 Read *In Memoriam* last night. Dark house by which once more I stand.

> *Dark house by which once more I stand,*
> *Here in the long unlovely street,*
> *Doors where my heart was used to beat*
> *So quickly, waiting for a hand,*

179

A hand that can be clasped no more.
Behold me, for I cannot sleep
And like a guilty thing I creep
At earliest morning to the door.

He is not here. But far away
The noise of life begins again
And ghastly through the drizzling rain
On the bald street breaks the blank day.

In the last stanza I'd scored out *He* and scribbled in *She* – again in the interests of accuracy. Tennyson was mourning a man.

I turned back to Christmas. All the ingredients were there tonight, so I told myself, leafing through the pages that had somehow held me together for an infernal year. All the ingredients – including no room at the inn.

Christmas Eve '93 More cards snowing through the letterbox, lying in thick white drifts in the vestibule. Clinical winds whistling under the door, sorting them into smaller piles. More cards than ever this year, an enormous sympathy vote. Rains had washed the white whales green but the white hand keeps coming back dusting those hills. So do the winds, cuffing the gulls, hurling them from the skies. Took winter jasmine from the garden, mixed with holly and mistletoe, and put them in the new vase up at Mortonhall. Poured two glasses of claret as always and listened to *A Child's Christmas in Wales* as we always did. Words, words, words. The magic had gone. It will never come again.

Christmas morning Phone bombillating like Mrs Prothero's dinner gong. Granny Graveclothes cursing me if the kids opened a single present before I collected her. Pig's arse. They'd have had to wait hours. The long gaunt shadow loomed and darkened the day. The cake stood in the centre of the table like a white marble monument on a grave. Miss Havisham's wedding cake, mice and spiders at its dead centre. We laughed and were jolly and each of us knew what the others were thinking.

Boxing Day Took a hard run up the glistening hill and looked down on the whitewashed city. How easy it would be to fake an accident, I thought. One slip, and ... Or perhaps if I ran hard enough in my current physical condition I could induce a heart attack and end it all here, up on the windy hill, overlooking Mortonhall. So the mind like Mephistopheles goes on with its disreputable suggestions. No control over this bastard brain – except to kick the surfacing thoughts in the face, back down to the wicked id, where the foul imaginings fester. By the time I showered and went back to bed for five minutes the kids were in on either side of me, the three of us sitting up in a row drinking coffee and thinking about her. Thank God for my kids. Merciful heavens, restrain in me the cursed thoughts that nature gives way to in repose. Or in running. As soon as reason switches off, the sharks swim free. Their eyes are dead to love, heartless as stones.

On and on. It made depressing reading. But right now I knew I'd give anything to step back into those terrible shoes tonight. To climb back into the skin of the man who'd lost his taste for living and turned his back on his city. And to tell him: things weren't so bad, you know. You'd seen nothing till you came to fucking Luc! There you really can see nothing!

Luc was left early by Stevenson to its own devices, whatever these might have been a hundred years ago. Now it seemed to possess neither devices nor desires. Luc was just another nowhere place. Morning had revealed it in all its disintegrating desolation. There was no shop of any kind in the village and that meant no breakfast. I was now out of provisions and thought mournfully of the tins of Bologna sausage with which Stevenson had loaded Modestine. A wiser man than me. I had simply taken a little along as a token to the spirit of the quest. I pictured Valvona & Crolla's delicatessen in Leith Walk in Edinburgh and would have sold my soul to be there now. Back I trudged to the garden to retrieve Anatole and to ask *madame* if she might sell me some breakfast. A strong breeze had got up and *madame*'s French undies were whirling at high speed on Anatole's temporary tethering-post, much to his alarm, but *madame* herself must have gone to work. It was Monday morning. I had to check my diary to be aware of this. There was no answer to my despondent knocking. Here too Stevenson had done better, waking at five in the morning to see standing by his bedside 'a stout homely wench' bearing a basin of new milk. Very nice for him. What I'd got instead was a whirligig of knickers. Absurdly, jealousy began to intrude itself, and competitive irritation. I left Luc with a hungry curse. It simply did not deserve the beautiful valley out of which I now followed the Allier, expecting a simple journey to La Bastide.

What I faced instead were yet more steep climbs, this time with an unexpected addition to my discomforts. The sun came out – the first time since Goudet that I'd seen it in a completely clear sky – and on the punishing climbs it hit me smack in the face, producing blistering sunburn on my fair skin. The charging waters glittered all over the landscape and I longed to leave Anatole and just plunge in, clothes and all, to relieve the smarting. I had the worst of both weathers. The rains had created streams where Stevenson had crossed dry land, rivers where he had stepped lightly over streams, and floods where there had been rivers. I found myself at the edge of a stream that had become a river and was now in rapid spate. Anatole made his decision: no bridge, no crossing. No way. I looked around. The flow disappeared into the landscape as far as the eye could see, stretching for miles. There would be no bridge – the river wasn't even meant to be there.

I tried all the tricks taught by Monsieur du Lac, including the bough held hard against the rump, heaving away and all the time dreading the backward kick in the knee or groin. It was useless. *I am a rock*, the donkey seemed to say in silent donkey-speak. *And I am an island*, I groaned, echoing Simon and Garfunkel and dismissing John Donne. I was marooned in France and going nowhere.

Until out of the blue came a *deus ex machina*.

Out of the green trees on the opposite bank, to be precise, and it took the form of a big shiny red tractor. The tractor contained another friendly farmer who at once saw my problem and its solution. *Attendez!* He disappeared into the trees, leaving the tractor running, and reappeared two minutes later. *Voilà!* A rope came snaking out over the river, landing with a splash at my feet. Under direction I tied the wet end to Anatole's saddle, having removed the panniers. Less than one minute later an outraged Anatole was standing – or rather stamping around madly – on the other bank, having been dragged at full throttle through the flood and almost drowned in the process. The tractor roared, the donkey brayed and the water thundered by. It was a diabolical din.

The following direction from the ingenious strategist

on the other side took me aback at first, till I saw the logic.

'*Enlevez vos vêtements!*'

What, *all* of them?

'*Bien sûr!*'

The freak river had swallowed Anatole up to his muzzle and there was only one way to ford this flood and keep my clothes dry. In addition to which there were the panniers. Five times I waded naked through the freezing torrent: first with one pannier, back again for the second, and finally over to the far side with my clothes carried guerrilla-fashion, on arms lifted like bayonets, well out of reach of the water crashing among the boulders and splashing in my face. I was just stepping out of the water and on to grass when three figures materialized out of the trees.

'*Bonjour, monsieur!*'

The treble chorus of *bonjours* came from the friendly farmer's friendly wife and, on either side of her, his two friendly teenage daughters, all of them creasing themselves. The worst part of it was that the repeated trips through the freezing flood had shrivelled my manhood to a tiny blue acorn. I was mortified. A piece of me, at least. What can you say, arms above your head, except *bonjour*?

Bonjour, madame. Bonjour, mademoiselles.

Coffee and eggs at the farmhouse put a golden glow in the autumnal stomach. The farmer's wife lamented that she was losing her daughters again tomorrow. They were returning to Paris, where they were students. I asked them what they were studying. *Art!* was the double chorus. *And perhaps we can draw you, monsieur, a life study? Now that you have already posed in the river you needn't be shy!* I joined in the joke but had no wish to remove my clothes a second time. I explained that I was following a strict schedule and that I had an important appointment to

184

keep – at Notre Dame des Neiges. This led to further hilarity. *At the monastery! You are going to join the monks! Mon Dieu!* In which case, they said, I'd better not risk a second modelling class. I might change my mind about the monastic life and it might *show!*

They were very liberated and intelligent girls and the increased mirth led, with my judgement weakened, to alcohol. The pastis appeared, the glasses clinked, and we were off. I went on from the farmhouse well fed and watered, dry-booted and smiling uncontrollably, wondering vaguely how Stevenson might have reacted to the idea of a life class with himself as nude subject – a spindly wisp of paint on the canvas. But less than a mile further on, the real world of the Cévennes came at me again. The route led up another badly swollen stream which came gushing out of a hill forest. The stream was careering downhill at a steep angle, which kept it reasonably shallow, but to be splashing through tumbling water on a bouldered gradient with a laden and nervous donkey was hard work, and, as so often in the Cévennes, I was as soaked by my own sweat as by the exterior wetness that weather and topography threw at me. The weather especially had the power to change the universe. And I lost count of the times the panniers had to come off to enable Anatole to complete a difficult crossing – and of course go back on again. It was all time, work and worry, not to mention toil and tears and sweat – yes, and even some blood. I picked up lots of grazes. By the time I reached La Bastide-Puylaurent I was utterly exhausted. The Cévennes, I acknowledged, had the power to elevate you and to throw you down without warning.

At La Bastide Anatole did a Langogne and refused to cross the busy bridge. I pulled every one of Monsieur du Lac's devilish anti-donkey tricks out of the hat: the long bridle, the blindfold, the ash bough, the stick across the rump. Useless. People stood around pointing and laughing. One couple were doubled up. I lost my temper, in English, of course, and swore at them. *Why don't you fucking help me instead of just standing there pissing yourselves, you feckless fucking frogs?* Though the alliteration was impeccable, aided by alcohol, this was really unforgivable. But I was hot, sweating, badly sunburnt, my feet freezing, wet and blistered. I was also frantic with thirst, probably on account of the pastis, and already utterly dispirited again. In the middle of the bridge, in the centre of La Bastide, I committed an even greater crime. I stood and cursed loudly and soundly the git of a writer who'd blazed this bastard of a trail by choosing to travel with a fucking donkey!

The locals laughed all the more.

Donkeys are tougher than we are. In the end I had to abandon the bridge and wander well out of my way to find one that was broader and less alarming to Anatole. So I came up to the monastery of Notre Dame des Neiges by the incorrect route, the main road, with buses and cars flashing past and their occupants all waving furiously (*Oh, regardes le petit âne!*), all of them headed eagerly for the monks' haven of solitude and silence. As you head up to the monastery a big brow of mountain frowns at you from the south. You are getting your first glimpse of the High Cévennes, giving you fair warning that the way ahead will get tougher still. This is no compromise country. And at Our Lady of the Snows you should take a deep breath, of both body and soul, and take on stores.

The white blocks of the monastic buildings are built on a hillside overlooking the Allier. Alluding perhaps to this unaesthetic aspect of the place, one of the brothers suggested to Richard Holmes that it was rather like a power station: best thought of as a sort of spiritual generator, pumping out prayers. I approached it in an alternative spirit, through the cool green cloisters of trees. To me it was a soothing balm. Stevenson felt again rather differently, driving his secular donkey before him and creaking in his secular boots and gaiters towards the asylum of silence. Rarely, he confessed, had he approached anything with such intense terror as he drew close to Our Lady of the Snows. And this sheer terror, he concluded, was the symptom of what it meant to have had a Protestant education. All Cummy's conditioning now came into play, and all the holy hellfire of her bigotry, emblazoned indelibly on to the infant brain of her charge and prey. Louis was now confronted by this first ever sight of Rome in its monastic uniform. This was none other than the perfectly affable Apollinaris. He might as easily have been Apollyon, the destroyer, the angel of the bottomless pit, who features in Bunyan's *Pilgrim's Progress*, much read from by Cummy. Stevenson made no such reference but I often wondered if there was an unconscious connection, verbally echoing his ancient terror of Rome, the great whore of Babylon. Father Apollinaris was planting trees, an innocent enough application of his industry, but Stevenson was unable to see it that way. Here was a hellish medieval friar, plucked straight out of one of the prints from his Sunday morning childhood reading, back in bell-beaten Edinburgh when the cold sea fogs came in out of the east, rain drenched the streets and the snow-powdered wind prowled howling southward from the firth and the Highland hills beyond. Calvinism and climate teamed up to colour all his future perceptions with lurid ineradicability. Hence the friendly friar took on a macabre aspect that the author was not ashamed to describe.

He was robed in white like any spectre, and the hood falling back disclosed a pate as bald and yellow as a skull. He might have been buried any time these thousand years and all the lively parts of him resolved into earth.

The wages of sin are death, Stevenson knew that from the age of two. And Rome meant death, he knew that too from Cummy. The language here betrays his fear of that death which is also deadly – leading to damnation. Interestingly too, it is the child's eye view that he employs when he recounts how he looked at Father Apollinaris 'as a boy might look upon a lion or an alligator'. There is self-mockery here, of course. Equally amusingly, Father Apollinaris looked at Stevenson with fascination. He had never seen a Scotsman before – we don't learn whether he had even heard of one – and Bohemian Stevenson, long-haired, haunted, spectre-thin and travel-weary, must have presented an unforgettable impression.

At first he was informed that there was no possibility of his being received at Our Lady of the Snows and I sympathized with his disgust, though he was at least offered the slim chance of a meal. But then as the conversation ran on and it became clear that Stevenson was not what he obviously appeared to be – some pedlar or tramp – but a man of letters, the monk's manner of thinking as to his possible reception began to change, leading to the literary man's rueful reflection that even a Trappist monastery is a respecter of persons, though God certainly isn't. The friendly father offered to plead his case for him with the Father Prior, even suggesting a little white lie. Perhaps they could pretend that he was a geographer? The truthful child of Cummy insisted on being introduced as an author, perhaps even a little nettled that a mere geographer appeared to enjoy a more exalted reputation here than a writer. 'Very well, then,' said Apollinaris, disappointed, 'an author.'

I had read various accounts of travellers who were refused admission to Our Lady of the Snows and am now in a position to advise future tramps of the road that if you are not actually on retreat, there are two sure pass keys: be a writer, or be a follower of Stevenson, that other famous writer – unheard of then but now familiar to all the fathers and brothers.

Apollinaris advised the Scottish author as to another possible pass key – his sleeping-bag. The monk was intrigued and entranced by this highly original bedstead with the green waterproofing and the blue sheep's fur, lying like a sausage across his donkey's back, and he begged him to show it to the Father Prior. It seems from the ecclesiastical records that Apollinaris, who had been nearly thirty years at the monastery when Stevenson arrived, was considered to be a good man, if a little simple and ingenuous. At any rate the Father Prior, charmed either by the author or his sack, proved equally affable. Modestine was led to the stables and Stevenson and his pack were received into Our Lady of the Snows.

I must have cut as wretched a figure as that other unheard-of writer, bedraggled and sunburnt as I was, to the brother who heard my explanations about who I was and why I was here. Through the gold-rimmed glasses I caught the faintest glimmer of irony from the handsome and intelligent face that looked at me with courteous detachment. My quest and therapy, together with any plans I might have for a book, suddenly seemed to be of little consequence in or to this place. Or any place for that matter. But the Père Hotelier assured me I was in time for a shower,

Vespers, dinner, some conversation with those on retreat, and lastly Compline – all of which will make *monsieur* feel better. And if *monsieur* would now care to follow him, he would show me in which of the fields I might most conveniently place my ass.

Getting my own ass into the shower was – like wisdom – the principal thing. Every drop was holy water. *Ye must be born of water*, the monks' great teacher said, and I stepped out of the shower born again. After which, with the luxurious feel of clean dry clothes about me, I made for the grocery department, where I bought brown bread and olives, sausage, rough country pâté, fresh white rolls, home-made butter, a pot of honey – and two bottles of wine, a white and a red. The monks are in the wine business as well as the God business. They make it into their own, ageing it in vast vats in the high-altitude mountain air, thereby reducing its acidity, a process, Frère Jean informed me with a wide smile, known as *bonification*. Yet another gift of *le bon Dieu!* Frère Jean, all eighty-one years of him in his brown habit and blue apron, was standing at a bar thirty paces long, the biggest pub in Christendom, cheerfully selling his wine among the hams and herbs and garlic sausages suspended from the ceiling in festoons of sheer temptation, the hanging gardens of Babylon the Great. Nothing whorish about this particular tradition. This was Lady Rome at home: domesticated, countrified, innocent, appealing – and yet seductive. I gave way as the amiable octogenarian offered me the opportunity of tasting almost anything I wanted to buy, liquid or solid. 'Try this in particular,' he said, spooning out on to a white roll a thick substance like coarse honey. '*Allez, allez! Goûtez, goûtez!*' I tasted – and told him I thought I'd died and gone to heaven. He smiled. 'No need to wait for that, my friend, you can eat as many as you wish. While you are still here!'

They were chestnuts, mortar-and-pestled into a paste. I nearly said that heaven would be an anti-climax after this but remembered to mind my manners.

Frère Jean was in his fiftieth year of the monastic life. '*C'est une bonne vie, une belle vie.*' Said with a big beam. And, he added, it was a great improvement on Hitler. He'd come here in 1945, having been a prisoner of the Germans till then. From one confinement to another in a sense, I asked? No, no, this was the true liberation. Other soldiers had gone back to civilian life, back to the traps of peace and plenty, and that was simply exchanging one prison camp for another. 'Because when you think about it,' he said, 'the world *is* a kind of camp, a prison. Life in it is not permanent – but every man has his term, his sentence to see out.' The real Victory Day was when he came to Notre Dame Des Neiges and gave himself up to God.

I listened to this with a mouthful of *marrons* and felt very wordly. He'd been up since four in the morning and had probably not eaten for eighteen hours. He looked as if he hadn't eaten since 1945. But here he was gladly dispensing food and drink, to wayfarers through a world that he didn't think much of, and yet was crammed with an abundance of good things. I ventured to remark that when God made the world, according to Genesis, he looked at it and saw that it was good. My friendly brother smiled a sad smile. 'And so it was,' he said, 'but that was before the Fall. Things are a little different now.' And reading my mind superbly, he added with all his former humour, 'in spite of a few pounded chestnuts!'

I found this old man so delightful I asked if it would be possible for him to give me a quick tour of the monastery. He thought for a second. 'Certain things are not permitted, my friend – but when you've been here fifty years certain things are overlooked.' Later that afternoon he took me along long echoing cloisters of shining stone and polished pine; showed me the chapter-house and chapel filled with silence and sunlight; a library like a medieval university; the wine-cellars and workshops and gardens where the brothers plied their chosen trades, beekeeping, bread-making, carpentry; and the huge kitchens where every-thing gleamed and ticked like a lighthouse. The sense of spotless order and incredible calm pervaded even this busy engine-room of the establishment. I expressed admiration. The monk on duty turned to me and said, 'You have to stand in front of your oven just as if you were praying. That way you can save the world. And what comes out will be the bread of life.' Finally Frère Jean showed me the graveyard, where the monks lay like soldiers of Christ under identical rows of crosses, sleeping their last sleep while waiting for the resurrection. They were buried right in the shadow of the church where the chanting of their brothers went over their heads, day and night.

'I hope to be deposited here soon,' said my guide.

He was smiling sweetly.

I asked him how his own day was organized.

Like everyone else's, he said. We rise before dawn, attend Vigils for an hour, read and meditate till seven, when we sing Lauds and celebrate the Eucharist. After Terce we start our chores and work on till noon. Then we eat something – in between two other offices of worship – and go back to work for the rest of the day. We have Vespers at half past six, a simpler meal, and the Chapter meeting after some private prayer. Compline is the final office before we go to sleep.

'Will you be attending Compline, *monsieur?*'

How could I have refused, even if I hadn't been wearing someone else's shoes? Someone who attended the same service and was the reason I was here. I asked about the vow of silence, for which the Trappists were famous. Had it been dropped? Everybody here seemed willing to talk. Frère Jean explained patiently.

'It's not so much a vow as an expectation, a requirement of our search for God and our inner conversation with him. It was a distinguishing feature of our Trappist brothers when they split from the Cistercians in the seventeenth century but now it's been greatly modified. You can hardly use the old-fashioned sign language when you're running a wine business and using computers. Even monks have to move with the times.'

Tourists were the other factor, he said, a feature of life unknown to the monks of long ago.

'Don't you find us a nuisance?' I asked. 'A distraction?'

'Not at all, *monsieur*. It's our duty. Every guest must be welcomed just as if he were Christ. After the summer there are few tourists in any case and we have plenty of snow and silence – sometimes from October to April.'

Finally, he said, there was the long winter fast, the vegetarian diet that lasted until April, accompanying the silence and the snow. It was only later that I realized he'd given up his own precious main meal of the day in order to show me around. I was both mortified and touched. I couldn't have hoped for better hospitality and at last found my experience in the Cévennes equal to Stevenson's.

Things had changed only superficially since he turned up with his donkey in 1878. In spite of Father Apollinaris's initial loquacity, the Protestant visitor quickly found out about the rule of silence and was even a little disturbed by what he called the 'ghastly eccentricity' of the sign language, the hooded figures raising their arms and flapping their fingers like giant spectral birds. But he found that all those brothers who had to wait on strangers were at liberty to speak, and after meeting the Father Prior, who refreshed him with a liqueur, he was given a good dinner and was asked if he'd mind having a conversation with an Irish monk who wanted to talk. It suited them both. The Irishman was delighted to find an English speaker and the Scotsman was glad to be given a tour and a run-down of the regime, such as I'd received from Frère Jean. He found the Waverley novels and Molière among Hebrew bibles. He found the brothers taking photographs, making cartwheels, studying literature, baking bread, binding books, growing potatoes and looking after rabbits, each to his own inclination. They were rising even earlier in those days, at two in the morning, and taking the two frugal meals a day, just like the brothers of 1994, and Stevenson noted that the great fast started some time in September and lasted till Easter, accompanying the snowfalls that cut them off from man, though not from God. Stevenson himself, who loved to talk, simply couldn't imagine how they suffered the silent isolation on those bleak uplands, a burden which he believed to be 'both appalling and petrifying to the soul', and he noted with some irony that although a notice had been posted begging visitors not to be offended by any abruptness in the tones of their silence-loving attendants, the note was entirely unnecessary. The brothers were absolutely brimming with words and ideas and would keep you buttonholed by the hour, he says. In spite of his personal and Protestant hang-ups, however, he was greatly impressed by the discipline and industry of these devoted servants of God and concluded that there were a great many people inclined to complain about their lot who could do a lot worse than take refuge in the silence of Our Lady of the Snows. There, he felt, they might learn something.

Stevenson himself learned things here, as Holmes

detected when he read the *Travels*. He learned, for example, that prayer is not just a matter of superstitious supplications formally arranged as words spoken to God, but may be a focusing of the mind and a reworking of attitude. Stevenson wrote three prayers himself, in one of which he refers to 'the love of women and the friendship of men', suggesting that he'd learned something in his loneliness in the Cévennes: an awareness of the importance of human relationships and responsibilities. As Holmes sympathetically perceives: 'Stevenson was telling himself quite simply that he was not made to be alone, either in the human or the divine scheme of things. Paradoxically the Trappists were teaching him that he belonged outside: he belonged to other people, and especially to the people who loved him.'

The prayers never made it, however, into the final published version of the *Travels*. 'A voyage is a piece of autobiography at best,' says Stevenson, but he clearly felt that this particular part of the personal story was just too confessional, carrying too much emotion perhaps and not enough art, and so he reverted to his darker view of the monastic experience:

I was wakened at black midnight, as it seemed, though it was really two in the morning, by the first stroke upon the bell. All the brothers were then hurrying to the chapel; the dead in life at this untimely hour were already beginning the uncomforted labours of their day. The dead in life – there was a chill reflection!

In other images he refers to them as *mankind's deserters, grave-clad prisoners of the iron mind, unsought volunteers of death*. And as if to escape these uncomfortable reflections he went Bohemian instead for the benefit of the reading public, pulling out of the air the words of a lewd French song:

195

Que t'as de belles filles,
Giroflé!
Girofla!
Que t'as de belles filles,
L'Amour les comptera!

This is not just a case of taking refuge in irrelevant bawdry. Fanny Osbourne – coquette, femme fatale, *fille de joie*, or the Circe of his earlier allusion, made at Fouzillac – was as far from the celibate isolationism of La Trappe as it was possible to travel in his mind. And he thanked God at that point that he was 'free to wander, free to hope, and free to love'. There is no question in my mind but that Stevenson made a major psychological breakthrough here, towards the object of his human affections, and that in a weirdly contradictory sort of way the monks had been partly responsible for this.

Dinner for me, in the post-Stevenson period, was good thick soup with bread, rice and roast beef, cooked with wine and herbs, and biscuits and cheese afterwards. Not exotic, but filling and flavoursome. Bottles of the monastery wine stood along the table, where I sat and ate with people on retreat from all over the world. Stevenson crossed swords here with two of the guests who attacked his Protestant ignorance, as they saw it, and he fiercely defended the religion of his mother – but there was none of that here, though they were all Catholics. The people around me preferred to talk about books. And to my surprise I found myself talking about my bereavement. I was not the only one there suffering from that universal ailment.

Time *will* heal you, in spite of what you say now, said Pierre (a lecturer in philosophy, I think). Time cures grief because in ten years from now you will no longer be the same person. So it's not the grief that dies – it goes away with the other person you once were. The same is true of quarrels. The offended can eventually forgive the offender because neither is the same person after a time. It's like nations coming together after two generations when they've been at war. We forgive the Germans for what they did to us because although they are still Germans, they are not the same Germans. There's nothing Christian about this forgiveness – it's pure logic. That's why people in love get divorced ten years on. Neither is the same human being. The chances are that they are always likely to change in different directions, not together, as there are so many directions possible for a human being. Only if there has been what your Shakespeare calls a marriage of true minds in the first place will they then evolve together, in harmony. That's very rare. But in the case of bereavement it's not so rare. It's common, believe me, things *will* be different. And you needn't feel guilty about wanting to be healed and lose your grief. It's like I told you: the grief doesn't get lost, it's always there. You just leave it behind with the other guy, like a suitcase or something. After you've stopped staying with that other guy you move on – and he looks after it for you. Permanently.

I recognized some applied Pascal in Pierre's small lecture, delivered with great tact and tenderness over the red wine of Notre Dames des Neiges, gleaming in the candlelight. Don't get stuck on the past, he went on to advise me. Or the future. That's the trouble with human beings. We're an illogical lot. Animals are more logical, though it's the logic of instinctive innocence. They don't wander about in times that don't belong to them, like we do. We're always running away blindly from the only time that does properly belong to us: the present. But the present is never the end we have in mind, with the result that we never actually live but simply *hope* to live, *dream* about life. It's perfectly logical too, you see. When a man is forever *planning* how to be happy, it stands to reason that he will never actually be so. Take my advice, my friend, be happy: live your life now, not tomorrow.

Pascal or Pierre, it struck me that Stevenson would have agreed with this. His whole life embodied this philosophy and he summed it up in his famous statement: to travel hopefully is a better thing than to arrive. It also struck me that I was inadvertently experiencing the grief counselling I'd scorned in Edinburgh. At the same time I told myself that this was a world away from the idea of a paid professional or even some unsalaried Samaritan walking into one's life and taking over the reins. I was listening to what was being said by this philosophical Frenchman having already journeyed part way through the Cévennes, and the journey so far had provided, in its uniqueness and in its exhilarating and at times frustrating loneliness, some kind of meaningful context for the words I was hearing. We still have to cope singly and for ourselves before we accept the helping hand. The dead, after all, are ours, not somebody else's. They belong to *us*.

Not that everybody at the table provided an intellectual spur like Pierre, not by any means. Some who took part in the spontaneous talk came out with the conventional pieties that no longer meant anything to me. O, Death, where is thy sting? That sort of advice. And revamping Arnold Toynbee perhaps, I said that my answer to St Paul's question would be St Paul's *own* answer: 'the sting of death is *sin*'. The sin of being so selfish that I'd felt suicidal after my wife's death. I hadn't wanted to survive the death of somebody with whose life my own had been so tied up that the end of hers had meant the desired end of mine. Death does have a sting, all right, I said, but not so much for the dead, who can't feel anything, as for the bereaved. Every time it strikes, death inflicts double casualties. Somebody loses his life, her life. And some survivor is left to take the brunt of the suffering.

'And that, I am afraid, is why human love is so tragic.'

Not Pierre – but Friedrich, a historian from Munich.

Speaking in perfect English, he assured me I was providing living proof of the theories of the Spanish thinker, Miguel de Unamuno.

'You should read his book, *The Tragic Sense of Life*. [I since have.] He says that love between two people is the most tragic thing in the world, born of illusion and giving birth in turn to disillusion. Why? Because it's a mutual selfishness. Each lover wants to possess the other and so to perpetuate himself or herself through the instrumentality of the other. But those who perpetuate their virginity perpetuate something far more human than the flesh. We become more human to the degree that we evolve away from our animal instincts, especially this desire to procreate and possess. It's a doomed quest in any case, as love is always looking for something else through the medium of the loved one. It never finds it, of course, and so it despairs. Or it finds it and then loses it when the other person dies – and loss is what causes unhappiness. So love is a tragically destructive experience, human love. Only God's love is truly creative.'

'Do you think a writer, an artist, is closer to God than a lover?' I asked. 'Because he is creating something eternal, out of some kind of love?'

Absolutely – was the answer. An artist uses his imagination, not his intellect. A true artist, that is. Reason is the real enemy of life, according to Unamuno. He says it is both nihilist and annihilating. It's a terrible thing to try to apply intelligence to life, like logarithms. Intelligence is deadly. The truly living, the absolutely individual, is strictly unintelligible. Reason has achieved only one triumph in the history of thought – to invalidate itself. Imagination is what matters. And the ultimate leap and triumph of the imagination is belief in God.

I wondered what Stevenson would have made of all of this. He'd have had more to say than I did, finding myself rather out of my depth among this gathering of deeply religious thinkers. There was a monk waiting on us, standing in the shadows. I recognized the Père Hôtelier with the flashing gold-rimmed glasses that concealed the completeness of his expression. Someone asked him what he thought of the last remark, that belief in God was the ultimate leap of the human imagination. He came forward a little, into the candlelight, and pondered briefly, though he looked as if he'd been through all this before and was gently indulging us.

'Faith, properly considered, is of course a form of imagination, since it involves a belief in a deity which you cannot *know* is there, not with your reason. Both imagination and faith are fuelled by and founded on suspension of *dis*belief. The difference between the two is that in the case of imagination there is usually an abundance of fuel to keep the mind racing. But faith can keep on running even when the fuel has run dry, when there no longer seems to be any reason why we should continue to have any faith left at all.'

Was he suggesting that a monk could actually have any doubts?

'Doubts? No, never. Wrestlings of the spirit, if you like, such as even Christ experienced in Gethsemane and on the Cross. He would not have been part man had he not known fear of death.'

But what about the monks themselves? Might even a monk fear death?

'Every man has his fears, whether he is a monk or a man of the world. For the monk death is the bell which calls him to meet God, and that meeting is what the monastic life has been all about and what it all leads up to. The monk sees death not as a rupture with life but as the door that leads to the true life.

'Having said that, there are, of course, certain private fears. There is the fear not of death, but of dying: the actual process of losing one's life. There is fear of pain and prostration and indignity. Monks are active men who take very little sleep. Of course it is a real fear, the thought of being deprived of your accustomed energy and activity and laid low. We are used to being useful.

'There is the fear of having to say farewell: the reluctance to leave the world and its wonders, nature and art, a loved environment and loved friends. To contemplate that all of that, the earth with its sights and sounds and shapes and scents, can still go on without you, does create in you I suppose a sort of rebellious frenzy that may amount to fear.

'There is fear of the unknown, of course, which scarcely needs any comment. And for some there may be fear of Judgement, though the monk hopes that through his efforts he has deserved Paradise and will not be weighed in the balance and found wanting.

'The greatest fear for many men is the fear of death as a precipice over which the generations merely tumble – endlessly, meaninglessly. The idea of that meaningless edge of and end to existence is the most appalling thing – and the most frightening. But maybe at the end of the day it would be more correct to say that there is no such thing as death: there are only *deaths*. And afterwards – an exceeding weight of glory. That at least would be the monk's view. Death in the abstract simply doesn't exist.'

A sermon extempore on death – mere meat and drink to a monk. Before the after-dinner conversation had started up I had asked those around me if anyone would mind my switching on my tiny tape-recorder so that I might return to Scotland bearing the benefit of the recorded wisdom of those on spiritual retreat. There had been no objections and every word was recorded. The Père Hotelier, however, had not been aware of the innocuous piece of equipment lying on the dinner-table among the plates and bottles and winking glasses. It was at the exact moment when he stopped talking that the tape ran out and the machine emitted a loud click. He looked at it with some surprise and I looked at him, wondering if I would be reprimanded for breaking some sacred code. I think I detected on his face the most enigmatic of smiles. Later, when clearing away our plates, he leaned into my ear and murmured, 'It's fortunate that *le bon Dieu* does not require a cassette-recorder and tapes. Can you imagine the logistics? It's difficult enough running *this* little place! But every thought is already recorded.'

It was time for Compline. We filed in, the lights in the chapel went out and the cowled humps stood etched against the whitewashed walls of eternity, the candles casting their flickering shadows on our faces. The singing began, tenuous and tender, a tentative probe into the silence. These kindly hosts had spoken to me freely and amiably, but now I could hear how they spoke to God in very different voices, voices of melting serenity that washed over me like the sea. I could see Frère Jean there, gaunt-faced under his white hood, his visitor-friendly beam replaced by an expression of focused devotion. Some looked even older than Frère Jean, and the most ancient of all was bent and twisted, both forwards and sideways.

Their ages must have ranged from nineteen to ninety. The youngest looked like Buddy Holly.

Protestant agnostic Stevenson was deeply moved by this nocturnal office.

> The plain whitewashed chapel, the hooded figures in the choir, the lights alternately occluded and revealed, the strong, manly singing, the silence, the sight of cowled heads bowed in prayer, and the clear trenchant beating of the bell, breaking in to show that the last office was over and the hour of sleep had come; these things had a flavour and a significance that cannot be rendered in words. Only to the faithful can this be made clear, to one like myself – who is faithful all the world over and finds no form of worship silly or distasteful.

That at least is what he wrote down in his journal, recording faithfully the mood of the moment as the diarist does. But yet again when he came to publish his *Travels* he struck out this positive passage, replacing it with one more compatible with his public persona. The admiration for faith has gone and we are left with an image of the confused if not distressed agnostic.

> I made my escape into the court with somewhat whirling fancies and stood like a man bewildered in the windy starry night.

As for me, I couldn't bear to come out once it was over and everyone had filed away. I stayed on in the darkness and silence for nearly an hour, recalling the echoes of that deeply spiritual singing. When I rose from my pew and turned to come up the aisle, I saw a solitary figure waiting patiently to lock up after me: it was Buddy Holly, barefooted in sandals and with hands clasped in his sleeves.

At four o'clock he'd be rising for Vigils at the start of his long day, but it had never occurred to him to interrupt my meditations. I was humbled and murmured apologies. He smiled. '*Cela ne fait rien.*' If I'd stayed until dawn I'm sure he'd have waited.

Outside the night was filled with the sound of crickets and the sky with stars. I stood for a few minutes. The terrible silences of Pascal's universe didn't frighten me here. I felt some peace. Up in my room I lay on my bed in the dark and fell asleep almost at once. Something woke me and made me sit up sharply. I peered at my watch. It was midnight, the exact time of my wife's death one year ago. It just so happened that following in Stevenson's footsteps had brought me to this monastery of all places, this spiritual oasis, on the first anniversary. But what had wakened me? An alarm clock in the soul? I felt, of course, as if she had sat by my bedside in this foreign country and wakened me just in time for the anniversary (she was such a faithful stickler for them), just as I'd sat by hers a year ago and had been unable to bring her out of that last sleep. I went to the window and opened it wide, listening to the crickets, still singing under the stars. They were shining with a warmth I hadn't seen in Luc around the head of the Virgin – even with a nimbus of stars her halo had been cold. But here in Our Lady of the Snows I could feel a halo of warmth all round my heart and head. And this for me was a turning-point.

The Braehead preachers of my old sea-town home would not so much turn as spin in their graves if I said that Notre Dame des Neiges was my salvation. Bible-boatmen, they steered a strict Calvinistic course through life and were every bit as fanatical as Cummy. An inkling of anything owed to idolatry was anathema to their ancestral Covenanting spirit. Curiously enough though, even Catholicism itself seemed to dissolve and disappear in this upland monastery. The Protestant's sense of Roman idolatry simply seemed irrelevant here. On the contrary, what I was most conscious of was a sense of real life going on, but geared to God at every moment. The phrase *le bon Dieu* spattered the monks' everyday conversation, as if He were to be met with anywhere in the premises, enjoying a quiet sit-down in the chapel or maybe having a beer in Frère Jean's bar. What I do know is that I arrived at Our Lady of the Snows sick in body and soul and that I left it feeling infinitely refreshed in both. I have little doubt that but for the hospitality and healing I was given there, I'd have abandoned the Cévennes the following day. That next day's march would have been sufficient to break me. I still refer to it as the march on Chasseradès.

The day began well enough, with breakfast served by Père Raphael and a stroll around the monastery woods and walks. I flagged down a passing brother, knowing well enough by now that the old vows of silence had given way to the smiling loquacity with which I'd become familiar. Did he happen, I asked, to know anything about Robert Louis Stevenson? 'Ah, Monsieur Steefsong!' He beamed and began to chatter, pointing out the line of birch trees that Stevenson had watched Father Apollinaris planting. They stood glittering in the sunlight. 'Yes, *monsieur*, you see the trees are doing well today, and Father Apollinaris, he's just over there.' Indicating with a wave of his wide sleeve the high-walled cemetery. I felt as if I'd just missed Stevenson, as if he'd left a day ahead of me. Only the maturity of the trees betrayed his long absence, and Apollinaris's. Time shrank in this place. Or expanded. I went along to say goodbye to Frère Jean. On the way I ran into Pierre and Friedrich, deep in peripatetic talk.

We exchanged pleasantries and said goodbye. 'And', said Friedrich, with a fierce handshake, 'may God *deny* you peace but give you glory!' Unamuno, no doubt. I left them and went into Frère Jean's place. His goodbye was more worldly ('One for the road, *monsieur?* On the house!') but in his own way deeply spiritual, offering refreshment to the wayfarer, for Christ's sake, as he would say. I said I hoped we'd meet again, knowing we never would. 'We shall, my friend – if not in this life then in the next.' I asked him if he really believed in this kind of literal reunion. '*Bien sûr, mon ami,*' he said simply, smiling irrepressibly, '*bien sûr.*' I drank his apéritif and saddled up Anatole with a feeling of happy regret, leaving the monks to their unhurried talk with God and their coming vegetarian fast through the season of the snows.

Back in La Bastide the sign to Chasseradès was clear. If I'd followed it I'd have been there by five o'clock but I stuck religiously to the rule of following the original route as far as possible. I wanted to be at Mont Lozère by 8.30 p.m. I also wanted to find the small hill that acts as the principal watershed of northern Europe, guiding the Allier north-westwards into the Loire and so into the Atlantic on the one side, while on the other side of the hill conducting the Chassezac boisterously south-eastwards through Chasseradès, into the Rhône, and so into the Mediterranean. A great parting of the ways with the headsprings only a couple of hundred paces apart at most. I'd made a note about that from a book about long walks in France and had seen the sign from a hired car when reconnoitring in the summer. But on the ground, on foot with Anatole, was a different experience altogether. I ended up hopelessly lost and ten miles adrift of my destination, Chasseradès. Light was now fading fast. There was scarcely a soul in the landscape and anyone I did meet didn't want to talk, looked blank, or gave me the wrong directions. Darkness came down like the flapping of a wing. A decision had to be made: camp or forced march? I decided to march for Chasseradès in the dark. I had no idea what road I was on but it was one never to be forgotten. It took me up some of the toughest climbs I'd encountered so far: up for hundreds of feet, plunging back down to the level I'd started from, then up again even higher still; through dense woods, following the banks of roaring rivers and along the edges of gorges and ravines, with everything blacked out, not a house, not a star, not a chink of light; over bridge after bridge at every one of which Anatole baulked and had to be tugged, shoved, cajoled and even whacked into co-operation. It was so black I couldn't even make out the road beneath my boots and at times, terrified, I was tap-tapping with my stick, Blind Pew fashion again, to ensure I wasn't stepping straight off some edge and plunging, donkey and all, into one of the rocky gullies that I could hear echoing far below.

Once again my back was sweating hard with the sheer effort of the donkey-driving added to the climbing, but my front was freezing cold where the night air hit me. I'd also run out of water and was dying for a drop. I could hear it all about me and below, gurgling over boulders, tumbling through the darkness, utterly invisible, none of it sounding remotely accessible. The assurances of Great-Aunt Epp kept echoing round the walls of my brain, coming through the keyhole of a chamber that still kept the memories from earliest childhood. *And when you're in hell you'll be crying for a single drop of water to cool your burning tongue. And not one drop of water will you get. Not one!* I'd discovered my worst physical weakness in the Cévennes: an inability to exist for long without water. It surprised me, for I'd run marathons back in

Scotland and had prided myself on what little water intake I seemed to require. The Cévennes have a way of finding you out. And you find out things in turn.

I didn't need the Cévennes to tell me about my cluelessness as to direction. I knew that before I came. I was sure that the road I'd chosen was not after all the road to Chasseradès and that I was now wandering aimlessly. Eventually the road did stop climbing and plunging, and after one last long steady ascent I found myself walking across the roof of the world, with long lines of hills lying like blind whales miles distant. At one point, far beneath them in the blackened valleys, a night train suddenly shot out of nowhere – a long yellow lizard of light hissing through the inky landscape in the opposite direction from me. My mind went into its usual mode, imagining the travellers on the train, only this time it wasn't for fun. I longed to be on it. I pictured its passengers, eating, drinking, reading, sleeping, talking, travelling in comfort from one known point to another, moving on to business, desire, friendship, family, love, along the shining rails of routine, security and civilization, utterly unaware of me, struggling alone here in the dark, lost, weary and more than a little afraid. That's when I started feeling sorry for myself.

The night wore on. I had no idea of the time and it was impossible to read the hour on my watch, it was so black. Then I became aware of a huge glow in the sky. Dawn? Not already. And it wasn't that kind of a glow. A village, then? No, it was a huge cone of light. It had to be a whole town, with hotels and beds and bars! Salvation! After another eternity of slogging I rounded a hillside and saw to my despair the source of the glow. There was an enormous hole in the earth that looked large enough and deep enough to have contained all of Edinburgh. Monstrous machines were at work on this construction site, dwindled by distance to the dimensions of insects, and in the glare of the giant arc lights I could see what I took to be the figures of men, moving like minute specks, smaller than ants, many hundreds of feet below. Human beings, contact, information, help – and all of it, like the water, completely inaccessible. There must have been an entry to this inferno but it would have required Virgil or Dante to find it. Probably it was miles away, off some other road. And as I stumbled along the lip of this vast quarry I noticed something else. The floodlights were an infinite distance away on my left, but in picking me out they had thrown my shadow on to the fields on my right. And there, accompanying me, was this weird silhouette: a bent figure hauling on a long line, and at the end of that line a long-eared, four-footed companion, laden with luggage. It was elongated beyond belief. A mad cameo. Which the donkey, which the man? It was impossible to tell.

After this great earthworks there was another plunge back into the blackness and it all started all over again – the soaring climbs, the plunging descents, the narrow bridges, the sudden drops, the increasing exhaustion, hunger and thirst. And the cold. I'd had nothing since Frère Jean's apéritif that morning. I knew I'd have to camp if things went on like this but Stevenson had reached Chasseradès at sunset and I couldn't bear the prospect of ending up half a day behind him at the start of the second half of the journey. I'd found it was very difficult to make up time in the Cévennes. I'd also found out just how tough Stevenson was. This legendary stork didn't fly across the Cévennes. He walked on his thin legs at the pace of a hardened soldier. So I soldiered on, groping my way up to the vague shapes of road signs, feeling with blind finger-tips for the hopeful sensation of a name, embossed or carved, only to find that each sign was a painted one, its directive invisible, or was not even a fingering post at all but a tree. I'd formed myself in Stevenson's own image for his trip – no compass and no torch. Now, as I stood shivering and staring helplessly at unseeable signs, I felt suitably idiotic. Had I not been so ridiculously pedantic in my approach to the journey I could have read them literally in a flash. I fell to cursing myself and, for some reason, the French, none of whose fault any of this was. I knew that and cursed all the more.

That's when the car lights came up behind me, piercing the blackness, the roar of its engine approaching so quickly that I was afraid it would flash past before I'd had a chance to catch the driver's attention. I stepped out dangerously, holding Anatole with one hand and waving madly with the other. The vehicle screeched to a halt alongside me and an astonished young man wound down his window and stared at me, a man out with a donkey in the middle of the night. I babbled crazily. *Je suis bien perdu! J'ai un grand soif! J'ai besoin d'eau! Où est Chasseradès, s'il vous plaît, monsieur?* And this is when I made yet another discovery: that if you don't pronounce Chasseradès correctly when asking directions, you will never find it. The word has four syllables, not three, and if you omit the final stressed *dès* you might as well ask the way to the moon. The young man, who had just finished his shift at the giant construction site I'd seen earlier, explained all this to me – '*Chasseradès, monsieur!*' – gave me directions and drove off. From what he told me I knew I still had miles to go but at least I knew now where I was headed and how to get to *Chasseradès*. He had offered to drive me there, leaving Anatole tethered to a tree, and to pick me up again in the morning when he returned to work, but I feared for Anatole: he was my responsibility, and in any case that would have been cheating. I plodded on.

I hadn't seen the last of the young man, though. Half an hour later his car lights appeared again, this time coming towards me. He leaned out of the car window and handed me a large plastic bottle. Water. Then, with a grin and a wave, he drove off before I had time to thank him properly – a man who was due back at work in the morning after a long shift but who had driven out of his way for an hour to give a thirst-crazed man with a donkey a drink of water in the middle of nowhere. And in the middle of the night. After his red rear lights had expired in the darkness I stood holding the water he'd brought me – not drinking it, just thinking. I was remembering an incident from the Old Testament when King David was holed up in a stronghold and the Philistines were holding Bethlehem. He longed for a drink of water from the well by the Bethlehem Gate, and in his desperation he gave voice to his thoughts. Three of his soldiers, without telling him, made their way through the Philistine lines and obtained the water – bringing it back heroically in a helmet, according to the illustration for children in my old bible. David looked at the water and blessed it as holy water, sacred to God. 'Far be it from me', he said, 'to drink this precious liquid that these men risked their lives for – to slake my thirst and indulge my weakness. It would be like drinking the life-blood of these heroes.' And he poured the water on to the ground, and the dust soaked it up. I thought for a long time about this story as I resumed my march. Then I stopped and drank. There was always an alternative response, I decided, to the act of kindness as recounted in the Bible. And basic human appreciation seemed to be in order on this occasion.

Then, quite without warning, I stumbled on Chasseradès – which apparently you don't see until you get there, even in daylight. This was the middle of the night, nearly three a.m. according to my watch, which I could now see by the light of a solitary street lamp. Even so I found a hotel and, beyond my wildest dreams, it was still open – people were inside, laughing and drinking. Then I woke up to the reality of the Cévennes in autumn. The hotel was full, there was no room to be had, there was no meal possible, there was no drink possible either, the hotel was actually closed. *Fermé!* The drinkers inside? They were just friends, having a good time, that was all. 'In other words,' I muttered to myself loudly but in English, 'you just can't fucking be bothered, can you?'

'*Monsieur?*'

'Never mind.'

How in God's name could a hotel ever be full up – in this godforsaken dump! If I hadn't cursed I would have cried as I unloaded Anatole and, after all that effort, freezing cold and again too tired to eat even one of Frère Jean's rolls, stretched myself out in my sleeping-bag for yet another night on the cold ground. Stevenson was snug in his inn, lying in an upstairs room with the window open. This could be the very building, I thought, and I wondered what he'd had for dinner. As I closed my eyes I noticed an upstairs window that was slightly raised. It was when I was vaguely picturing a long-haired shadow looking out at me that I fell instantly asleep.

Into a wilderness of dreams.

I was a medieval nun, apparently, and I wanted to go to God. I was, after all, one of the brides of Christ. Seemingly my wish was granted and I was taken up by a spacecraft far beyond the stars to the outermost corners of the universe. So far so good. But then the thing went horribly wrong. I had been deceived. There was a circle of cruel hands and grinning helmeted faces. I was dragged from the spacecraft and pinned to a very small planet, not much bigger than myself, and left hanging there in space in an attitude of crucifixion, left to die. The spacecraft sped off and became a speck among the distant stars. What

212

struck me as soon as it left was the absolute darkness and the intense, unbearable cold. This and the absence of oxygen. The cold and the airlessness were killing me fast – I knew it would not be a slow death. But the real horror was the realization during the dream of what it all meant. The icy blackness, the void, the want of oxygen, all told me that there was indeed no God, no immortal soul, that the souls of the departed had simply been obliterated. And as the blood froze and crackled inside me and the veins snapped like rods of red ice, the full terror of that thought hit me in the chest and I woke up with an appalling pain and a feeling of sick panic. I thought it might be a heart attack brought on by the battle for Chasseradès and I blundered out of the sleeping-bag, thinking that if I were on my feet I could somehow fight it better. As if it were a boxer.

Eventually I calmed down, realizing just how much of the dream content was related to both the physical hardships I'd just suffered and my recent stay at the monastery. And I crawled back inside the bag – only to find myself dancing on a stage of some sort, a high eminence, but narrow and confined, little more than a stunted column really. There was a large old-fashioned clock standing with me on the stage. It was shaped like a gravestone, a sort of grandfather clock reminiscent of a coffin. It was the grandfather clock from childhood, which had always frightened me. I used to imagine that my ancient relatives would be buried in it when they died and that the slow sombre ticking would be heard emanating from their graves. Tick, tick, tick. Eternity, eternity, eternity. Hell, hell, hell! As I looked closer, however, I realized that this was no grandfather clock but was in reality the tombstone that its shape suggested, a tombstone with a clock face instead of an inscription.

Suddenly my wild dancing made it sway. It toppled from the stage, striking Pushkin and crushing the cat completely. I leapt from the stage, screaming, to find that he was not actually crushed but that the tomb-clock had gashed his head deeply and bloodily. Then began a mad car race to the vet's. Would he be brain-damaged? But by the time we reached the vet's Pushkin had turned into Patricia. I panicked. I should have driven not to the vet's but to the doctor's. I tried to take off for the surgery but saw that the clock-tomb was now in the car with us, lying along the back seat, and the sheer weight of this had crippled the suspension.

I was immediately ejected from this wreck in which Patricia was left trapped and dying, and I floated upwards on my back. Into the stars. Then I righted myself, turned over and started flying above an Edinburgh leprous with snow. Far beneath me the treetops stood out like spreading black cancers and I could see the stones of Mortonhall wearing their white mantles. By this time I was the snowman, accompanied by music and by Jonathan in his dressing-gown. But my swimming strokes died out and I started to fall. We weren't going to make it to Christmas. Where was Catriona? The dream ended before I could crash and I woke up, as I thought, to an Edinburgh Sunday and the smell of bacon, relieved that it had all been a nightmare, that she was not dead after all. The same old trickster of a brain, twisting the knife. Vaguely I was aware that they were frying up breakfast in the inhospitable hole of a hotel, yards from where I was stretched out on the ground. I screwed up my eyes. The window where I'd seen the long-haired shadow last night looking out at me was now half open.

In the morning the shadow rose at the innkeeper's call at its usual time ('*Hey, Bourgeois, il est cinq heures!*') in a roomful of sleepy railway workers and blue translucent darkness. He was given new morning milk and hot coffee while I lay in my dew-drenched sleeping-bag and drank some of the water from the well by the Bethlehem Gate. He set off early over the plateau, plunging suddenly into the ravine of the Chassezac, 'a little green ribbon of meadows well hidden from the world by its steep banks with here and there a buried village smoking among the broom'. After making some black coffee on the tiny stove and munching one of Frère Jean's rolls and garlic sausages, I too plunged in after the shadow, obediently dogging its heels, but I saw no sleepy little villages smoking in the valley. Nor did I hear cowbells and cockcrow, or the shepherd's horn, or the sound of an autumnal flute. All had passed away with the shadow.

Feeling a new energy and urgency after his stay at the monastery, Stevenson left the road and took a steep short-cut through the woods. 'Should anyone follow the example of my tour,' he says here (he'd be amazed at the inadvertent prophecy contained in this suggestion), they should beware of the donkey! Modestine objected strenuously and vociferously to this unexpected toil.

As for me, I was by now used to this sort of strain, though Anatole adopted the Modestine viewpoint and the panniers had to come off and be put back on a couple of times. The shadow ahead of me then went over the Montagne du Goulet, following no special road, as none was marked, only upright stones posted sporadically to guide the drovers, and with only a lark or two for company. The Goulet is not a spectacular summit – it is something of a non-event in fact – but from it you can see the next real challenge, the great granite continent of the Lozère, rising to four and a half thousand feet. I came over the Goulet through even denser pines, up steeper climbs and along rougher-than-ever tracks, strewn with boulders and sharp flints, rutted and gouged, soggy in some stretches (my boots sinking up to the ankles) and in other sections flooded with streams in spate, cascading down at me from nearly perpendicular gradients, almost from the skies. It was the hill of Purgatory for both man and donkey. Up and up it went endlessly. How could a hill go so high without running out of air? Yet it seemed nothing compared to the night march on Chasseradès. After eight and a half miles you arrive at Le Bleymard, which you come to through another ghost-hamlet, Les Alpiers, after which you cross the Lot, a modest stream at this point. As usual I could find nowhere to lunch and Frère Jean saved me again. Coming out of Bleymard I passed the poor-looking rows of holiday homes for low-income city families, soulless vacation retreats taking over, while the shepherds and farmers retreat in reverse to the soulless cities, leaving behind the beautiful mountains of the Cévennes.

This is the point in the journey at which I felt closest to Stevenson and his quest, sensing the increased urgency – not merely to press on but to find an experience, to find himself, to see less darkly through the glass, to know something for sure. I felt the same sensation, desperately anxious to arrive at the Lozère, which he'd reached before sunset. This was where the shadow I was following had spent his famous night under the stars, thought about human love, and decided in his own mind and heart that his future belonged to a woman – felt this in his soul. You find yourself by losing yourself.

Although it was already late he deliberately set out to scale a portion of the Lozère along a stony drove road, passing ox-drawn carts piled high with fir trees for winter burning and that looked on the gradients like rampant dragons, clawing the air. Such were the images imprinted on his mind by these surreal silhouettes – the imagination and the adrenalin both now running high. When he reached the top of the woods he found a path among the pines that led to a dell of green turf, refreshed by a tiny streamlet, just a spouting of water over some stones. Here he camped, fed Modestine her supper, buckled himself into his sleeping-bag, fed on bread and sausage, chocolate, brandy and water, and as soon as the sun went down, pulled his cap over his eyes and went to sleep.

In his journal he reflected on the spiritual experience of sleeping *à la belle étoile*.

Night is a dead monotonous period under a roof; but in the open world it passes lightly, with its stars and dews and perfumes, and the hours are marked by changes in the face of nature. What seems a kind of temporal death to people choked between walls and curtains is only a light and living slumber to the man who sleeps afield. All night long he can hear nature breathing deeply and freely; even as she takes her rest she turns and smiles; and there is one stirring hour unknown to those who dwell in houses, when a wakeful influence goes abroad over the sleeping hemisphere and all the outdoor world are on their feet. It is then that the first cock crows ... cattle awake on the meadows, sheep break their fast on dewy hillsides and change to a new lair among the ferns; and houseless men who have lain down with the fowls open their dim eyes and behold the beauty of the night.

At what inaudible summons, at what gentle touch of nature are all these sleepers thus recalled in the same hour to life? Do the stars rain down an influence, or do we share some thrill of mother earth below our resting bodies? Even shepherds and old country-folk, who are the deepest read in these arcana, have not a guess as to the means or purpose of this nightly resurrection. Towards two in the morning they deduce the thing takes place ... we are disturbed in our slumber only, like the luxurious Montaigne, 'that we may the better and more sensibly relish it!' We have a moment to look upon the stars. And there is a special pleasure for some minds in the reflection that we share the impulse with all outdoor creatures in our neighbourhood, that we have escaped out of the Bastille of civilisation and are become for the time being a mere kindly animal and a sheep of nature's flock.

That hour came to Stevenson as he lay there utterly alone and exhausted in his sack at four and a half thousand feet on Mont Lozère under the faint silvery vapour of the Milky Way. It was 2 a.m., the hour of the monks, and he was very thirsty. He gulped down ice-cold water from his tin and smoked a rolled cigarette – nobody could roll one thinner than the spidery Scotsman. The stars were just beyond the black fir tops, and he could see and hear the quiet silhouette of Modestine contentedly munching the moist grass. There was no other sound except the quiet conversation of water and stone as the stream ran over its pebbles. As dawn drew near he lay lazily smoking and examining idly the sheen of the silver ring which he wore (he confessed) to be like a gypsy. Each time he raised and lowered his cigarette he could see it gleaming, and with each whiff the palm of his hand glowed redly and became the highest light in the entire landscape.

The deliberately highlighted hand, with the symbolic

silver ring on it, clearly reveals at this point in his journal jottings how his mind was moving towards the whole point of this experience and its mystical significance: an acknowledgement to himself that he belonged to the woman he described elsewhere as a fellow-gypsy, and that his future happiness depended on marriage to this particular female. Reflecting that he had never in his life 'tasted a more perfect hour of life', he went on to confess more to his private journal than he finally decided to reveal to his readers.

> O Sancta Solitudo! I was such a world away from the roaring streets, the delivery of cruel letters, and the saloons where people love to talk, that it seemed to me as if life had begun again afresh, and I knew no one in all the universe but the almighty maker.

The overtly religious tone of this is far from accidental, coming so soon after his experiences at the monastery. At the same time monks are men alone with God, and Stevenson quickly admits that this is not his ultimate aspiration.

> And yet even as I thought the words I was aware of a strange lack. I could have wished for a companion, to be near by me in the starlight, silent and not moving, if you like, but ever near and within touch. For there is, after all, a sort of fellowship more quiet than even solitude, and which, rightly understood, is solitude made perfect. The woman whom a man has learned to love wholly, in and out, with utter comprehension, is no longer another person in the troublous sense. What there is of exacting in other companionship has disappeared; there is no need to speak; a look or a word stand for such a world of feeling; and where the two watches go so nicely together, beat for beat, thought for thought, there is

no call to conform the minute hands and make an eternal trifling compromise of life.

This was the road to Damascus revelation, the personal high point of his travels. This is what he had come to the Cévennes to find out. And yes, this was a marriage proposal, made in his mind, to Fanny Osbourne. But it was also partly a message to his family, especially to his father. After all the rows over religion in 17 Heriot Row, the prodigal son, in his post-monastic release from Black Dog, had stood before God on Mont Lozère. He would never return to the formal pieties which he had shaken from his feet along with the cold shackles of the Edinburgh rain. But he had already stated at Notre Dame that he considered no form of worship silly or distasteful and perhaps now he felt he had come as far along the road as it would ever be possible for him to travel to meet his father and his father's God. This night on Mount Lozère was the double central experience of the whole trek across the Cévennes. Even the prodigal donkey played its part in the symbolic spiritual journey.

And this, I suppose, was the moment I'd dreamt of in my schooldays, forgotten, and dreamt about again: this famous night among the pines and the stars. I followed the trail eagerly up into the sky, ringed by cairns and crests and buffed by still cold breezes, tugging at Anatole as he stopped to drink from the tiny twirling wells of water springing from the turf – reminiscent of Stevenson's watered green dell, and building up to it, so I imagined. I was following Holmes too, among others, and I stopped with Anatole to taste the experience, water so sweet and cold and refreshing, as Holmes says, like pure peppermint, that it seemed to spring from the source of life itself. The moment of truth was almost upon me.

The actual reality of what I faced on top of Mont Lozère is something I can hardly bear to describe. I found a French playground for tourists: two huge hotels, packed with climbers and holidaymakers from all over the world, swarming like wasps among the mountain slopes. I was so bitterly disappointed that I was ready to swap the solitary night among the pines, impossible now, for a hot pine-lotion bubble-bath and a clean bed, with a hot breakfast in the morning. Nothing doing, naturally. They were booked out, overrun by Germans and Japanese, and when I did make the famous camp it was among not pines but a babel of radios and laughter and cackling foreign tongues, punctuated by the sporadic rifle-cracks of ring-pull tops being torn off beer cans. By that time I was past caring. I went along to the Hôtel Lozère where I wrote up my journal and knocked back several cognacs in swift succession, inducing equally brisk reflection on the state of play so far. I was tired and once again pretty fed up, also homesick and desperately missing the children, but still in the game. And what about travel? The man said that the great affair is to move. So it is. But my mind kept on returning to Notre Dame des Neiges, where the cell-bound monks were on the move every day, from earth to eternity, travelling hopefully, travelling in the ultimate hope: a greater voyage than any that even Stevenson made. Or any mere geographical traveller. A man must keep moving in his mind and soul. Otherwise he goes dead.

Returning from the hotel with a bottle of cognac, I poured a libation to Stevenson who knew what it was to drink alone here when missing a loved woman. And I poured out a second libation, Peel Terrace style, to the woman I still missed and loved. The raucous sounds around me gradually died away towards dawn and I heard in my brandy-befuddled brain the Stevenson sound of a century ago: somebody singing to himself as he footed it through the valley down below. And the shadow in the other sleeping-bag leaned over in my direction and whispered to me some words that I might note down in my journal.

There is a romance about all those who are abroad in the black hours; and one wonders what may be their business. But here the romance was double. This glad passenger, lit internally with wine, who sent up his voice in music through the night; and I on the other hand, buckled into my sack and smoking alone among the fir woods four thousand feet towards the stars.

We shared other words too – about two women, the love of whom, and grief for whom, had brought us together, to meet in this place. The shadow then leaned closer still and offered me, a non-smoker, a cigarette to share. I had brought along the necessary equipment, of course, rolling-papers and tobacco, and the resulting cigarette was as thin as the shadow. In the absence of pines and stars, and surrounded by sleeping campers, I smoked this solitary cigarette with him and watched the smoke disappear into the blackness as we communed.

About our respective women. He'd known the moment he'd entered the room that this was she.

'Was it like that for you too, my friend? *Un coup de foudre?*'

'The same. I was a student teacher in Edinburgh and she'd already been teaching five years – a little older than me, just like your Fanny.'

'A mother figure, would you say?'

'Who knows? I know that I fell for her. And worked it so that I'd be appointed to the same school.'

'Go on.'

'I wasted no time. Started there in August, asked her out in September, got engaged in the spring and married the following year.'

'And were happy after that?'

'Ever after. Except that nothing's for ever. But there was never anyone else for either of us. It was impossible. We were one person. A single soul.'

'Like the lovers in John Donne's poetry.'

'We like sepulchral statues lay – and we said nothing all the day. It was exactly like that. We didn't even have to speak – just like you said a moment ago, the two minds chimed together. And that's all right. So long as –'

'So long as you're together?'

'I used to teach Donne's poems to my pupils. When we did "A Valediction Forbidding Mourning" I'd tell them that true lovers don't need their bodies. Their love is so mysterious that they care less than the rest of us about eyes, lips and hands. And when they're apart they don't miss these anatomical irrelevances. Death is the ultimate separation but even death can't part them, not essentially.'

'Do you believe that?'

'I used to.'

'And now?'

'Now I'm not so sure. But up until less than a week ago I'd abandoned the belief, I felt so stricken, so desolate. Now I'm almost starting to feel there's a coming together again, after a year of being cut off.'

'Talking helps.'

'It depends who you talk to.'

'And your children – what do you think they feel now?'

'It's difficult. Like the love that existed between

their mother and me, our togetherness as a family was something special, as it should be in every family. And again that's fine up to a point.'

'So long as the family stays together?'

'So long as the group stays intact. But we were too tight-knit as a unit, I can see that now. Reprehensibly perfect. Not nearly enough outside influence. And the other thing is that my wife was the linchpin. In practical terms I was a passenger. And although I blamed her mother for everything I confess I was at fault too. I didn't take enough of the strain. There was always a twinkle in her eyes, you know. I should have noticed that one day it went away, the laughter died out. She'd stopped smiling and I never knew it until it was too late.'

'Do you have a picture of her?'

Walking along the shore one day, over in Fife, she'd picked up a broken old herring basket that the waves had washed up on the beach. She hoisted it up on to her shoulder in the style of one of the old fishergirls of yester-year – and smiled. I snapped the moment with a cheap little camera. Now I slipped the photograph from my wallet and looked at the familiar scene, glowing faintly by the light of a roll-up, high on Mont Lozère: the sea, the sands, the smiling woman with the broken basket on her back, the long trailing lines of wickerwork etched against the sky. My companion studied it for a long time before speaking.

'Do you remember that line of Cowper's about his mother's portrait?'

'*O that those lips had language!* You don't feel the force of that till you look at a picture of the one you've lost.'

'There's a poem on the back.'

'I wrote it several days after she'd died.'

'May I?'

'Of course.'

'This would be a good place to read it out loud – quietly of course.'

'Everyone seems to be asleep at last, thank God.'

'You read, I'll listen.'

> *A broken creel and the sea on her shoulder –*
> *she closed her eyes and laughed*
> *at the tangled lines that time had told her*
> *all things turn to, unwoven for her fun.*
> *Join with her then, rejoice, be daft*
> *and happy if you dare, hold her,*
> *enfold her, repay that smile. No one*
> *has her now, her hand, her hair; the boulder*
> *on the beach is more my wife*
> *than this stopped picture of a life*
> *unreachable, a lass unwrinkled in laughter's craft,*
> *too blithe, too young: a woman clothed with the sun.*

A woman clothed with the sun. Louis liked that image. That's how I saw my woman too, he said. The hue of heather honey, the hue of honey bees, shall tinge her golden shoulder, shall tinge her tawny knees. And I told him I thought we were lucky men to have had such partners, and that we'd compare more notes in the morning.

But when I woke again at sunrise, the ghost had gone ahead of me again, had scaled the Pic de Finiels and crossed the Lozère, reaching Le Pont-de-Montvert by 11a.m.

He woke before first light, dressed, fed Modestine, downed some hot chocolate in the blue darkness and strolled about the dell smoking a cigarette before sunrise. A long steady sigh of wind poured out of the cold quarter of the morning and the sun came up, lighting the way ahead of him to the last steep climb. Giving way to a sudden

225

fancy, he decided to pay for his night's 'lodging'. The room had been fresh and well-aired, the water excellent, the ceiling and tapestries inimitable, the view second to none. Whom to thank? The implication is that he was in debt to the Creator for this liberal entertainment. Eccentrically, therefore, he scattered coins on the turf as he left the place, rendering to God what he hoped would not fall to Caesar, and in this half-laughing but semi-serious way left enough money to cover the bill. Then he began to climb the Pic de Finiels, noticing with some surprise that for the first time in the entire trip Modestine of her own accord broke into a jogging trot. I started to run too, deciding not to follow the ghost quite so closely at this point, the game having changed. He'd gone round the east side of the peak and I made straight for the top, meaning to go over the summit and meet him on the other side. When the peak finally came into view I tethered Anatole to the turf with a spike and broke into a run, covering grass, boulder, bog and scree at the pace of a man gone mad. The days back in Edinburgh when I'd run up Arthur's Seat three times a week, the city beneath my flying feet – they were paying off now. They carried me to the high point of the physical journey, a moment of unprecedented exhilaration, when I suddenly saw, stretching ahead of me as if on a vast canvas, exactly what Stevenson had seen: wave upon wave of peaks and ridges, rolling southwards like a sea.

This was the morning of the Great View and I was standing shoulder to shoulder with Stevenson – no longer a shadow, a ghost – sharing it with him. The two donkeys male and female, Anatole and Modestine, nickered in delighted recognition. The two authors shared another solitary cigarette and stared in awe – silent upon a peak in Darien. For this was the moment when he felt 'like stout Cortez when with eagle eyes he stared on the

Pacific' and in that second he took possession in his own name of another quarter of the world. The Pic de Finiels commands a view over all of lower Languedoc to the Mediterranean Sea. Some even claim to have seen white ships sailing by Montpellier. And apart from that magical shimmering patch of sea in the far south, you can also on a good day see the Alps to the east. That is what is capable of being seen across the indecipherable labyrinth, the land of intricate blue hills below your feet.

Not that it was quite like that. My own journey had been plagued by bad weather, it was not a clear day and there was no question of seeing the Mediterranean, but all the same it was spectacular and uplifting. The clouds were crossing this sea of mountains like long slavering Chinese dragons. These were the Cévennes of the Cévennes, the visionary highland country that I'd read about in Stevenson and in Holmes, my Old and New Testaments, when you walk against the sky like a prophet and watch the world unfurl. Six thousand feet up in the air very nearly, I turned to look northwards, saw the hills that were now behind me and realized how far I had come through the Cévennes; also how far I'd come from my previous existence, the old life. Wherever I turned I was ringed by peaks, hemmed in and yet liberated by one extraordinary experience. It was a moment that made up for absolutely everything.

With great reluctance and a certain *tristesse* I came down off the peak and took the path over Mont Lozère marked by standing stones, a very ancient path which soon disappeared into a wilderness of narrow tracks that quickly grew rougher, sometimes ending up as the beds of streams, sometimes simply fading out altogether. Anatole came through the rocks and ruts like a little hero and to my amazement I emerged correctly on the Stevenson road round the hill. I'd crossed the Lozère. From then on it was

227

a slow sedate trek down through the long plunging valley of the Tarn, where I could see all the chestnut terraces Stevenson wrote about, on one of which he now spent his worst night camped out on a cramped and steep ledge, his hand on his revolver much of the time. I gathered some chestnuts for roasting later. A hundred years ago they were a staple of this district, eaten fresh, put into soups and stews, ground into flour for bread. I also saw my first and only adder, a deadly looking weapon, sticking like a brightly decorated dagger in the middle of the road. In that mass of bracken and boulders, I thought, there would be hundreds of them lurking. It put me off the thought of yet another camp. I'd no wish to imitate the uneasy sleep on the narrow chestnut terrace and in any case I felt I'd earned a good night's rest. I came down with tremendous relief into Le Pont-de-Montvert.

A deceptively serene place, revealing little of its violent past, beyond a plaque or two. Here the Inspector of Missions the Catholic Abbé François du Chayla, the oppressor of the Protestant rebels (the Cevenols or Camisards), used his house as a prison and torture chamber, thrusting live coals into the hands of his victims and forcing them to shut their fists, screaming, on the flaming fuel: his method of persuading them that their Protestant beliefs were heretical. It was on the night of 24 July 1702 that his personal regime of bloody oppression was halted. A band of psalm-singing Camisards, fifty strong, surrounded the house where the Abbé was staying, guarded by about a dozen servants and soldiers. They were led by the inspired Spirit Séguier as he was called, an insurrectionist with the looks of a prophet, breathing death and carrying fire. The archpriest ordered his soldiers to fire on the mob. They burst the doors with hatchets and a ramming beam and quickly overran the lower storey but couldn't take the upper floors, bravely guarded by du Chayla's men. The Camisards were determined. They torched the place and everybody aloft came swarming down the outside walls on knotted sheets under a river of bullets. The Abbé himself fell, broke his thigh and crawled into a hedge, from which he was dragged, begging them not to damn themselves by killing a priest. It seemed a good reason for sparing his life, except that in the course of his career he had provided them with many stronger reasons that told in the opposite direction – and these he was now to hear. One by one, Séguier striking first, they stepped up to him and stabbed him. 'This is for my father, broken on the wheel. This is for my brother in the galleys. That for my mother or my sister, imprisoned in your cursed convents.' Each man gave his reason as he struck his blow and drove the dagger home. Caesar on the Capitol with his thirty-three wounds took second place to this. They left his house in flaming ruin and his body punctured fifty-two times. History does not record whether, dying under the hail of dagger-thrusts, du Chayla was stabbed methodically enough to allow him to hear every last one of the reasons for his death before he finally expired.

Séguier's career after that was brief and bloody. Two more priests and whole households were slaughtered on his orders before he was captured. He died where he had murdered du Chayla. At Le Pont-de-Montvert less than three weeks later his right hand was struck from his body and he was burned alive. These events fascinated the Scottish author, nannied by the indoctrinating Cummy, whose Covenanting ancestors were the religious equivalents of the French Camisards: an author who had written his account of the Pentland Rising, a similar Protestant stand, when he was just sixteen. Fixing the comparison in his mind as he entered Le Pont-de-Montvert, Stevenson says that 'it was here that those southern Covenanters slew their Archbishop Sharpe' (du Chayla's Scottish counterpart). He would also have heard from Cummy at an early age the story of the murder of Cardinal Beaton in St Andrews by Protestant avengers, and du Chayla practically quoted Beaton's last words when he begged for his life on account of his priesthood.

These images were all in Stevenson's mind as he stood looking down on the maze of mountains before descending into Montvert, and although some writers have dismissed his long section on religious history as something written up later to fill out the book and irrelevant to his preoccupations at this point, this is to distort the truth. Stevenson never stopped carrying these religious preoccupations around with him – they were always part of his spiritual luggage: one of the burdens that Modestine *didn't* bear. The very biblical-looking landscape, also setting up parallels with and images of Scotland, acted directly on his memory and imagination. He couldn't choose but to remember the exiles, the executions, the galleys, the dragonnades, the whole historical processes of various cleansings, religious, political, social, economic. He would remember the notorious 'killing time' as dramatized in novel form by Sir Walter Scott in *Old Mortality*. He would remember the Highland Clearances. He would remember Glencoe. These things were dear to his heart.

Standing by myself in the 'Cévennes of the Cévennes' and seeing all these hills, quivering with history, it was impossible not to reflect on the events they hosted, in an age that suddenly seemed like yesterday, although it began in 1685 when Louis XIV revoked the Edict of Nantes which had given Protestants freedom of worship. From then on they had to fight for their beliefs against the troops of His

Catholic Majesty, and thousands of Protestant mountaineers took to the hills, to escape the persecutions and to fight for their religious rights. Nearly five hundred villages were burnt and their entire populations exterminated. These were the Wars of the Camisards that I had read about at school. Many of these 'pastors of the wilderness' spent their lives preaching in caves, burying the dead, carrying out secret marriages and baptisms, and eking out miserable winter existences in their bleak mountain hives. When captured they were sent to the galleys or were broken on du Chayla's wheel. The murdered oppressor's foundation still stood as I came into Montvert and I could see the terrace garden into which he dropped to face his executioners rather than the flames.

As I looked at the plaque an old man tottered by with his tiny granddaughter. She looked as though she was the one taking him out for a walk. She stopped to stroke *le petit âne* and her guardian spoke about the Camisards under my prompting. Hundreds of them were caught and killed in the forests round about here, he said, and in the caves where they made their weapons and gunpowder and looked after their wounded. Then when the Boche came here during the war the Maquis used the same caves. There's one further on called the Cave of Sorrow. You should visit it. You can feel things in it. You can see why even the Maquis didn't like to live there for too long. The Camisards are still there, you see. Everybody knows that.

It was irresistible, even if Stevenson had never visited it. The old man's directions were good and I came to the Cave of Sorrow. Can mere stocks and stones retain memories, impressed there by strong emotions? Yes, it did have an atmosphere, though perhaps I was the one who brought it along with me. The leaves were falling outside and another old man was busy pruning. Why was

231

everyone so old? Back in Fife they'd felled her favourite wood the summer she'd fallen ill and she said later that she'd seen it as an omen. We'll to the woods no more – the laurels all are cut.

This was enough to make me feel depressed again, remembering the old life, the liveliness and laughter and loyalty, the warmth and truth and the abundance of good sense. I missed it all over again with suddenly renewed longing: the clink of ice in our gin-and-tonics, handed to me at tea-time with a wicked wink, the kids enjoying their Chinese carry-outs on the sacred Friday nights. For a long time after her death Fridays were impossible. Unable to eat or drink without her I'd spend as long as I could in the supermarket, shopping for the rest of the week. I'd mark papers. Anything to avoid the walls, the suddenly shut door, the sheer shock of being abandoned. Weekend in no man's land over, I'd then barge into school bellowing 'T.F.I.M.! Thank fuck it's Monday! Back to the trenches! Now let's go and see about this 'ere war!'

Thinking about it now made me understand just how much harder I must have made it for the kids. I felt the tears coming. This was the Cave of Sorrows all right. And standing there in the gloom I closed my eyes and said their precious names to myself, bringing them as close as I could. That was when I felt the back of my neck go cold and the light brush of a hand on my shoulder. I cried out as I whirled about, instinctively stumbling back to the entrance and staring into the back of the cave. There was nothing there. Of course. But I remembered Rita, an old neighbour who'd called and asked me if I'd care to go with her to the Spooks – her endearing term for her weekly spiritualist meetings. Nothing to lose, I thought at the time, seeing as God's *in absentia*. And nothing came of it either. Never mind, Rita had said. Time is a great healer. And so it is, I remember thinking – but what happens when you don't want to be healed? So much for the Spooks. But here in the Cévennes, though I'd seen no ghost, I'd summoned up remembrance of things past, and it was a healing and a resurrection of a kind. The Cave was not all sorrow.

I was even more fascinated by the Tarn river crashing uncontrolled through the town. I had read in advance about its water and there it was, just as described – thrillingly clear and cool with a strong hint of crème de menthe or green ink. Over the spindle of a bridge was the Hôtel des Cévennes, where Stevenson had dined and had drooled over Clarisse, the amiable cow, who had waited on him. The language of his journal, unacceptably sexist for today's consumption, revealed his intense sexual loneliness at this stage and his longing for Fanny now that he had committed himself to her in his mind.

I walked in through the open front door. Empty. Dining-room, kitchen, guest-rooms, bar – I wandered through all of them and found no one. So I left the panniers propped up against the bar and went back over the bridge and into the street to ask for information about the invisible owner. '*Ah, Jeannot des Cévennes,*' they chorused, '*tout le monde le connaît!* You won't find him anywhere right now. He's out in the forests, foraging for his mushrooms – his speciality! But you don't have to worry about that. Just go right in and make yourself at home. He won't mind.

Ten minutes later I was standing in a long hot shower, thinking of the joys of sleeping in a bed that night after sitting at a table, with a knife and fork again, eating a dish provided by a master chef. This was a sudden splash of civilization, the first since leaving Le Monastier, apart from the oasis of the monks. I came out of the shower, dressed and went downstairs. The radiators worked, there was hot water in the bathroom taps, my wet clothes were drying, I was shaved. Tomorrow, I told myself, I will eat breakfast sitting on a chair. Tonight I would drink to Le Pont-de-Montvert, where my fellow Scot rested before his night camp. Just for once I was going to let him have the ground and I was going to take the feather bed of civilization. After all, he had spent only three nights sleeping out: all the others had been spent in inns, apart from the monastery. So far, apart from the monastery, I'd slept in only one hotel, in horrible Langogne, so I was going to make up for all that, starting now.

My host, when he arrived with two armfuls of weird-looking fungi, did not disappoint. Monsieur Jean Camus, Jeannot des Cévennes, was a smiling and relaxed restaurateur, and a genial genius to boot. Later that evening he transformed his treasures of the forest into truly magic mushrooms, exotic enough to demand the best Bordeaux, which I invited him to share. There were no other guests. With each glassful he grew more enthusiastic – on the subject of mushrooms. Sadly my schoolboy French from the class of '62, in spite of Herbert Soutar's right arm, proved unequal to the gastronomic technicalities thrown at me in an idiolect that ran faster than the Tarn.

During the night the rains returned. I woke up wafting on a winy sea, wondering what was bellowing in my ears. It was the Tarn, of course, thundering past my open windows over its big clean boulders. No time for moss to grow on these hard-swept stones. I got up and opened the windows wider to let the torrent rush through the room and lay again in the roaring refreshing darkness, thinking of my fellow-writer encamped miserably in the Tarn valley on a narrow chestnut terrace where there wasn't even room to stand Modestine as well. The unhappy ass was perched on another little ledge fifty feet higher up, making a meal out of a pile of chestnut leaves. Anatole was in the garden of the Hôtel des Cévennes, happily munching the heads off the genial Jeannot's geraniums. They were almost over anyway, on this last day of September. I kept waking up with satisfaction, though I sympathized with the friend in the sack who kept turning and turning nervously, his hand on his revolver, alarmed by the strange rustling that he could hear even above the bellowing river and the chatter of the frogs. The night was alive with ants and mosquitoes and rats, and with mysterious noises of the sort that might have been made by human fingernails scratching at his pillow from beneath, fingernails clawing out of the ground. He admits that he was shaken by this and couldn't get back to sleep. 'I perspired by fits, my limbs trembled, fever got into my mind ... I was only conscious of broken, vanishing thoughts, travelling through my mind as if upon a whirlwind ... ' Modestine didn't help matters by stamping about overhead and rolling down stones on her master. He climbed up to make sure she was still safely tethered, smoked a cigarette, watched a couple of stars set, and fell asleep at last.

When I finally woke and went down for *petit-déjeuner* I found Monsieur Camus sitting in his kitchen playing chess with himself. I explained to him that at this junction in his journey Stevenson had turned west to Florac, making a forty-eight-mile detour from the direct route south over the mountains. Many travellers ignored this irrelevance and pressed on due south. I, however, wished to follow my friend as exactly as I could, but it was a long digression for a donkey. What would the roads be like? *Merde!* Main road all the way, busy traffic, concrete, tarmac, an ass's definition of hell. But why didn't I do it without Anatole? By the sound of it, my donkey and I had been pretty faithful to the Cévennes experience up till now. No one, least of all

Monsieur Steemson, would blame me for completing that pointless part of the trip *sans âne* and then returning to the hotel to pick up Anatole and resume the route due south. Anatole could continue to be staked out in the hotel's back garden – 'where in any case', said Monsieur Camus ruefully, 'he seems to be enjoying my geraniums'. The suggestion was a good one and I took it up. I left Anatole in his own private little *pré* and went donkeyless to Florac.

Through gorges of dizzying depths and Wordsworthian awesomeness – 'black drizzling crags that spake by the wayside' – through all of which the Tarn crashed like some maddened crocodile, tearing out the terrain. I passed La Vernede, where Louis breakfasted, the daunting castle of Miral, Cocures, and the church of Bedoues, looking like Macbeth's castle, complete with its quota of temple-haunting martlets. Quasimodo might just have peered out of the belfry. Then – at the euphoric pace now affordable by shanks' pony – it was into Florac. An old decrepit dirty dive with sleazy-seeming quarters, low menacing arches, claustrophobic back courts, rusted shutters on rotting old houses, and many a Fagin's den lurking up closes, with small dark windows behind which God knows who or what lived out their low sly lives, more primitive than the fauns or ferns. The rain poured down on this vile slumland and over it soared the streaming black crags of the gorge: a fearsome crenellation, as grim as anything seen by Gawain on his deadly quest to find the Green Knight. It made me shiver. All I really wanted here was a coffee, but every place was shut – except for the bars, whose unshaven denizens scowled at me when I peeped through their doors. Thank God I didn't bring Anatole here. They'd have eaten him. I got out fast and started to make my way back to Montvert, footsore and tired after an inexplicably ugly day. Stevenson had liked Florac ('as perfect a little town as one would desire to see') and had been attracted by its handsome women. Suddenly the soulmate in the sleeping-bag, the friendly flickering shadow, was no longer so easy to identify with. He was off on his own again, gone.

Out of interest I checked with Holmes, whose diary I remembered as recording his homesickness and tearfulness around this stage in the journey. And here was Stevenson slipping away from him too, hurrying on to his goal, leaving the travelling companion to fend for himself and define his own destiny and destination.

> The original journey becomes brief, disjointed, dreamlike and in places highly emotional. Though he travels with increasing speed and purpose he is sunk in his own thoughts, physically driving himself – and Modestine – towards the point of exhaustion.
>
> As I followed him I was aware of a man possessed, shut in on himself, more and more difficult to make contact with. The narrative of the trip became at the same time more intense, more beautiful, and on occasions almost surreal ... The general descriptions take on a visionary quality: strangely awestruck meditations on the huge shadowy chestnut trees overhanging his route; the dusty track glowing eerily white under the moon (it is noticeable how often now he seems to be travelling after dark).

There is the dream-like night among the pines, the troubled camp with the drawn pistol. And more of this sort of thing to come. The Stevenson journal records the darkening anxiety, but it is only by making the journey yourself that you can feel the traveller's fear on your own pulses and follow him now with trepidation. We were separating in some sense, Stevenson and I, there was no

237

question about it, we were no longer on the same wave-length – or for the moment, at any rate, even the same route. I left him in Florac immersed in his religious meditations and his private sexual longings, and returned to Le Pont-de-Montvert determined to spend another quiet night in this refreshing watering-hole beside the tumbling Tarn. I wanted to draw one more deep breath, one more draught of civilization, before taking Anatole over the Montagne de Bougès, the steep and thorny way to Cassagnas. This is what most Stevenson followers do. But I'd do it having done the Florac detour as well. I'd return to Edinburgh having followed him every step of the way – and more. I'd also, I noted down in my journal, have feasted in some style.

It was only then, looking at the word 'feast' and glancing at the date in the diary, that it registered. One year ago today I had buried my wife. How could I have forgotten? Was that the real reason I'd been depressed in Florac? Unconsciously remembering that awful day, that awful night. And yet it had been a tapestry in relief, the funeral feast. Joy and woe are woven fine, as Blake once put it. A clothing for the soul divine. Another old shag put it differently. Eat, drink and be merry, for tomorrow we die, and as we've all got to go there, let's live while we're waiting – and wash her down with good strong wine, the way the monks of Notre Dame wash down the body of their Christ. And may the force – whatever that is – be with her.

We tried hard. And the one absent friend, the special guest who couldn't come that day – she was the one most present. On everybody's lips and in all our hearts, the shattered mosaic of her life providing a piece for every one of us, bright splinters of her sticking in our minds like little mirrors. The things she'd said, the things she'd done. It took three ministers to rebuild her in words, a mosaic of celebration, rather than lamentation, recalling her to our midst as a teacher, a colleague, a wife, a mother, a friend. She was remembered for her laughter and her loving kindness, her forthrightness and wit. Above all for her devotion to her husband. She had created the conditions that enabled him to function as an author – not the neurosis and misery of myth, but stability, fidelity, harmony and love. Too late – I thought at the time. The usual story. Unthanked and unappreciated, except in the funeral oration. Water unmissed till the well ran dry. And it was hard to believe she wasn't still here, in the kitchen, the engine-room of the house, seeing to everybody's needs, as always. Our honoured hostess.

I kept it going well into the night, obeying the plangent voice of the poet inside me. Kick up the fire and let the flames break loose. Prolong the talk on this or that excuse. But the voice also warned me what to expect next – when the last guest had stepped into the windy street and gone. And there it was again – the instantaneous grief of being alone. That was the worst moment yet. One year later the hole in the heart was still there. But it was covered over. And I had eaten with pleasure again.

After an early breakfast of hot black coffee and croissants with raspberry jam, I said goodbye to Jean des Cévennes, fed Anatole some fresh bread, and left Le Pont-de-Monvert on 1 October at 9.15, knowing that for the first time in the trip I was now the one ahead. Another tired donkey and tired donkey-driver would not be leaving Florac till late in the afternoon. The late start was on account of Stevenson's staying on to write up what he referred to as 'this disgusting journal'. The phrase hints at a measure of self-contempt, tells of his anxiety and uneasiness, his longing to be elsewhere, six thousand miles away, to be precise. I stopped on my own journey more than once to look into his journal and I saw into the psychology of a man desperately missing his soul-mate: an all-consuming, all-colouring state of mind that I recognized all too easily. Stevenson admitted, as he went into the valley of the Mimente, that he couldn't blame the landscape for the gloomy state of his mind. 'The scenery was fair enough . . . to please the heart of the tourist.' There were rocky red mountains, eaten by the elements into a fantastic and delicate lacework; oaks and chestnuts studding the steep sides of the gorge; a red millet field, apple trees jewelled with ripe fruits, a pair of little hamlets – and even a picturesque old castle.

> But black care was sitting on my knapsack; the thoughts would not flow evenly in my mind; sometimes the stream ceased and left me for a second like a dead man; and sometimes they would spring up upon me without preparation as if from behind a door. I was alternately startled and dull.

Again I hardly found it difficult to recognize the mood swings, the nervous anxiety bordering on panic, the almost surreal perception that the abstract has become concrete and that inanimate objects have taken on a sinister life of their own, as they did for me back in Edinburgh during that black year. The knapsack has now become the burden of his soul, the weight of original sin, like the symbolic baggage carried by John Bunyan's hero, Christian, in *The Pilgrim's Progress*. That archetypal traveller from his earliest childhood reading came back to haunt him now as he travelled, all these years later, through the valley of the Mimente, a man too long on his own. Due to the late start from Florac he had to think about camping out again after about ten miles. I myself am an early riser, like Stevenson, and I identified very easily with the depression that comes from the feeling that the best part of the day has already gone, related perhaps to the larger neurosis that life itself is slipping away and that you have to quicken the pace, that the Grim Reaper finds it more difficult to hit a moving target. It's part of the psychology of travel, which is a micro-symbol of life.

Still 'black and apprehensive', he looked around for a place to sleep in the steep and stony gorge, while the shadows lengthened and the valley filled up with the sound of the herdsmen's horns, calling the flocks home. He found a little hollow under an oak, fed Modestine, spread out his sleeping-bag, slipped down to the river to fill up his water can and dined in the dark. Afterwards he lay smoking a cigarette and watching the faint glow of moonlight on the hilltops. Momentarily he was calm again as peace fell from the stars like dew on his soul. Only those who have slept *à la belle étoile*, he says, can understand the healing spell they exercise on a troubled mind. But the mood of contentment was short-lived. A dog began to bark, breaking open the comfortable silence of the dark. It was more than just an auditory annoyance. The dog was the guardian and symbol of a civilization into which he could not at that moment enter and to which he did not belong. He was a tramp, that was all, a benighted traveller, shut out from the charmed circle of family life sitting round the table behind closed doors: food and drink, fun and laughter, companionship, love. And the dog's bark represented 'the sedentary and respectable world in its most hostile form'. Then the wind got up, combining with the canine to keep him awake. All night it blew up the valley, gusting strongly, and all around him and over him the acorns fell pattering from the oak, his one-poster bed for the night.

Meanwhile I was facing the prospect of sleeping out myself – on the Montagne du Bougès. Soon after I left Le Pont-de-Montvert the Cévennes landscape played its usual trick and the path I was following quickly ran out among the inevitable wilderness of tracks, the amazing maze that renders any map irrelevant. Even by Cévennes standards it was baffling, and I began to mutter to myself that things couldn't get worse. I should have kept quiet. Down came the fog to obliterate any idea of direction. All I could see as I drifted on with my donkey were tall trees peering palely at me through the cold gloom – and more of those evil red toadstools that grew fat in this forest, where I felt such an incompetent alien. Then the trees thinned out and I found that we were on high open moorland with dozens of tracks disappearing into the mist in all directions.

Suddenly some shots rang out and shapes like Greenland bears loomed through the thick whiteness. They were hunters. I hailed them, asking for directions to Cassagnas. They stared at one another – and back at me. There was no road to Cassagnas, they said. I pointed out that *all* roads lead to Cassagnas – or Ardnamurchan, or Rome, if that is where you want to go. Just point with your finger – that way Paris, this way Cassagnas. Their fingers stayed on their guns and they moved off, muttering and shaking their heads. Then one of them, the one who had looked the most unhelpful and aggressive, returned through the thick white swirls and advised me – earnestly and with unmistakeable sign language – to lie low: quite literally, flat on the ground. There were many hunters out today after the wild pigs and if I or my donkey were mistaken for one in the fog I could quite easily get myself shot. Anything that moves or grunts, basically, is fair game.

My bowels could have dropped out and hit the Montagne du Bougès. The *chasseur* vanished into the mist and shortly afterwards there were shouts, and more shots cracked out, not far off. I made to throw myself flat but stopped, wondering what to do about Anatole. He could be in real danger and there was no way I could communicate to him the benefits of his lying on his side for a while. With utter stupidity I hooked my arm around his strong neck and tried to bring him down by force. His response was immediate. He bucked and kicked and broke loose, knocking me to the ground. A moment later he was off, galloping into the mist, which swallowed him up in seconds. For the first time in the Cévennes I felt fear, real fear. Also rage and bewilderment, and sheer horror at what I had done. I saw Monsieur du Lac's face in the mist. *J'accuse!* His best donkey, missing or dead on a barren mountain, miles from home. What about the panniers? He was carrying food, drink, bedding – everything. A few moments ago I had been despairing at the thought of having to camp out again, of being benighted on this misty mountain moorland. Now I was standing absolutely alone, shaking and chill with panic. The survival bag had gone along with everything else, and I was destitute and donkeyless, knowing that if I did just stretch out on the ground I'd be likely to die of hypothermia. For the first time in the Cévennes I realized how much I'd come to depend on Anatole, not just as a porter but as a companion. The prospect of a night on a bare mountain together with all the other embarrassing inconveniences that would follow even if I *were* to survive the experience overcame my fear of taking a blast from a French shotgun and I chose a track at random.

It led quite unexpectedly to a better road and – a wild surge of joy – to Anatole! A docile shadowgraph of donkey materializing in the mist, miserably nibbling the short shaven grass that grew by the roadside. Through a miraculous keyhole in the fog I glimpsed what looked like a little black hamlet. Not only had Anatole been found, he had found the way out. I grabbed his rein and capered round him, wildly. Anatole, *je t'aime! Veut-tu m'épouser? Tu es très joli! Je t'aime! Je t'aime!* No response. Only when I expressed my gratitude in the form of one of Frère Jean's now mouldy rolls, did he show some appreciation of this sudden spring of love.

But the surge led to a short-circuit. The hamlet we had stumbled upon by divine asinine intuition was three thousand feet above the main road, with no way down for a man with a donkey other than by making the long slow march round the mountain – away from Cassagnas at first, and tortuously back again. Surely there had to be a way. I knocked on door after door. *Is there anybody there, said the traveller?* Never an answer. This was like being trapped in the Country of the Blind. It was the familiar Cévennes story – a ghost hamlet of holiday homes, with not even the ghosts for company or direction. There was nothing for it but the slow downward spiral, followed by a sore slog to Cassagnas twenty-five miles from that anonymous hamlet in the clouds. It took nine hours, darkness fell, and my feet were in a bad state by the time I reached the Hôtel Stevenson – which was closed for renovations. I stood and stared at this unbelievable spectacle. Even the ironic symbolism couldn't wring out of me a bitter laugh. The Stevenson – closed. He was warm in the sack, under an oak tree, somewhere in the valley of the Mimente. A dog was keeping him awake and acorns were stinging him into irritation as the wind howled up the gorge. He had his own problems, and I had mine, but if he came this way now he'd find no welcome. There was nobody around here to care that I was *doing* Stevenson and that I'd only two more days to go. Why should there be anyone, after

244

all, and even if there were, why should anyone care? We all wander through the world on our own, at the end of the day. And at the end of this day there was the usual blankness. I'd reached Cassagnas ahead of him, to no purpose. I saw him smiling in his sack, surrounded by a blue narcotic haze.

Then the cavalry arrived. Well, the infantry at least. A party of mushroom hunters. They were students, headed for a *gîte* after their day's work and they invited me to join them – one more would be no problem. I fell in with them gratefully and two hours later found myself on the receiving end of a course of leek, potato and onion soup, pâté and terrine, lamb and potatoes, green beans, cheese – and endless bottles of good rough red country wine.

The students were intrigued by the notion of this journey of mine and after the meal we sat around chatting and drinking cognac from various hip flasks. Would it be possible, I asked, for them to sing me a song of the Cévennes? For my journal and for myself of course, after the journey – emotion to be recollected in tranquillity.

Led by Hélène (an Edith Piaf sound-alike but much more beautiful to look at) they sang me a song which haunted me then as now: not a vintage piece from the cellars of the folk traditions, like the songs of the Auvergne, but a song called 'La Montagne', written and composed by Jean Ferrat. Eccentric words, unimpressive without the music, but with melody – a sad and beautiful song of depopulation.

> *Ils quittent un à un le pays*
> *Pour s'en aller gagner leur vie*
> *Loin de la terre où ils sont nés*
> *Depuis longtemps ils en rêvaient*

De la ville et de ses secrets
Du formica et du ciné
Les vieux ça n'était pas original
Quand ils s'essuyaient machinal
D'un revers de manche les lèvres
Mais ils savaient tous à propos
Tuer la caille ou le perdreau
Et manger la tomme de chèvre

Refrain:
Pourtant que la montagne est belle
Comment peut-on s'imaginer
En voyant un vol d'hirondelles
Que l'automne vient d'arriver

Avec leurs mains dessus leurs têtes
Ils avaient monté des murettes
Jusqu'au sommet de la colline
Qu'importe les jours les années
Ils avaient tous l'âme bien née
Noueuse comme un pied de vigne
Les vignes elles courent dans la forêt
Le vin ne sera plus tiré
C'était une horrible piquette
Mais il faisait des centenaires
A ne plus que savoir en faire
S'il ne vous tournait pas la tête

Refrain . . .

Deux chèvres et puis quelques moutons
Une année bonne et l'autre non
Et sans vacances et sans sorties
Les filles veulent aller au bal

Il n'y a rien de plus normal
Que de vouloir vivre sa vie
Leur vie ils seront flics ou fonctionnaires
De quoi attendre sans s'en faire
Que l'heure de la retraite sonne
Il faut savoir ce que l'on aime
Et rentré dans son H.L.M.
Manger du poulet aux hormones

Refrain . . .

The swallows in the song, symbolically leaving, were an image, I suppose, of the economic autumn that had descended on the Cévennes since Stevenson passed through. The stream of human life that had refreshed his sojournings in villages and inns had now almost run dry. And yet the mountains were still beautiful. And though she was no longer in it, the world itself was still beautiful.

Everybody eventually dispersed – some a little drunkenly. There were bunks in every conceivable corner and cranny, up to the rafters. It was a case of taking your pick. First I made my way down to the showers. This was one advantage of a *gîte*-sleep I was determined not to miss. Stumbling through the darkness I came into the dimly lit shower area to the sound of pattering water and the hot hiss of steam. Someone was already there. That hardly mattered. It was a large communal area and there seemed to be no other takers, apart from myself and the guy already in there. I peered through the steam. And stood gaping. It wasn't a guy. It was *la belle Hélène*, showering as naturally as if she had been a man. Clearly she wasn't. I continued to stare. And as I did so I felt something I hadn't felt in a long time, a thick blind surge of desire, urgent and unexpected. She

247

saw me through the steam-clouds and smiled.

'*Bonjour!*' I stammered.

'*Bonsoir, monsieur!*'

Ah yes, of course, *bonsoir*. Must be losing my sense of time.

'Was there something you wanted to ask me?'

I must have been still standing there, staring.

'Yes, I'm sorry – but later, when it's more convenient.'

Later she reappeared in sweater and jeans. I asked her if she would translate for me the words of the song, 'La Montagne', recorded on my dictaphone.

'*Bien sûr.* But it will have to be done right now – the group is leaving early in the morning.'

After she had written out the words we went to look at the stars. It was a mild night and we lay stretched out on some dry hay, gazing up at them, some last cognac between us. She thought it was a terribly romantic thing to be doing – taking a donkey across the Cévennes in famous footsteps and pursuing a personal ghost. I said it hadn't felt particularly romantic up until tonight – but now it was different. We drank the last of the cognac. Tonight's stars and brandy made up for the lost night among the pines. And the starlit companion, so longed for by Stevenson, was lying next to me. *Find someone. Be happy. Live life.* It was two o'clock in the morning. But it was not the hour of the monks.

We were both wakened early – Stevenson by the same dog that had disturbed him during the night. Reaching the point of complete exhaustion, he saddled up for one of the longest days yet, a trek of twelve miles. He left at once but by the time he reached Cassagnas I had gone, having said goodbye to Hélène and already singing in my head the words of her song. She left early with the mushroom hunters and there was nothing to keep me in Cassagnas, no hotel, no café, no shop and, as far as I could see, no people. Stevenson found the usual conversation and cuisine under its cluster of black roofs. Then, a little after two in the afternoon, he struck out in search of me. By that time I was already on the summit of Mont Mars, waiting for him. He crossed the river to the southern side of the Mimente valley 'and took a ragged path up a hillside of sliding stones and heather tufts'. By the end of the afternoon he finally made it up the long escarpment and over the crest where he found me ready to share the view with him, and the words to describe it. We were now on the separation of two vast watersheds: behind us all the streams were bound for the Garonne and the western ocean; before us was the watershed of the Rhône. Here, as from the Lozère, you can see in clear weather the shining of the Gulf of Lyons.

It was the same view. Only the details of a century were different. Long before Stevenson's time 'a man standing on this eminence would have looked forth upon a silent, smokeless and dispeopled land. Time and man's activities have now repaired these ruins; Cassagnas is once more roofed and sending up domestic smoke.' The words record what he saw as he stood there. Standing by his side, a century on, I noted once again the silence, the smokelessness and the depopulation. Economic forces had finally achieved what the Sun King's dragoons couldn't – the social devastation of the High Cévennes, as lamented in Jean Ferrat's sad sardonic song. Have you heard this one, Louis? And I sang it to us both on the summit of Mont Mars. There was nobody else in the world to hear it, only us and our two donkeys, momentarily reunited. *Pourtant que la montagne est belle . . .*

> *Ils quittent un à un le pays*
> *Pour s'en aller gagner leur vie*
> *Loin de la terre où ils sont nés*

Autumn had indeed come – and darkened the skies.

And yet it remained essentially the same view. No need for me to describe it. Louis's words, always better than mine, spoke for us both at the time, and still do.

> It was perhaps the wildest view of my journey; peak upon peak, chain upon chain of hills ran surging southward, channelled and guttered by winter streams, feathered from head to foot with chestnuts and here and there breaking out into a coronal of cliffs.

The sun was about to set, sending a misty light drifting across valleys that were already plunged into darkness. He said he would rather have looked down on a nice simple plain, confessing he was sick of the journey now and wanted it to end. But, positive as always in the end, he conceded that 'the hills also were a field of travel' – nothing is impassable to the determined traveller – and away across the highest peaks to the south-west lay Alais (now Alès), his destination. His mind was there already. He was thinking about letters from Edinburgh and elsewhere that would be waiting for him. He'd written to his mother, among others, from Le Monastier in September, describing his plans and advising where mail should be directed.

> You must not expect to hear from me for the next two weeks; for I am near starting: Donkey purchased – a love – price 65 francs and a glass of brandy. My route is all pretty well laid out; I shall go near no town till I get to Alais. Remember, Poste Restante, Alais, Gard.

I was thinking of Edinburgh rather than Alais, eager for the end of the affair, and St Jean-du-Gard was the end of the donkey trail. Our minds were already moving in different directions as we shook hands and separated on the summit of Mont Mars, though we took the same road now to St Germain-de-Calberte, eight miles or more distant. But we were agreed about one thing –we saw not a single human being all the way there. Only Stevenson heard the voice of a woman singing among the trees – some sad old endless ballad about love. Maybe he was put in mind of Wordsworth's similar experience when he heard a girl singing in the Highlands, an endless, melancholy strain, immortalized in his poem 'The Solitary Reaper'. At any rate Stevenson's language echoes Wordsworth's:

> *Will no one tell me what she sings? –*
> *Perhaps the plaintive numbers flow*
> *For old, unhappy, far-off things,*
> *And battles long ago.*

The voice Stevenson heard was, of course, the voice of Fanny Osbourne, singing from six thousand miles away. She was one of the 'unhappy far-off things' that he was preoccupied with now, as he had been every step of the way. And I found some notes jotted down in the log-book I'd prepared for the trip, telling me how the sadness of that unknown voice still lingers over the lonely landscape with its sparse poor farms, stretches of tough goat-grass and crucified scarecrows, now an occasional irrelevance in fields where no crops grow. But Stevenson, as he listened to the singing, insisted on the interpretation that suited his absorptions and his mood.

What could I have told her? Little enough; and yet all the heart requires. How the world gives and takes away, and brings sweethearts near only to separate them again into distant and strange lands; but to

251

love is the great amulet which makes the world a garden; and 'hope, which comes to all' outwears the accidents of life and reaches with tremulous hand beyond the grave and death.

Easy to read this and see what he meant when he said about his *Travels* that much of the book was mere protestations to Fanny; and that every book is in a sense a circular letter to a man's friends, containing private messages of love for their eyes only. While he was thinking along these lines night fell and the white dusty road glimmered in the moonlight. He felt like a drink. The last of his brandy he had emptied out at Florac, unable to bear the taste of the stuff any longer, and so he gulped down a good couple of mouthfuls of Volnay, in the moonlight, drinking to the moon until he could no longer feel his limbs. This put him in a good mood as he followed the winding silvery road with its warm wind, whispering music and dancing shadows, and came down among masses of chestnuts into St Germain-de-Calberte. Everywhere was shut up and asleep, steeped in silence. Only from a single open door did he see some lamplight spilling on to the road. With his headful of Volnay wine, lucky Louis got himself into an inn just in the nick of time, as the landlady was getting her chicks to bed. The fire was out and had to be rekindled. This caused a certain amount of grumbling but at least he didn't go supperless to roost.

My day failed to measure up to his. After he left me on Mont Mars I got lost among roads that radiated as ever to all points of the compass. This led to more hours of blind voyaging, hemmed in by trees, the only sound the ghostly crash of chestnuts, falling like huge green sea urchins through a deep ocean of leaves. I passed under wet, sweating black crags, went by derelict houses, left behind me whole villages sunk in ruin. I felt like the plague passing through – King Death. I should have ridden a pale white horse instead of walking alongside a donkey. I knocked on doors, squinted through keyholes, saw only specks of dust silvering the sunbeams, only the usual ghosts thronging the hallways, swirling up the stairs. Whoever *lived* here? Or died here? I might as well have knocked on the doors of tombs.

Until I finally found St Germain-de-Calberte. It was held in the palm of a hillside, looking just like a pretty label on a wine bottle, a world away from the depressing aura of dereliction and decay I'd just come through. I arrived excitedly, allured by the terraced gardens, lush with vines and flowers, the quaint little church. I felt like Aeneas, shipwrecked on a coast he fears may be inhabited by barbarians. Then he sees some figures carved in bas-relief, and comes out with the most famous lines in Virgil: *Sunt lacrimae rerum et mentem mortalia tangunt.* These men know the pathos of life – and mortal things touch their hearts. This is civilization.

What a mirage! It turned out to be just another ghost-town, merely prettified. The only other difference was that the ghosts of this town actually appeared on the streets. That's all they were, though – ghosts. An old man sitting on a bench, hands knotted over his stick. I said *bonjour* and might as well have saved my breath. An even older specimen was standing outside the church gates crossing and recrossing himself endlessly, as if expecting Arma-geddon. *Bonjour, monsieur.* The fish-eyes bulged, the fish-mouth opened soundlessly, and a toothless scowl was all I got: an expression of outrage that I had actually spoken, broken the silence of this tarted-up cemetery. The apoca-lypse could hit this place and it would never even notice.

It had one bar – which was shut. One *gîte* – which they said was full up, though there wasn't a sign of a solitary guest. The owner was English, the first English voice I'd heard on my travels and a sign that things were coming to a close. She was an ageing hippy who'd come here after the sixties but seemed to have lost her people-love en route. Not so much as a cup of coffee was offered. Not a flower given in peace.

I came outside again to find another lady who'd stopped her smart car to admire Anatole through the driver's window. She simply loved donkeys. Had I been out for the day with him? Quite a wheeze round here, to take a donkey into St Jean-du-Gard, though that was a bit of a trek, which was why she'd never done it. I explained I'd come all the way across the Cévennes. Oh, how marvellous! *Voyage avec un âne* – how I love that book! (She liked Jane Austen too. And Nancy Mitford. And Catherine Cookson.) It's all so romantic. Ooh, how lucky you are!

And she drove off with her silent daughter, leaving me in the deserted street to contemplate just how lucky I was and how romantic I felt. I did think about camping for the night on the village football pitch but it was waterlogged. Footsore as I was, I marched on and found a *gîte*, at Pont du Burgen, near St Etienne, where I was the only occupant. I lit a fire with pine cones, put in some chestnuts to roast, and toasted one of the exotic mushrooms of Monsieur Camus. He'd have been horrified by its preparation, or lack thereof, but it tasted delicious stuffed with the hot *marron* mush. I didn't have even one mouthful of Stevenson's Volnay but I'd kept back, as a master-stroke, a last bottle of red wine from Our Lady of the Snows. This set the world to rights, and the last of the cognac from the flask made it disappear altogether. I threw some logs into the enormous grate and went up to bed near the rafters, telling myself that I was still just a little ahead of Stevenson, about twelve miles maybe from St Jean-du-Gard and the end of the road. In the morning I'd be saddling up for the last time. As I lay high up under the huge beams, wood-smoke from the fire filled my dreams, and all night long something seemed to be rushing over the roof. My head was roaring with the monks' wine and with all the waters of France.

I awoke to the same sights and sounds as my old partner of the road: the crowing of cocks and the long shadows and slanting lights of early morning. He looked around him at St Germain and later, when writing the *Travels* back in Edinburgh, indulged in more of his historical reflections on the place in the context of the religious struggle. But none of that was his real concern this morning. He recorded the deep enjoyment he felt in this peaceful place, then added: 'But perhaps it was not the place alone that so disposed my spirit. Perhaps someone was thinking of me in another country.' And followed this up with yet another paragraph of protestation to Fanny. He talked with a pair of Catholics, continued his religious reflections, and 'what with dinner and coffee it was long past three before I left St Germain de Calberte. I went ... through St Etienne-de-Vallée-Française ... and towards evening began to ascend the hill of Saint-Pierre. It was a long and steep ascent.'

Anatole and I knew just how long and steep it was. We were there before him, having left in the early morning. We had it easy for the first few miles and took it easy too, gathering strength. Then we left the road to make the last arduous climb upland over the Col de St Pierre. It turned out to be the rockiest and steepest yet of the entire

255

journey, and the hardest for Anatole, who had to get into the gear of a mountain goat. Rocks lay like elephants and camels in our way and sudden leaps over rushing water were required. But it led to the view of our destination, St Jean-du-Gard, tucked away neatly below. We stood for a long time, looking down. It was as if Anatole recognized the view. Maybe he'd done it before, with some other crazy writer, and was already thanking the gods of donkeys that he'd soon be back in the fields with his friends in St Martin-de-Fugères. He looked round only once. So did I. Not hard to see who was standing there.

> Modestine and I – it was our last meal together – had a snack upon the top of Saint-Pierre. I on a heap of stones, she standing by me in the moonlight and decorously eating bread out of my hand. The poor brute would eat more heartily in this manner; for she had a sort of affection for me, which I was soon to betray.
>
> It was a long descent upon Saint-Jean du-Gard.

Coming down is always harder and poor Anatole had to be dragged all the way. Sometimes he fell and I was terrified he'd break a leg. The panniers came off repeatedly. By the time I had got to the bottom I was feeling heartily sick of it all – mountains, forests, boulders, rocks, bogs, torrents, cataracts, rain; days and nights and sheets of rain; sick of the shut doors, the derelict villages, the deserted farms; not to mention the aching joints and freezing feet, the clothes stiff with old sweat – and the endless series of zigzags which I'd mostly followed blind, plunging like whales and rising again, never sure of where they were taking me. But at long last I caught a glimpse of St Jean-du-Gard through the trees, and after a last flat anti-climactic mile along the main road, it was suddenly over.

I went down to the river and took off my boots, letting the clear cold water of France bathe my battered feet for a full half hour. Life was sweet, bitter-sweet. The tears were making clean runnels down my not too clean face and I quickly splashed a shower of cold liquid sunlight over my head, ashamed at the spectacle I was presenting: a tramp sitting on a rock with his feet in the water, crying into the river, his donkey standing by the bank, looking lost. But sweet to stand in these stiff clothes, barefoot at the bar, drinking chilled beer, knowing that all the sodden filthy gear was about to come off for the last time. This was the first establishment that had accepted anything as unlikely as a Visa card. I'd emerged from more than mere mountains. Centuries were behind me. The barman was amused by my anxieties about the acceptability of plastic. He spoke some English – '*comme une vache sud-africaine,*' he apologized, in response to my own standard ice-breaking excuse: '*Je parle français comme une vache espagnole.*' There were cars parked outside from Germany, from the States. There were neon signs in the town, waiting to flare up in the evening and obliterate *les belles étoiles*, push back the mountains into the darkness, into unspecific time. There was pop music playing on the radio. I was back in the real world.

Was I? In St Jean-du-Gard on the morning of 4 October Modestine was declared unfit to proceed. But a carter had seen her bowling along at an uncharacteristic trot as she came into the village, and he spread a useful notion of her capabilities. Bargaining hard all morning, Stevenson was delighted to sell her, saddle and all, for 35 francs – and no glass of brandy. He had also purchased his freedom. But he wept when he sold her and had to say goodbye. To be freed at last from something that has stood between you

257

and solitariness, between you and the end of something, doesn't always leave you with the feeling you'd necessarily imagined or expected.

It was not until I was fairly seated by the driver and rattling through a rocky valley with dwarf olives that I became aware of my bereavement. I had lost Modestine. Up to that moment I had thought I hated her; but now she was gone, 'and oh! the difference to me!' For twelve days we had been fast companions; we had travelled upwards of a hundred and twenty miles, crossed several respectable ridges, and jogged along with our six legs by many a rocky and many a boggy by-road ... As for her, poor soul, she had come to regard me as a god. She loved to eat out of my hand. She was patient, elegant in form, the colour of an ideal mouse, and inimitably small. Her faults were those of her race and sex: her virtues were her own. Farewell, and if for ever –

Father Adam wept when he sold her to me. After I had sold her in my turn I was tempted to follow his example; and being alone with a stage-driver and four or five agreeable young men, I did not hesitate to yield to my emotion.

Some writers have doubted Stevenson's sincerity here, but how many of them took a donkey through the Cévennes? Stevenson yielded easily to emotion. I too shed tears when I parted with Anatole. He'd endured a hard slog, some of which had been caused by my incompetence. He'd kept me from total loneliness. A bond had formed on my side at least. Even now, years later, I think about him, wonder if he'd recognize me if I ever returned to the Cévennes, wonder if he is still alive, out to grass.

There were other emotions. The challenge was over, the life that had consisted of travelling each day with no other objective than to leave one point and arrive at another, to keep on going. I'd inhabited a world in which there had been a suspension of decisions, where the only problems had been to do with eating and sleeping and finding the way ahead, the nuts and bolts of living. To travel hopefully is a better thing than to arrive. Now that I'd arrived I felt a crushing sadness. And woven into it, the wild delight of being able to say, along with others, that I had done it! Had followed him! Had crossed the Cévennes with a donkey. Had pushed myself further than ever before. Or was ever likely to again.

Monsieur du Lac drove down with his wife to collect us and whisked me from place to place while I sat dazed between them, unable to believe that the responsibility for turning a corner, choosing a road or checking the route or the time no longer lay with me; that there was no donkey to saddle up; that I didn't have to take a single step. We saw the Museum of the Wilderness, where the names of those who lost their lives in the Camisard Wars were written round the walls in letters of gold: a very early war memorial.

Next day we left St Jean-du-Gard in his great rust-rotten red bus, its interior an alarming collection of exposed wires, with a bent poker for a gear stick and its exterior eaten away at the wheels. His chivalric ancestors, bold knights, would have been terrified by their descendant's chosen means of mobility. It roared like a monster all the way to Le Monastier, Monsieur du Lac usually keeping both hands *off* the wheel to gesticulate to his wife. Between them sat Figaro, their St Bernard, seemingly more in charge of the wheel and definitely looking the most trustworthy of the four of us. The fifth member of the party, Anatole, was in his box, being towed back up through the Cévennes with a lot more speed and sound and fury than he'd known on the way down. It was a weird sensation to be driving back north like this, flashing so swiftly and effortlessly along the route that had caused both of us so much trouble and hardship.

At Monsieur Pradier's, where a celebratory dinner had been prepared, they all looked at me as I entered, the conquering hero – and pointed at something about my person, roaring and gasping as only the French can do. I thought my flies were open. In fact they were indicating my belt and shouting, '*Deux! Deux!*' – two notches at least – two notches tighter! It turned out to be a stone per notch. I'd lost two stone in twelve days. Now was the time, they said, to put it all back on again in one go. That was easy. Every taste of France was on the table: apéritifs, salmon, *charcuterie*, quiches, rabbit in a marinade, cheeses, sorbets, coffees and cognacs – and gallons if not galleons of gorgeous wine. '*Allez, allez, allez!*' was the constant cry from *chère* Madame Pradier, the goddess of the feast. Naturally the entire *voyage* had to be recounted, the highs and lows of mind and mountain. Then did I strip my sleeve and show my scars . . .

'*Et un chanson, mes amis, un chanson, s'il vous plait!*' I begged Monsieur Pradier, whose strong melancholic singing voice I recalled with admiration, and he obliged us with a perfect rendition of Hélène's haunting lyric.

> *Pourtant que la montagne est belle*
> *Comment peut-on s'imaginer*
> *En voyant un vol d'hirondelles*
> *Que l'automne vient d'arriver*

After which they drove me by request to the Hôtel Provence. I couldn't face Madame Fayole's ancient eyrie again.

Before leaving Le Monastier next morning for Lyon airport there was one last thing I had to do. I strolled along to the Place de la Poste and looked across the valley of the Gazeille to the start of the romantic trail, winding its way quietly into the Cévennes. I stood for a very long time staring at that quiet track, leading out of so peaceful a valley. It was steeped in sunlight and silence. I hadn't known when I stepped along it a fortnight ago, just what it had been leading to – all those experiences, now past, and yet present, and part of my future, to be carried with me wherever I went. I asked myself if the same man had come back as had disappeared into those trees two weeks since. Had I learned anything about Stevenson? About myself? About travel? Had I changed? All the images and impressions came crowding back in on me – the slogs through the rain, the night marches, the fear in the fog, the view from Finiels, the elation and isolation, the huge harmony of Notre Dame des Neiges, the night full of crickets and stars, the night full of Hélène and her song of the Cévennes, the peaks and valleys of triumph and disaster – and the imposters that they were.

Much of the time I hadn't been thinking at all about the wife I'd lost or about my youngsters, abandoned in Edinburgh. I was concentrating instead on my miseries, the inconveniences that the less cosseted Stevenson took for granted and did not even bother to record; thinking about how nice it would be to be warm and clean, well fed and well watered. I remembered from Homer how the shipwrecked Odysseus and his men made fires on the beach, ate good red meat, drank good red wine – and only

261

then did they sit down and weep for their dead friends, the comrades they'd lost at sea. The belly had to be filled first, so that the grieving could go ahead. Such is human nature. I'd learned to love and long again for the home I'd despised for a year as being no longer of any account to me. I'd come to yearn for my children. I'd thought a lot more about living, not dying. The journey through the Cévennes hadn't been a mere escape, or even a satisfying therapy. It had been a catharsis and a confrontation, a voyage of self-discovery. In getting from A to B and back again under difficult and even dangerous circumstances, you come back to what was your starting point a different person, to find that the point no longer remains in time. It's not only that your perspective has altered. The person you were no longer exists and hopefully you are now a better person.

On a lighter note, Stevenson wrote that 'if a man knows he will sooner or later be robbed upon a journey, he will have a bottle of the best in every inn, and look upon all his extravagances as so much gained upon the wholesale filcher – Death. We shall have less in our pockets, the more in our stomachs when he cries: Stand and deliver.' On life's journey you are certainly going to be robbed at some point, and for most of us at more than one. First of your loved ones, then of life itself. So keep moving, Stevenson advises, and drink life to the lees. And keep the Grim Reaper on his toes.

What else? You can't freeze-frame someone in whose footsteps you are following, whether it's a dead writer, or a lost partner, or child, or friend, just as you can't always make the geographical journey with physical exactitude. Time turns landscapes round, gives them different shapes. Ghosts are travellers too and get lost, or sometimes make themselves elusive, letting you go at last, setting you free. You get lost yourself – and end up finding more than the right direction, much more. And you can copy the spiritual journey more closely if you are travelling in something of the same spirit as the people you are pursuing. It's the inner odyssey that counts. Stevenson wasn't treading an untrod track either because he too was following himself – and a woman, and his family and friends, and the God he couldn't quite let go. In some sense also he was getting away from all of them, including himself, finding an escape route that paradoxically led back home, to the point of departure. So it is a trail flickering with ghosts – your own, and those left there by the man who made the trail famous. And there are the ghosts of others who have gone ahead of you for serious reasons. Tourists don't leave ghosts, they leave crisp packets and ice-cream cartons. But then tourists, as Louis would have said, are no travellers. Tourists are intent on arriving and departing. The real travellers, says Baudelaire, are those who leave for leaving's sake, not to make for a destination. Their hearts are light as balloons, they never diverge from the path of their fate and, without knowing why, they always say, 'Let's go!' The true traveller, as Louis put it more famously, is travelling hopefully. And that is a better thing than to arrive. I found that out in the Cévennes. You can't find it out from a dictionary of quotations. Or even by reading *Travels with a Donkey*.

So much for philosophy. From a purely personal viewpoint I would have to say that when I came out of the Cévennes the pivot of the universe had shifted once again. I left Le Monastier, in Stevenson's phrase, 'a miserable widower' and arrived in St Jean-du-Gard remarried – to life. It may seem an absurdly large claim that twelve days had turned me around to that extent. But experience, as somebody once said, is as to intensity, not as to duration, and I doubt whether I have ever lived so intensely as I did in the Cévennes. It was an experience of exhilarating extremes, of highs and lows, reflecting the geographical peaks and valleys of the literal journey. The trouble with life as I had lived it (and as most folk in any civilized neck of the woods live it) is that it lacked those real physical extremes that make you appreciate both what you've got and what you are; and, if you have lost something, just how much you still have left to live for.

Even the hunger and thirst I felt in the Cévennes were nothing to what millions suffer daily on this planet, but for my own cushioned carcass they were enough. You have to hunger and thirst after your own redemption. How can you understand the force of that biblical metaphor unless you've known genuine hunger and thirst? There's a story about a man who asked the Buddha how to find salvation. The Buddha took him on his shoulders across a river. Halfway across, he toppled him, holding him under water till he was all but drowned. When he brought him up again and he broke the surface, choking and spluttering, the Buddha asked him, 'What did you most crave down there? Was there anything you particularly wanted?' The man gasped back at him in disbelief. 'Air, of course! Air, air, air!' 'Well then,' said the Buddha, 'when you *want* salvation as desperately as you wanted air just now, you'll find it!'

I crossed many a river in France. Nobody pushed me in – but I believe I pushed myself to the point where I wanted life again. Salvation, if you like to call it that. And a return to normality. For Stevenson the Cévennes worked the trick. He married Fanny Osbourne and he exorcised some ghosts. In the Cévennes too I exorcised my own evil spirit rather than the beautiful spirit of the loved one – expelled the Mr Hyde that had been pushing me to the

264

brink. I managed to lay my wife to rest, psychologically. I was no longer a miserable widower.

A few days after my return to Edinburgh a package arrived for me through the post. It had been sent by airmail and I recognized the French stamps with a surge of interest. When I opened the jiffy bag I was disappointed. There was no letter, no indication as to the identity of the anonymous donor. It was a videotape of a French film, *Tous les matins du monde*, recently released. Intrigued, I sat down to watch it.

The phone rang more than once. I think the doorbell went. I never answered. I was transfixed. It was a film about a man whose wife had died. He was Monsieur de Sainte-Colombe, the seventeenth-century composer and player of the viola da gamba. In the spring of 1660, one afternoon, he was at the bedside of a dying friend who wanted to say goodbye to life in style with a glass of wine and some music. That same spring afternoon, as her husband played his friend into eternity, Madame de Sainte-Colombe died. When the musician returned home he found her already laid out on their bed to greet him. She was exquisitely beautiful.

From that day on he plunged himself into mourning and remarried himself to his music, pursuing a set of ascetic ideals from which he never wavered. He couldn't get over his wife's death, he loved her so much – so the murmured voice-over hauntingly recounted. That was when he composed the eerily evocative *Tomb of Sorrows* containing the plangent piece called 'Tears' – and all subsequent arrangements were composed and played with her in mind as he thought ceaselessly about her and of the things he had loved her for: her liveliness, her laughter, her sound advice, her chatter, her physical beauty, the hips he had held, the belly that had given him two children. And he passed on to his two daughters his elegiac philosophy of exposition. Each note should end dying. With each stroke of the bow someone you love vanishes into the shadows. Mysteriously they fade from sight, leaving tears in your eyes – tears that become translated into notes of music. A music totally informed by love and death, the two things that change all things.

Gradually he shut out the world, viewing it only by the bright flame of the torch we light for the dead. He sold his horse and built himself a cabin in the garden of his country house and into this he retreated to play and compose, practising up to fifteen hours a day. He devised a new way of holding the viol and added a seventh string to give the instrument a deeper sound and a more melancholy tone. It was said he could imitate the full range of the human voice, from a young girl's sigh to an old man's sob. He had withdrawn completely into his art and had become as mute as a fish, expressing himself only through horsehair and catgut.

Songs and laments arose under his fingers and when they haunted him he jotted them down in his red book to be rid of them. But he was haunted by more than music. His wife's memory never dimmed. Her image was always in front of him, her voice always whispering in his ear. She drank wine from the glass he left out for her, she shared his food, his loneliness and his grief. Time failed to cool their bedsheets. And these ghostly encounters were his only joys apart from his music. Otherwise he was full of confusion, austerity and rage. Every night was that same night. Every chill was that same chill. He no longer took any pleasure in language, in conversation, no longer wanted the company of people or books. His friends were his memories, his life-

266

blood his music. He had quite simply renounced all that he had loved on earth.

Except for his two daughters, Madeleine and Toinette. He brought them up as best he could and devoted all his leisure time to teaching them the viol. In time they became fine performers with their father and the Sainte-Colombe three-viol concerts were soon all the rage with the aristocracy. The King got to hear of them and sent his own violist, Monsieur Caignet, to summon the composer to come and play at court, with a view to being taken on as a royal musician if His Majesty was impressed.

The interview did not go well. Monsieur Caignet was a competent musician but on this occasion his phrasing left something to be desired.

'Sir, you live in ruin and silence. People envy your wildness and the green woods above you. All very fine. But the King wishes to hear you play. If he likes what he hears then I'll have the honour of playing beside you at court.'

Sainte-Colombe was equally direct.

'Sir, I live my life among grey wooden boards in an orchard, to the sound of seven viol strings and my two daughters. In my court are willows, streams, whitebait, elder buds. Enough for me. Thank you for your offer, but no.'

'Sir, you don't seem to understand. You really are a complete wild man. Don't you understand? His Majesty's wish is an order!'

'Yes, you're right, I am a wild man. I'm so wild I believe I belong only to myself. You can tell the King he was too generous when he glanced at me!'

And Monsieur Caignet, the King's Violist, found himself being bundled unceremoniously out of the composer's cabin, his plumes quite literally ruffled. Outraged, he assured the savage musician that he'd be back. With a royal delegation.

As indeed he was, King's horses and all. Including Father Mathieu to try out his persuasive powers where Caignet's had failed. Unfortunately these turned out to be even less diplomatic. The cleric was a fat bully.

'Sir, you hide your name among turkeys, hens and little fish! You obscure a talent God bestowed on you in vainglorious poverty! It's time to burn your coarse country clothes, your outmoded ruff, time to procure a fashionable wig and to accept the King's bounty!'

It was a hard pounding but Sainte-Colombe pounded even harder.

'So you think my clothes outmoded, do you? Wrong, sir! It is I who am outmoded! I like sunlight on my hand, not gold. My public are chickens and geese, thank God! I prefer my hens to royal fiddles, my pigs to your absurd manners, your huge wigs!'

This went down even less well and tempers flared.

'You bumpkin, you'll rot in your mud! Rot like a plum in your orchard!'

'Very well, I'll rot! Now get out! Get out and leave me! Leave me alone! I tell you your palace is smaller than my cabin, your public less than one person!'

The King liked that reply and he let the violist be. But he ordered his courtiers to avoid his concerts. The shades closed thicker and darker round the Sainte-Colombe residence. Not that this mattered to him. He had dispensed even with words. Music, after all, exists without words and is not entirely human. It doesn't exist for kings either, or for gods or gold or glory or silence or sorrow or love. It is something on its own – a drink for the shadows, a wafer for the unknown. That is how Sainte-Colombe now saw it.

And he grew even more isolated as the years went by. Once he dreamed of sojourning in deep water. In his mind he left the sunlight altogether and slipped beneath the green surface of the lake. After that he felt his anger fading. Deep inside himself he felt that something had ended.

But the time came when once a month his daughters had to put a cloth between their legs, first Madeleine, then Toinette. They grew up and grew beautiful. The younger one embraced life, learned to harmonize, learned to laugh. She married the local viol-maker's son.

Madeleine inherited instead her father's single-minded, self-punishing obsessiveness, his refusal to let go. She had an unhappy love affair and, driven by unswerving austerity and grief, wasted away to a shadow and hanged herself in her bedroom. Hanged herself with one of the ribbons from the fine shoes that her former lover had given her.

For six months after that Sainte-Colombe never spoke a word.

By this time he had long given up on life. Even, in a sense, on his music. Instruments, scores, exposition – the material expression of the art no longer mattered. He was music. He was living entirely in his head. He was a ghost, speaking only to old shadows that no longer moved. He had come to see that death is not nothing, contrary to what many believe. Death is everything because it is the sum of everything it steals from us. It is all the worldly pleasures bidding us adieu. Life, to be sweet, has to be cruel.

So the film, with its haunting script, depicted with exquisite tenderness the tragedy of two people who let themselves be destroyed by sheer sadness, by clinging to the memory of a love that had nowhere to go. One love had faded, the other had been ended by death. Both had run out of time – which is too precious to waste. Each day dawns only once. *Tous les matins du monde sont sans retour.*

I was struck to the soul by my experience of this film and by many of the details that spoke so tellingly about my

269

own situation – the extraordinary episode of the wine-glass, for example, and its symbolism. One must leave a drink for the dead, a refreshment for those who've run out of words. Perhaps the script simply went back at that point to Omar Khayyam, as I had done. Even so the parallelism shook me.

Let Love clasp Grief lest both be drowned. The film sent me back to *In Memoriam* and to this line of Tennyson's. Grief, going off on its own, unchecked by love, takes you down a deadly path. And love, out of control, is what my monastery friend from Munich called it, citing Unamuno: the most tragic thing in the world.

I replayed this cinematic masterpiece over and over, absorbing both its beauty and its lesson – a French lesson that had come free and unsolicited and which played a huge part in rehabilitating me over the months that followed. I knew that if I'd seen the film a year ago I'd have identified myself wholly and uncritically with the suffering Sainte-Colombe and ignored the central lesson. A year on, and with the experience of the Cévennes behind me, it came as an educating influence. I never found out who sent it, but it was yet another mysteriously healing balm that came out of the Cévennes. I began again to eat and drink with some appetite, to read with and for pleasure, not merely to mirror my loss. I managed to speak to her again in the manner we used to speak to one another when talking in bed, finding it not difficult to discover words at once true and kind, or not untrue and not unkind. I returned to my job and taught again with passion and concern. By the time spring came, persuading myself that what will survive of us is love, I was quoting even Larkin (still on the syllabus) with a kind of half regretful enjoyment, if not joy:

The trees are coming into leaf
Like something almost being said;
The recent buds relax and spread.
Their greenness is a kind of grief.

Is it that they are born again
And we grow old? No, they die too.
Their yearly trick of looking new
Is written down in rings of grain.

Yet still the unresting castles thresh
In fullgrown thickness every May.
Last year is dead, they seem to say,
Begin afresh, afresh, afresh.

Begin afresh. Very early one spring morning, well before dawn, I drove again to No. 2 Marchmont Street to stand outside our first flat – sleep had continued for a long time to elude me in the middle hours of the night. And this was something I felt I had to do, a sort of touchstone of the grieving process. I couldn't have believed that a street could be so full of this sudden presence. Perhaps it was all in my mind. But the aura of peace and warmth and joy was unmistakeable. I went home again and looked up *In Memoriam.*

Doors where my heart was used to beat
So quickly, not as one that weeps
I come once more; the city sleeps;
I smell the meadow in the street.

I hear a chirp of birds, I see
Betwixt the black fronts long-withdrawn
A light-blue lane of early dawn,
And think of early days and thee,

271

And bless thee, for thy lips are bland
And bright the friendship of thine eye;
And in my thoughts with scarce a sigh
I take the pressure of thine hand.

And I did walk hand in hand with her after that, not in the sense of being possessed – which is what I had been, but in the spirit of one of the card messages which a friend had sent me after she died. Now at last I was able to accept its message. It was the piece which begins with the words: Death is nothing at all.

Death is nothing at all
I have only slipped away into the next room.

I am I, and you are you.
Whatever we were to each other,
that we still are.

Call me by my old familiar name,
speak to me in the easy way
which you always used.

Put no difference in your tone,
wear no forced air of solemnity or sorrow.
Laugh as we always laughed
at the little jokes we enjoyed together.

Let my name be ever the household word
that it always was,
let it be spoken without effect,
without the trace of a shadow on it.

Life means all that it ever meant.
It is the same as it ever was:
there is unbroken continuity.
Why should I be out of mind
because I am out of sight?

I am waiting for you,
for an interval,
somewhere very near,
just around the corner.

All is well.

And there was one more message that meant a lot to me. It contained an anonymous poem.

If I should die and
leave you here awhile,
be not like others sore undone,
who keep long vigils
by the silent dust, and weep.
For my sake turn again
to life and smile,
nerving thy heart
and trembling hand to do,
something to comfort
other hearts than thine.
Complete these dear
unfinished tasks of mine.
And I, perchance,
may therein comfort you.

Complete these dear unfinished tasks of mine. Most of us die wishing we had completed personal business, instead of leaving important matters undone. I knew exactly what my loved one's uncompleted tasks were, the only ones that ever mattered to her apart from me: our two children, who were so relieved to see me back safely from the Cévennes that I can safely say that the Cévennes worked for them too. All three of us came through. I had a long way still to go in bringing them up but I no longer felt I was doing it entirely on my own. Somewhere along the route between Le Monastier and St Jean-du-Gard she had joined me again. Or rather I had allowed her to join me. I can't pin it down to a night among the pines as Louis did. But I know it happened.

If anyone deserves the last word it should be Louis himself. In his Dedication to the published *Travels with a Donkey* he wrote that 'we are all travellers in what John Bunyan calls the wilderness of this world – all, too, travellers with a donkey; and the best that we find in our travels is an honest friend. He is a fortunate voyager who finds many. We travel, indeed, to find them. They are the end and the reward of life. They keep us worthy of ourselves.'

That we are all travellers we all know. In what sense exactly we are all travellers with a donkey, the man who drove Modestine through the mountains and whom Modestine drove mad, didn't say. I believe I know what he meant, the man whose own body had been subject to a huge amount of strain – a world of illness and of travel.

Let my own last word, then, be about donkeys.

Hamlet, in his suicide soliloquy, calls us donkeys by implication when he asks *Who would fardels bear/ To grunt and sweat under a weary life?* The metaphor is shared by the Duke, Vincentio, in *Measure for Measure* when he likens life to 'an ass whose back with ingots bows'. *Thou bearest thy heavy riches but a journey, And death unloads thee.* Perhaps most startlingly of all, St Francis of Assissi. He died, like Louis, in his forties, worn out by his self-imposed austerities, and begging forgiveness of 'my poor brother *donkey*, my body' for having driven it so hard, and for all the hardships and privations and abuse he had loaded on to it. The cerebral haemorrhage that prematurely ended the life of Stevenson was unquestionably brought on by the strain of overwork. From that point of view we should all try to make the journey for the donkey challenging but kind; hopeful, but no harder than it need be because, if you look at it in this way, every one of us is indeed travelling with a donkey. And there are many Cévennes in the lives of men.

'La Montagne'

One by one they leave their land
to make their fortunes,
heading far from the places of their birth.
For ages they have dreamt of it –
the allure of the city and its secrets –
cheap plastic furniture and a night at the flicks!
For the old folks life was nothing special,
they just sat there stupefied,
wiping their lips
on the backs of their sleeves.
But at least they could hunt down a partridge or a quail,
and knew how a good goat's cheese should taste.

   Refrain:
No matter how beautiful the mountain,
Autumn comes –
and already the swallows
are darkening the skies.

With perfect grace
they made their way
right to the very tops of the mountains.
All those days and years –
still they were noble of soul, spirited thoroughbreds,
gnarled as the ancient root of the vine.
As for the vines, now they run wild in the forest.
Their grapes will be gathered no more.
It was only a rough country plonk anyway –
but it was the stuff centenarians were made of!
And it came in such floods –
they drowned in sheer delirium.

Refrain . . .

They didn't have much — just a few goats and sheep.
One year would be fine,
the next not so good.
They knew no holidays or days off.
The young girls dreamt of going to the balls —
it's natural to want to live your life.
A life in which they'd all be salesgirls or cops,
earning enough to see them through
comfortably to retirement.
Ah, but dreams may be deceptive --
and see how they ended up, stuck in their tiny rented
flats,
with chicken for dinner — well stuffed with hormones!

Refrain:
No matter how beautiful the mountain,
Autumn comes —
and already the swallows
are darkening the skies.

Acknowledgements

THIS BOOK COULD NOT have been written without the help and support of a secret army of people who helped me both to and in the Cévennes. In particular I want to thank Elizabeth White and Mairi Hedderwick for their reconnaissance skills and personal support. Without them I should never have got there in the first place. Nor would I have survived the first day had it not been for my scouts and guardian angels, Anne and Eugène d'Esprémenil, and their friendship, while the entire Cévennes experience would have been a pale shadow of itself had it not been for the warmth and enthusiastic assistance of Monsieur Jean-Frédéric Pradier and his wife, and also Jo and Marie-Rose Exbrayat. I can never sufficiently thank those I have named. And there are others: Jim and Maggie Braithwaite and Alex and Morven Peden, who were among those who looked after my children while I was in France; numerous friends and colleagues who helped me when I needed it most; Dr Viktor Kolesnikov, who sowed a seed and fixed a washing-machine; André du Lac, who taught me how to drive (and survive) donkeys; and the four-footed man himself, Anatole, my companion of the roads and hills who, unlike Modestine, treated triumph and disaster just the same, as the imposters that they are.

Special thanks to my agent, John Beaton, who did not fight shy of relaunching the career of a writer who had not written for a decade – and it is because of John that I am now thanking all those at Profile who also had the courage to take me on, especially my editor, Gail Pirkis, together with Ruth Killick, Kate Griffin and the entire outfit headed by Andrew Franklin. Their warmth and enthusiasm and indeed their concern to put writing itself at the top of their priorities are virtues I thought had ceased to exist among publishers.

I want to take this opportunity of saying how grateful I am to Dr Fiona MacLaren for support above and beyond the call of general practitioning; to the staff of the Royal Infirmary of

Edinburgh and the Edinburgh Western General Hospital for everything that they did; to the monks of Notre Dame des Neiges for the soothing balm of their upland retreat, where I turned a hard corner. And of course I am especially grateful to a certain long-haired maverick Scotsman, a one-time fellow-citizen of Edinburgh, who inspired me as a storyteller when I was a young child and as a trail-blazer when I felt the urge to follow in those famous footsteps.

Footsteps. That brings me to Richard Holmes, my thirty-year predecessor, and to a host of literary debts. *Footsteps* was an inspiration equal to Stevenson's. Of the many other biographers of Robert Louis Stevenson, apart from the old stagers, Furnas and Daiches, I want to make special mention of Jenni Calder, Frank McLynn and, in particular, Ian Bell. Their influences will be apparent to many and I acknowledge these gratefully.

Finally, readers of this book will understand and appreciate the extent to which I was held together and sent on my way by the voices in my head from a chorus of writers whose words insist on being overheard – Philip Larkin, Pablo Neruda, Bernard Levin, Adam Nicolson, Jean Ferrat, Alain Corneau, Pascal Quignard. And Pascal himself, of course, and Miguel de Unamuno, philosophers whom I met not quite face to face, but very nearly, in Our Lady of the Snows; and many others whose names I can't acknowledge simply because we have communed together so long they have become inseparable from my own thoughts and the words that emerge. All of them have their say in this book and where I allude to them and quote them I also salute them endlessly.

And even if it could be, that would not be the end of my gratitude. How could I fail to express my undying thanks to my children, Catriona and Jonathan, for putting up with their father when he had lost the place for so long? And to dearest Anna, who helped me find it again – and who gave me the confidence to write this book at last.

The author and publisher would like to thank the following for permission to reproduce copyright material:

Extract from Jean Ferrat, 'La Montagne', words and music by Jean Ferrat © 1980 Productions Alleluia © 1964 Productions Gérard Meys, 10 rue Saint-

Florentin, 75001 Paris; extract from Philip Larkin, 'Trees', in Philip Larkin, *Collected Poems*, published by Faber and Faber Ltd; extract from *Selected Poems* by Pablo Neruda, translated by W. S. Merwin, edited by Nathaniel Tarn and published by Jonathan Cape, and used by permission of The Random House Group Ltd.